SATAN'S SUMMER IN THE CITY OF ANGELS
THE SOCIAL IMPACT OF THE NIGHT STALKER

Photographs from the Collection of

LOS ANGELES PUBLIC LIBRARY

PHOTO FRIENDS
of the LOS ANGELES PUBLIC LIBRARY
PUBLICATIONS

with Additional Images from the Los Angeles County Sheriff's Department

AN ENTIRE REGION—MILLIONS
OF PEOPLE—WERE TERRIFIED,
LEFT SLEEPLESS AND TOOK ON
BEHAVIORS OUTSIDE THEIR NORM.

SATAN'S SUMMER IN THE CITY OF ANGELS
THE SOCIAL IMPACT OF THE NIGHT STALKER

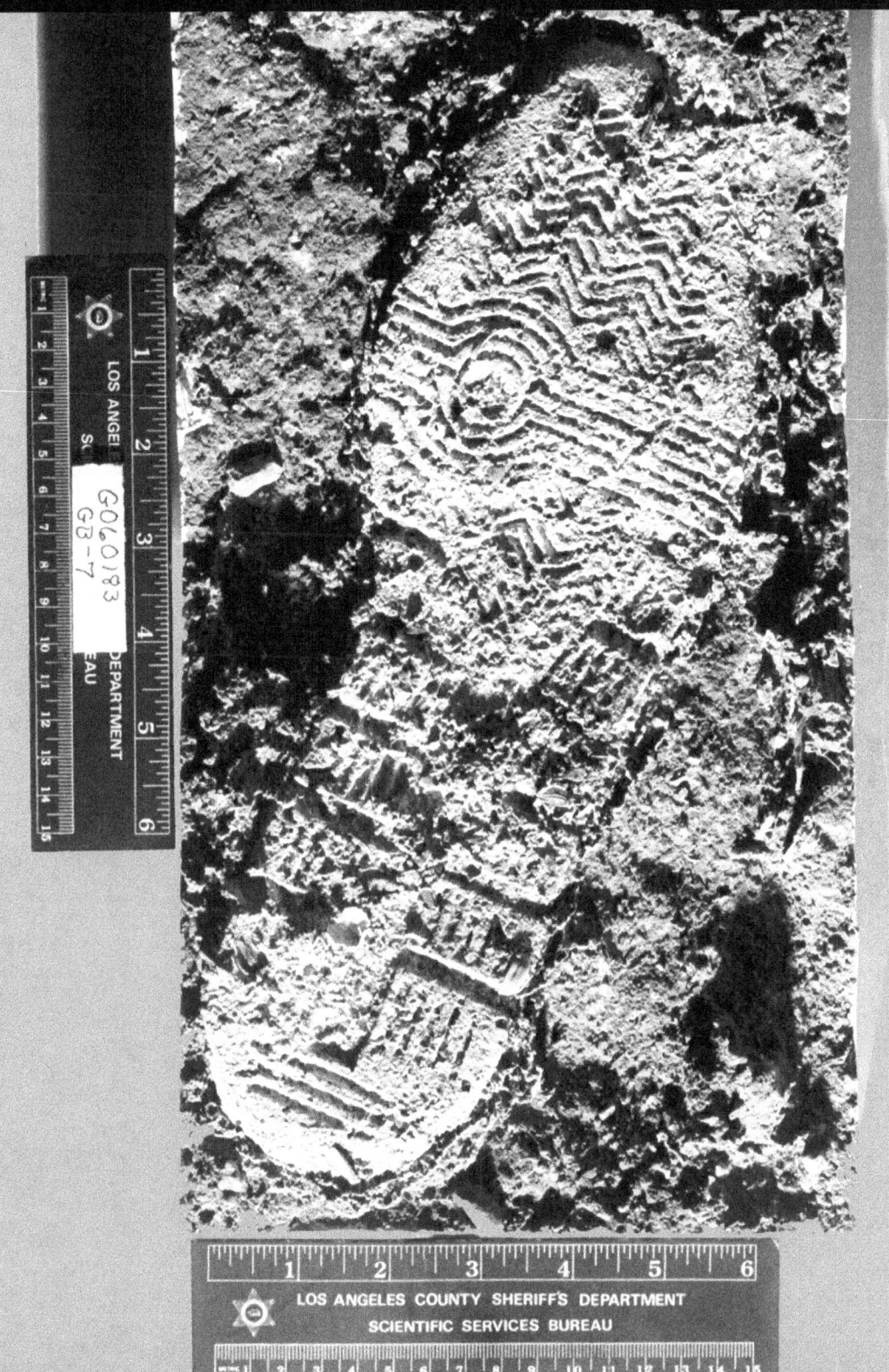

GLYNN MARTIN   FOREWORD BY JAMES ELLROY

For Mom and Dad

Dedicated to Kraus and Hays

Incredibly talented cops,
great partners
and even better friends.

CONTENTS

DE NIGHT STALKER
BE COMIN' AT JOO—
HE GONNA MAKE YOU DO DE
BAAAAAAAD BOOGALOO!!!!!

FOREWORD

It's the achy eighties, kats and kittens. It's that sicko summer people still talk about. There's a baleful beast on the priaphic prowl. He's a pad creeper, a slasher, a shooter, a perv for all seasons. He takes lives, he lets blood, he lays waste. You've been waiting to score the skinny on Ricky Ramirez's reign of terror. You've been gorching for the inside story, told as only a seasoned law enforcement professional can tell it. Here it is—Glynn Martin's *Satan's Summer in the City of Angels.*

I'm putting my imperious imprimatur on this book. My pustulent paw print will adorn every copy. Glynn Martin and I are hellhound hermanos. Glynn served on LAPD for 20 years and later served as the executive director of the Los Angeles Police Museum. We co-authored the archival-photo book, *LAPD '53*, and had a blast ballyhooing this turgid tome all over El Lay and environs. The pix in this book are just as skankily scarifying. This book should carry a dystopian disclaimer: "Caution—noxious nightmares may result!!! Read at your rapacious risk!!!" Glynn's got a pulse-pounding sense of suspense. This book demands to be read in one seditious sitting. It's also a trenchant treatise on FEAR. The human cost of the Night Stalker's rampage was hellaciously high—and Glynn charts that cost in heartbreaking fashion.

Satan's Summer in the City of Angels.

The torrid text.

The law enforcement insider's perspective.

The pithy social critique.

Paparazzi-esque pix from the Los Angles Public Library collection and the photo archive of the Los Angeles Sheriff's Department.

In calamitous conclusion:

Strap into Glynn Martin's terrifying time machine. The sicko summer of '85 awaits. The Night Stalker will greet you with beastly bared fangs.

James Ellroy
December 13, 2018

I WAS A COP IN HOLLYWOOD
WHEN THIS DIABOLICAL DRIFTER
TORTURED THE GREATER LA AREA
IN THE SUMMER OF 1985.

INTRODUCTION

Photo Friends of the Los Angeles Public Library is a nonprofit organization tasked with the care of the LA Public Library's expansive collection of photographs, and offering programs which highlight the collection while generally promoting the art and craft of photography.

Or, at least that's my take on things after serving on the board of directors for a number of years.

It was during the course of my board service that the board, advised by the very talented Senior Librarian Christina Rice, realized that the photo collection held much promise for fund-raising. Many of the directors found a subject in their wheelhouse, and created image-based books. The books sell well.

Problem is, I was, and remain, devoid of the artistic talents held by all of my fellow directors. So, I asked my colleagues if there were enough crime photos to support a book. I had some experience in this regard, having worked with famed author James Ellroy to create the bestseller *LAPD '53*. Christina immediately informed me of the series of images related to the Night Stalker case.

Bingo, Jackpot, Bullseye, or whatever term fully reflects how much the suggestion resonated with me on both a personal and a professional basis.

I was a cop in Hollywood when this diabolical drifter tortured the greater LA area in the summer of 1985. My father's photo appeared in the *Los Angeles Times* following a double murder in Glendale, where I was raised, and my father was serving the police department as the Detective Bureau Commander. I recalled my worries for friends and neighbors. We didn't need another Hillside Strangler in our quaint city. Glendale seemed to be the only listing in the phone directory for serial killers of the day, particularly those who trafficked in ritual murder.

When it was decided that I would do the Night Stalker book, it was clear other images would be necessary to illustrate the story. So, one of my published colleagues, Joan Renner, suggested we contact a mutual friend from the Los Angeles Sheriff's Department, Mike Fratantoni. Both had lent their gifted assistance to the *LAPD '53* project, so working with the both of them on another benefit book would undoubtedly be enjoyable. Mike contacted Sheriff Jim McDonnell about the project and obtained clearance for the use of case photographs taken by Los Angeles Sheriff's Department photographers.

Mike and Joan put me in touch with one of the lead investigators from the case, retired Lt. Gil Carrillo. His interview was fascinating and confirmation as to why this case was ultimately solved. Carrillo sought and found the important details during his tireless pursuit of Richard Ramirez. He is due significant thanks for the efforts that brought about the arrest and prosecution of Ramirez, as well as for the lengthy interview he granted Joan and me. The story of the series of horrific crimes perpetrated by Ramirez couldn't be resolved without a good guy. That was Sheriff's Homicide Investigator Gil Carrillo.

In some senses, this book is a metaphor. It took a multi-dimensional partnership to solve the Night Stalker crimes, and ensure justice was served. Elements of that same partnership were present 3-plus decades later to revisit and detail the social impact of those crimes, and not a full recounting of the crimes and investigations. This was done in the courts and in Philip Carlo's book, *The Night Stalker: The Life and Crimes of Richard Ramirez.* Our goal was to recall a regional reaction to the horror wrought over one summer by a disciple of Satan who decided to summer in a City of Angels.

I thank all involved, especially James Ellroy who generously contributed the book's introduction and my former LAPD colleague, Sheriff Jim McDonnell. Mike Fratantoni, who the Sheriff wisely tapped to advance the Sheriffs' museum, was extremely accommodating and helpful. Ditto Gil Carrillo. The main part of this story is absent without Gil's incredible recollections.

The contributions of Christina, Glen Creason, Ester Petschar, and my long-time author friend Kathy Kristof, better expanded the story beyond my professional perspective. Thanks for helping me and Photo Friends!

Photo Friends President Amy Inouye and Senior Librarian Christina Rice assisted in many ways. This book is just a part of the publishing program which has been wisely envisioned and administered by both. Thanks to my fellow directors Kim Creighton, David Davis, Lynell George, Kathy Kobayashi, Dennis Kopp, Eric Lynxwiler, Tom Meyer, Cindy Olnick, and Tom Zimmerman for supporting the publishing program, and allowing this oddly off-topic sub-ject to be included in an otherwise-less gruesome series of books.

And then there is Joan Renner, a fellow Photo Friends board member, friend, historian, and committed Angeleno. Joan helped from the start and never waivered in her support for this book. This could not have been done without her considerable talents and efforts, so I extend my many, many thanks!

Glynn Martin

"I DIDN'T LIKE THE WAY ONE EVIL MAN WAS ABLE TO CHANGE THE WAY MILLIONS OF US LIVED OUR LIVES," WROTE *LOS ANGELES TIMES* STAFFER STEVE EMMONS ON THE DAY FOLLOWING THE ARREST OF RICHARD RAMIREZ.

SATAN'S SUMMER, 1985

This observation by Steve Emmons (opposite) and much of his commentary are ample motive for the publication of this volume. Much has been written, and screened, about the serial killer dubbed the "Night Stalker." Evil incarnate understates his criminality. Likewise understated was the social impact his crimes had on the greater Los Angeles area. Other areas and other good and unsuspecting folks also endured the attacks that sadly vibed during the summer of 1985.

No one is ready to attribute that summer, or any other season, to the Night Stalker. The vile being would undoubtedly accept the gesture as a compliment, much like the case name the media finally settled upon. Ramirez had murdered, raped, robbed, assaulted and terrorized many by the time his criminal appellation was fully applied.

An August 13, 1985, *Los Angeles Times* story still mentions the Valley Intruder, or Valley Invader, or Walk-in Killer before the story gets to *Night Stalker*. The final entry stuck, but it was way late in terms of the number of crimes for which Ramirez would ultimately be held responsible. Additionally, his remaining known crimes wouldn't be committed in Los Angeles, where this "Name the *CREEP* Contest" seemed to be thriving in newsrooms.

Days later, the Night Stalker was in custody, but the worries and wonderment continued. Was he acting alone? Doors and windows were still being locked, exterior lighting continued in otherwise quiet quarters of LA. Women were slow to returning to their nighttime forays from home or work. Even though the skinny scumbag was in a downtown jail, people still worried. It was part of the social impact Ramirez's gruesome handiwork etched into LA some thirty-odd years ago.

This state of affairs, *this* phenomenon, *this* criminal consequence is explored herein, and told through a reflection on the crimes, the capture and the trial of one of the most despicable humans to ever set foot in the Golden State.

Sleep safely now, the bad man is gone.

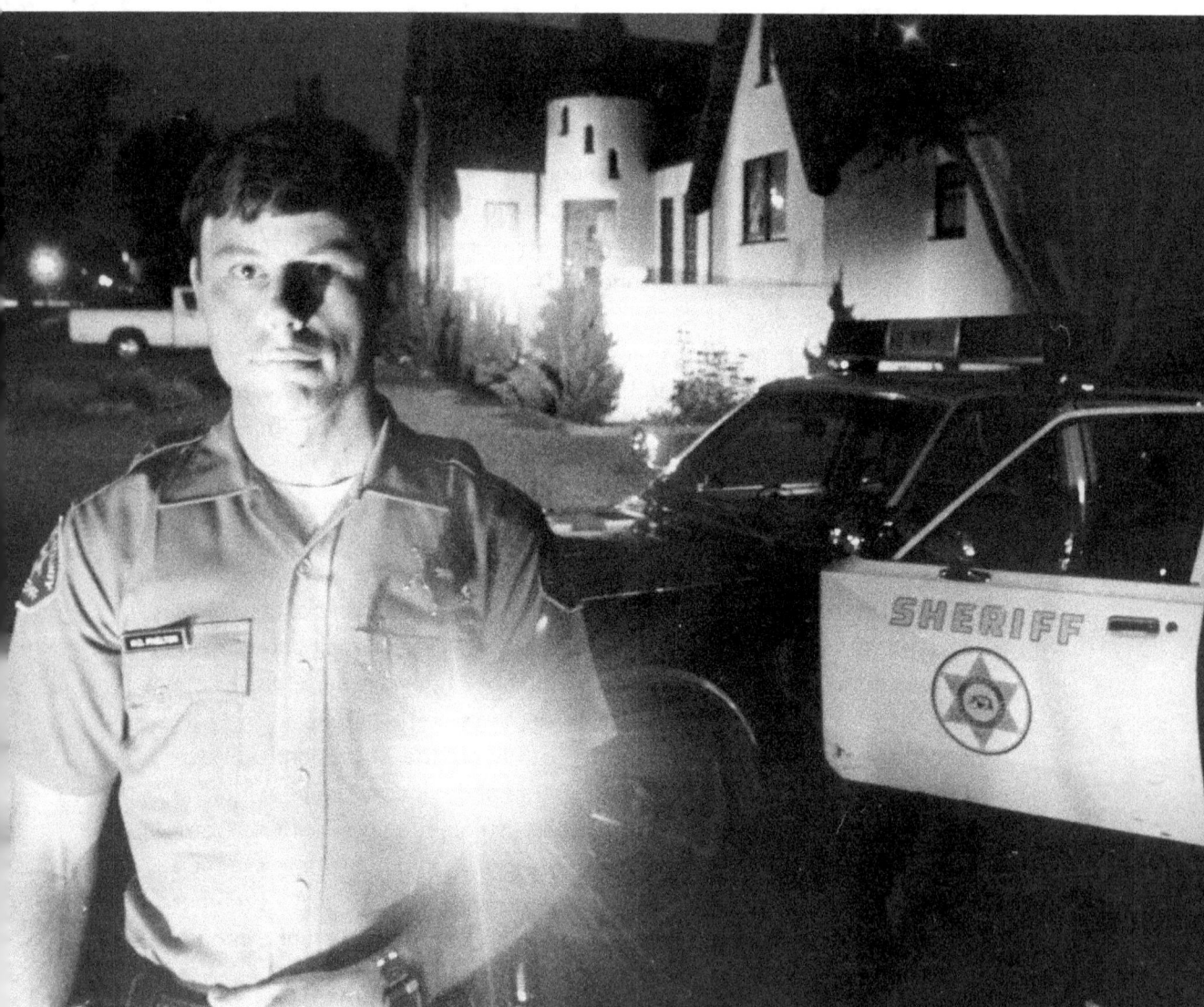

There were nearly 100,000 violent crimes in Los Angeles County during 1985. This staggering number included more than 1,000 murders. None caused the county to tilt to the edge of fright like the series of murders ultimately proven to have been committed by Richard Ramirez. (Michael Haering/Herald Examiner Collection)

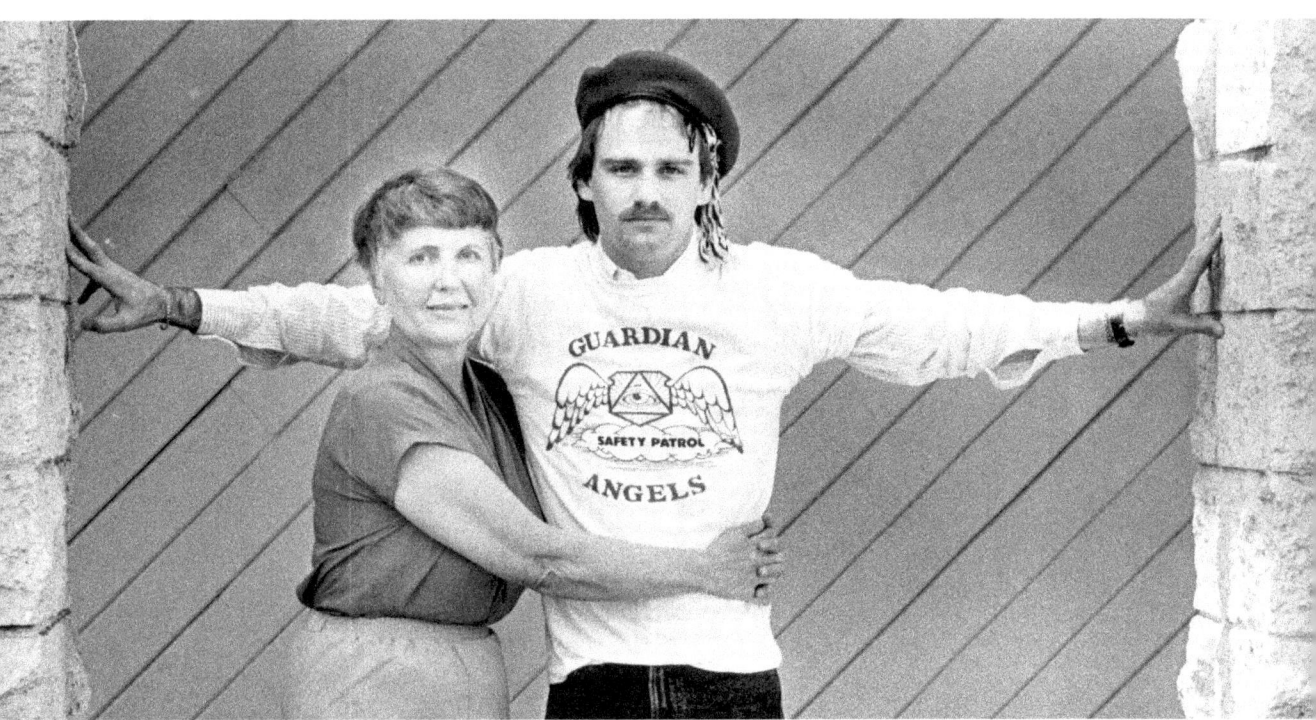

A group claiming to be Guardian Angels tasked themselves with a mission somewhere between vigilantism and an unlicensed security function. (James Ruebsamen/Herald Examiner Collection)

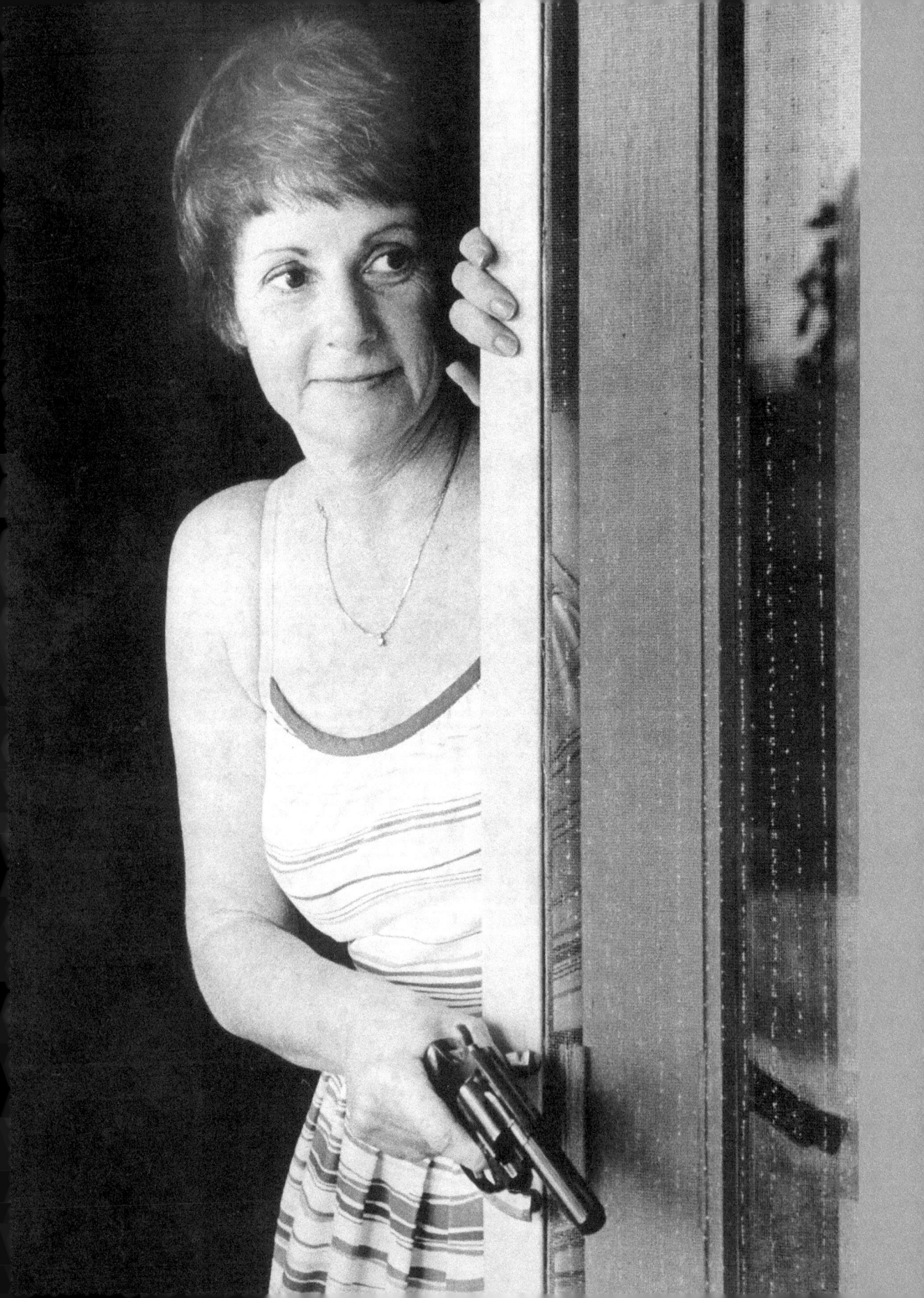

That's not to say unlocked doors and windows are tolerable, they're not. Opportunists still lurk among us, and somewhere another emaciated goth-like peeper is seeking more than just a chance to skulk the hallways of a still and darkened suburban home.

Could these actions further drive the concern, the paranoia and the other components of the social impact that came and went during a single calendar year? Doubtful, but to better understand what went on, examine the text and the images from the crimes and the courtroom once temporarily inhabited by a drugged and driven devotee of the devil who passed through popular culture as the Night Stalker.

Do all of this knowing that law enforcement effectively massed its personnel once the evidence and *modus operandi* demanded special attention. A task force led by the Los Angeles County Sheriff's Department was formed to identify and arrest the person or person(s) responsible for a series of crimes to include multiple sadistic murders. Homicide detectives from a number of jurisdictions that had experienced similar crimes were represented. Among those was the Glendale Police Department, where my father oversaw all investigations. LAPD contributed investigative and forensic resources to complement the thousands of us in and out of uniform that were busily creep-seeking. Juggling the many investigations and multiple agencies were two monstrously talented investigators from the Sheriff's Department—Gil Carrillo and Frank Salerno. Both pursued a single purpose, and did so passionately. They would identify and hold accountable someone they had never met for crimes nearly innumerable and positively unspeakable.

Calming public fears was likely an ancillary goal of those involved. Informing LA's denizens that the best and brightest homicide cops were on the case did not seem to resolve communal safety concerns, however. As was widely reported, gun sales increased sharply.

Friends I made later in life recalled the fears and actions stirred in them by the Night Stalker.

Linda Hada lived through the brutally hot Northridge summer with two young children sequestered in a small two-bedroom house sans air conditioning. Windows were closed, bedroom doors locked and for an added measure

Opposite: Persons unexpected took up arms.
(Anne Knudsen/Herald Examiner Collection)

SEEMINGLY THE GAME CHANGER
WAS THE NAME ISSUED TO THE
CREEP RESPONSIBLE FOR THE SERIES
OF MURDERS, THE NIGHT STALKER.
INTEREST WAS IMMEDIATELY ELEVATED,
AS WERE THE CONCERNS OF THE
GENERAL POPULACE.

of safety, the family dog camped at the foot of her bed, serving as a K-9 early warning system. She enjoyed no comfort in her own home, and not just because of the San Fernando Valley summer. Like so many women, she feared an attack. And in the midst of those fears, it happened on a different street in Northridge.

Sharon Padgett trusted that she wasn't paranoid. Still she wondered if her home was of a similar profile to those where attacks had occurred: suburban, close to a freeway and light in color. It was the murders of couples while in bed that truly impacted the Santa Clarita resident. Her husband was sent to purchase and install window locks, as well as locks for the bedroom doors. She next dispatched her husband to purchase a shotgun in order to defend against uninvited visitors in the darkness.

Even with these additional security measures in place, Sharon Padgett began eyeballing people in parked cars. It was all fear-driven. By her own admission she was truly scared. And not just by the crime spree. She was concerned about her own level of fear.

Calm didn't return to her home until the shotgun her husband Mike purchased was loaded and bedside. But there was still that worrisome edge that would remain until true calm was delivered by an ass-whoopin' crowd in East LA who latched onto Ramirez.

Elsewhere yard lights were installed along with fences, gates and virtually any real or perceived security measure. Dogs, as previously mentioned, were enlisted as safety aides more so than companions.

I was working LAPD's Hollywood Division, where I saw firsthand this killer's impact on LA. So, too, did I see it at home.

Most people make it through life without a connection to the most heinous crime, *murder*.

Like virtually all cops in Los Angeles, I didn't.

I saw all manner of dead.

Shot, stabbed, thrown from the roof of a parking structure, skull crushed with a television, beaten brutally and then killed by hypothermia delivered by cold water from a garden-hose jammed in a rectum.

I even captured killers fleeing murder scenes.

Hell, it was a tough time in Los Angeles. Murders numbered about a thousand per year, so there were plenty in that lethal lot to lock up.

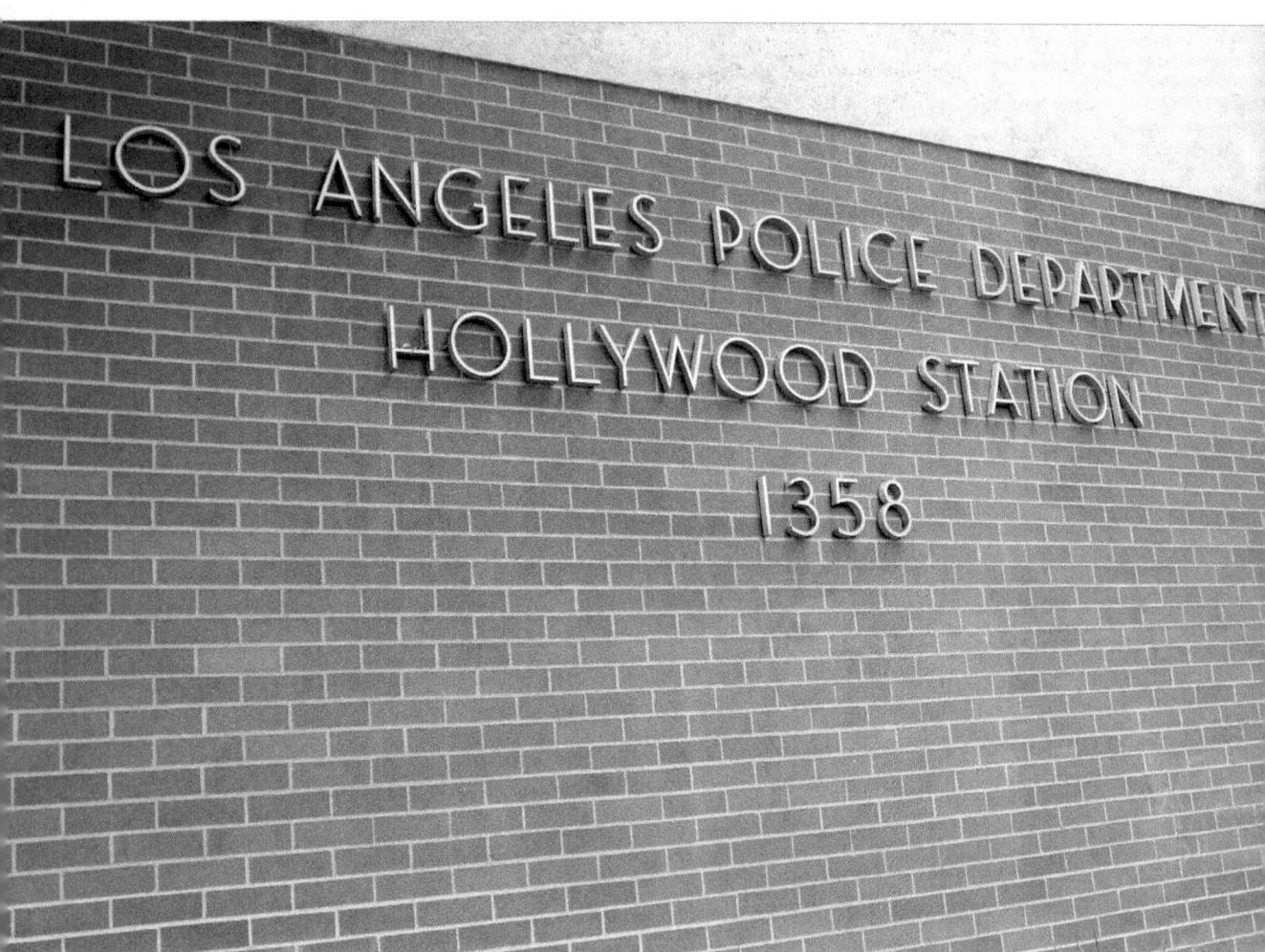

Hollywood Station. (Glynn Martin)

Hard to believe the difference a few miles makes. I grew up in Glendale, a suburb that kisses LA's borders in a bunch of different places. A major cemetery "lives" in both cities. Look for me there when the time comes. I was born blocks from there. The LAPD station I retired from is a grave stone's throw from the cemetery entrance. In my 58 years, I never strayed too far from sprawling Memorial Park. It's not that the rolling hills of Forest Lawn have been an anchor to my existence, nor is the massive graveyard my life's centerpiece either. A recurring theme, possibly. A constant? Nope, that would have to go to Glendale at large.

It's where my dad worked.

He was a cop, too.

We had about twelve years of overlap in our respective careers. These were different careers—vastly varied experiences served concurrently with a number of intersections.

The first notable crossroads arrived with an El Paso-raised drifter. Of course, we didn't know about the roots of this evil Texan during the mid-1980s, but his presence would become known in both of our police careers and well beyond. Ramirez brought an overdose of death to the county, early in my career.

Well before this series of murders stands one of the earliest recollections from my childhood. That would be the televised image of JFK, Jr. saluting at the funeral of his father. Presumably this was my first exposure to a murder, albeit on a black-and-white television set. There's a big gap between the Kennedy assassination and my next go 'round with the grim reaper. This one directly involved my Dad's police work and tangentially touched my existence as a USC freshman working in retail sales at a newly-minted mall—the Glendale Galleria.

The murderous punks, Angelo Buono and Kenneth Bianchi caught the singular *nom de meurtrier* "Hillside Strangler." Their rise to infamy preceded the common descriptor befitting the two—*serial killer*. Yes, that's singular, as the original case theories believed the killings were committed by a single, inhumane being. If serial killers is more appropriate, then so be it. They were murderous, unholy low lifes deserving of far more indecent descriptors.

Lives claimed, lives ruined, lives terrorized . . . not the way it was supposed to be in Glendale. It was one of the nation's safest big cities in the seventies.

That's why we lived there. That's why murder hadn't intruded on the lives of my family, my neighbors and my school chums. They're still my friends, some forty-plus years later. Sure, we went off to different colleges, but we managed to stay in contact through the course of our studies, our work and our family-raising.

In the months following our graduation from Crescenta Valley High School, my connection to murder resumed. It was 14 years since that televised hand salute to JFK. A dead teen was found in the parkway near the home of a fellow CV alum. The corpse was found in the unincorporated area of La Crescenta, so Glendale Police Lt. Glynn Martin wasn't involved. At least not in an official capacity.

We were living a couple of miles from the scene, which was closer to my junior high school than to CVHS or to our house. A lot of kids I grew up with

City of Glendale Police Department. (Gordon Dean/Valley Times Collection)

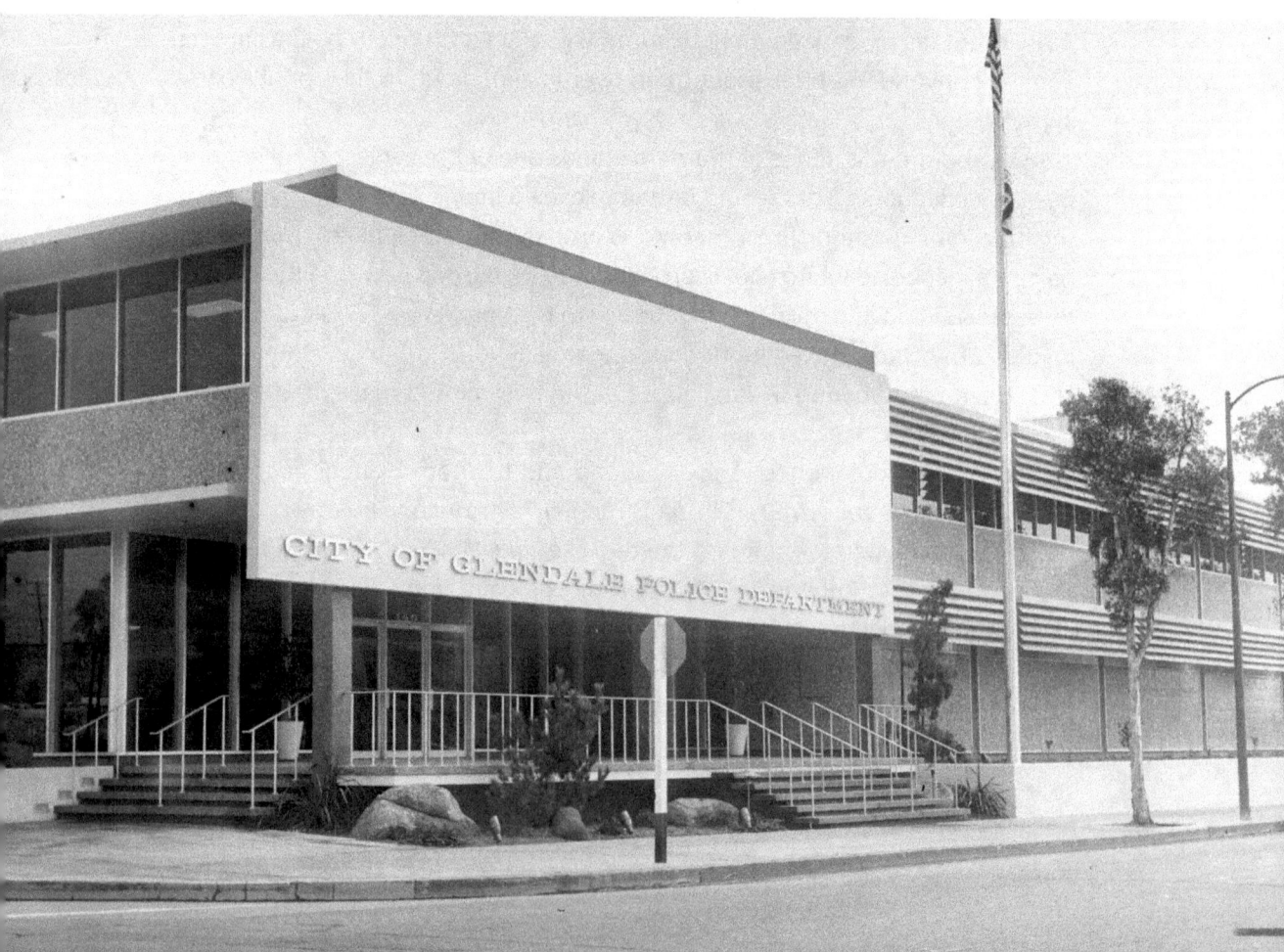

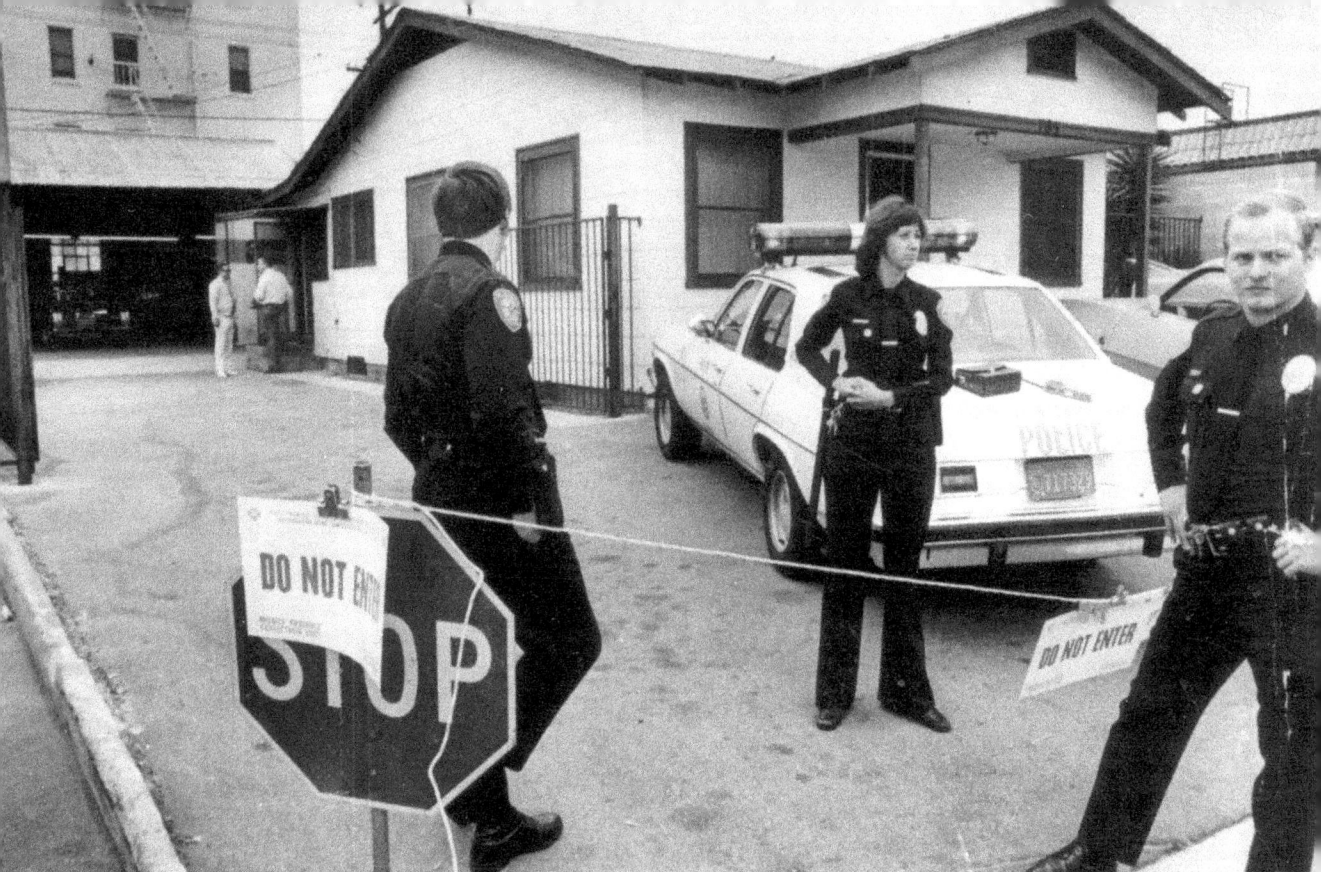

Glendale Police search for evidence at the home and upholstery shop of one of the Hillside Stranglers, Angelo Buono. (Mike Sergieff/Herald Examiner Collection)

lived nearby; one of my lifelong friends lived just 3 or 4 blocks from there. He was at UCLA, and might well have been hosting a blender party in his dorm room. It was November 1, 1977.

Five days later, the body of another female murder victim was found near a Glendale country club. Glendale PD joined the investigation. As more murdered females were found, a task force was formed. Homicide detectives from the much larger law enforcement agencies—the LA Police Department and LA Sheriff's Department—were joined by Glendale. It was likely the first time a task-force approach to LA murders had been used since Special Unit Senator concluded its work on the Robert Kennedy assassination.

Glendale feared for itself. Brutally murdered women weren't what the "Jewel City" was known for. Even though it was the third largest city in the expanse that is LA County, it suffered none of the maladies known elsewhere in the county. This was a safe place with a historically low crime rate and a homicide rate that was virtually nil.

Talk of the murders dominated conversations that were otherwise Mayberry-like. Doors were bolted and windows locked. If a city of more than 100,000 could batten its hatches, Glendale silently and systematically did so. Part of that ran through Glendale's popular indoor shopping area, where I was selling dungarees with a group of mostly teenaged high school and college kids. When the mall closed at 9 pm, the female employees were escorted to their cars by the males from our store. The garrulous co-ed talk expected of this group took on a tone of morbidity mixed with insecurity.

Dad went about his work without much comment. He was a couple of ranks above the detectives working the Hillside Strangler case. Still, he had responsibility as their supervisor, and he lived in the city with his wife and teenage boys. When the case broke, I recognized the places on the news footage. The upholstery shop tied to one of the killers was across the street from the batting cages frequented by all of us who played youth baseball. The shop was also just a few blocks from my job at the Glendale Galleria, and Dad's office at GPD.

In terms of our family history, this seemed to be serial killer prelude.

The next multiple murderer to operate in Glendale saw both Glynn Martins involved in very different ways. I was a three-year LA cop assigned to Hollywood station. Dad was the Commanding Officer of Glendale's Detective Bureau. By this time, in 1985, he'd been in the business for 27 years. I had just moved out of the condo he was renting to me and began my first and only stint outside of my childhood environs. I was living with a police academy classmate in a house in Walnut that we bought together. He, too, was assigned to the special problems unit in Hollywood. Our detail was the replacement for LAPD's old felony cars. Some days we worked in uniform, others in plainclothes, but always in an unmarked police car, and always at night. Largely we were charged with interdicting street felonies like car thefts, auto and residential burglaries, and street robberies. We also did a tour making hand-to-hand drug purchases from the scores of street dealers that had become Hollywood's undesirables.

This was down in the gutter police work. Nearly all of us with this assignment played on the station football team. At 6'0" and 200 pounds, I was physically in the middle of the pack. My partners were large men committed to doing dangerous work at a dangerous time.

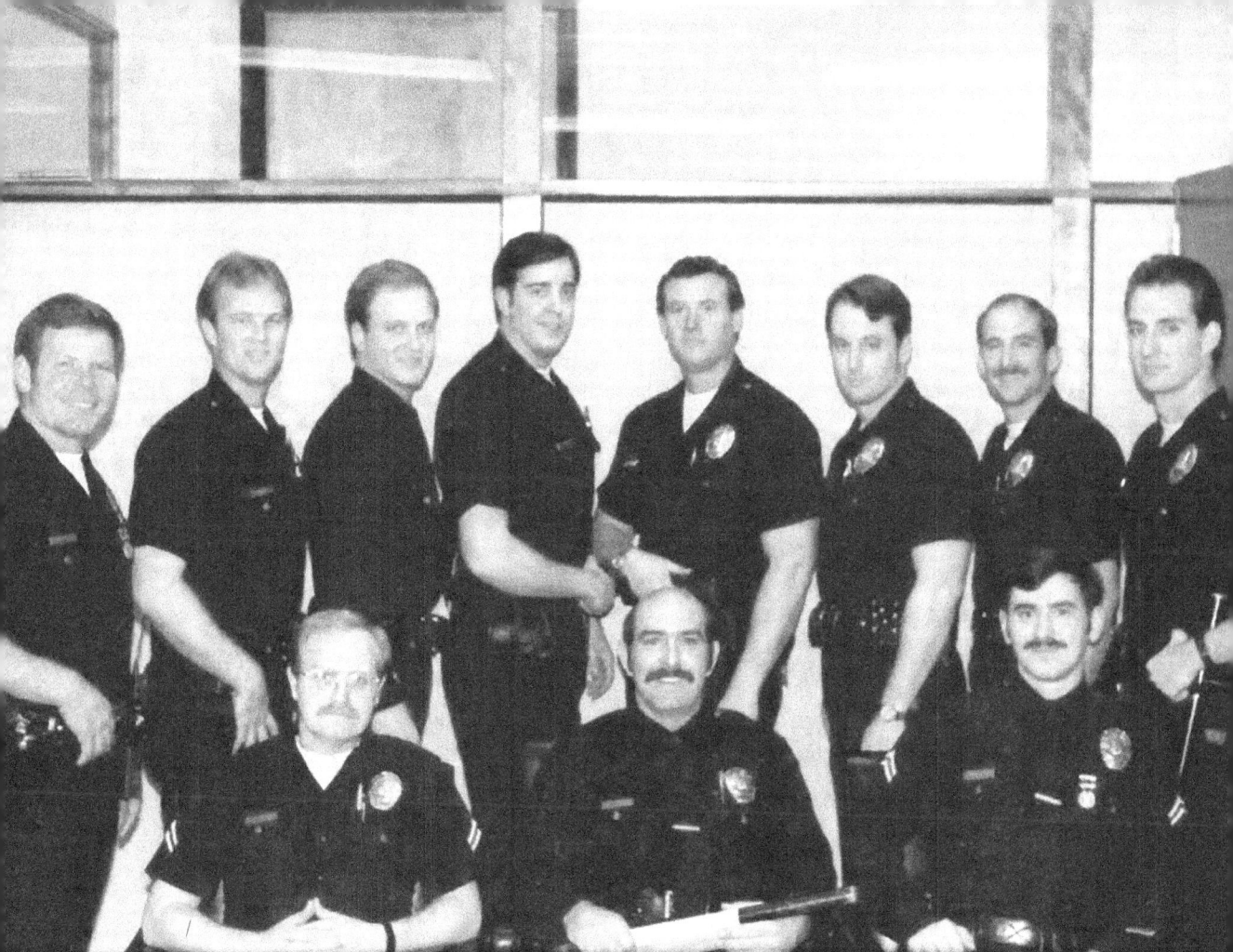

The Special Problems Unit of LAPD's Hollywood Division, 1985. Standing, L to R: Sgt. Bob Good, Jim Hays, Mark Strohmeier, Bob Kraus, Wally Carr, Glynn Martin, Mike Fesperman, Jim Pagliotti. Seated, L to R: Fred Davis, Butch Moore, Steve Biczo. (Author's collection)

All of us worked to pretty up Tinseltown prior to the 1984 Olympics. We all held our breath for those couple of weeks. Virtually all of us were assigned to Olympic venues, then we returned to our Hollywood roles so we could re-apply lipstick to the pig.

As expected, the post-Olympic exhale saw many of the suppressed criminal influences retrench and prosper. Hollywood Vice was still making thousands of arrests. Streetwalking prostitution wasn't just comprised of unbathed women in shabby dresses. Working the special problems detail, in this part of LA, at this time in history, was the greatest on-the-job training that any cop could ever want. Mostly we were a very tight-knit group. We worked hard and we played hard. The post-shift get-togethers were had at local bars and other locales known to us with nicknames each had earned, like an as-yet unnamed stretch of dirt off Barham that is now a Warner Bros. parking lot.

When word of another serial killer came our way, our work, and that of all of us in Hollywood, initially remained the same. It was business as usual, if there ever was such a thing when patrolling Hollyweird. Then came the series of murder victims. Seemingly the game changer was the name issued by the *Herald Examiner* newspaper to the creep responsible for the series of murders—Night Stalker. Interest was immediately elevated, as were the concerns of the general populace. Sightings of the Night Stalker were phoned in to dispatch. Police cars responded. It was Hillside Strangler redux. Those nasty events had just cleared from residents' memories. The fear factor reset—immediately—and nearly immediately ratcheted up.

So did the police response. In a time when LAPD was very judicious in the use of lights and sirens, Night Stalker sightings were dispatched Code-3. People on the street stopped cops and inquired about their safety. A police sketch artist created a color composite that went out to all of us. We had something to show the inquiring public, and something to tell them—keep your doors and windows closed at night. Sure it was the heat of an LA summer. Better to sweat uncomfortably than to bleed fatally.

The lockdown advice was shared far and wide. We talked to our friends and families about it. Late one evening my LAPD partner and I decided to check on a longtime friend, who lived in an apartment bordering Hollywood. During the Hillside Strangler ordeal she was a co-worker who I had escorted to her car. I attended USC with her and her sister, both of whom remain good friends today. En route to her place, my partner and I cruised a series of alleys diligently checking darkened carports and ensuring gates to apartment complexes were tightly closed and windows completely shut.

As we passed the assigned carport, her car was parked in its designated space. We swung the unmarked car around to the front of the building and parked. It was but a few steps to the only door of the ground floor apartment. It was some time after a dark midnight.

We knocked. No answer. We knocked again, still no answer.

A twist of the doorknob revealed an empty apartment. Both of us saw it. Instinctually, we drew our handguns and flashlights and entered the abandoned rooms. No one living here, and of odd importance, no one dead here, either. A strange finding, but a conclusion that ranked well above what could have been. Better to find empty closets than a butchered body. We stepped out into the courtyard before heading to the manager's unit.

She had moved upstairs, we were told, and came to her new front door lickety-split. I was awash in the type of relief that often generates a scolding. I tempered my remarks and accepted her gratitude for our continuing concern. She cared that we cared. She knew the risk and was doing what she could.

It was a different story in the household of Captain Martin. Mom was spooked and Dad was honoring his commitment to case confidentiality. Most of my Hollywood duties kept me at work deep into the night, if not early into the morning. Post- shift activities usually meant I slept for most of the day before heading back to LAPD digs on Wilcox. When I really needed to sleep, I unplugged the telephone, or simply doused the ringer.

But not every day was a phone-free day. With two cops in the Walnut house, both of whom were frequently on call for court, the phone was usually plugged in. Had it not been, Mom may well have driven out to Walnut to question me about the goings-on in her own home.

"Your Dad has a gun in the house!" It came at me while I was still mentally cursing the telephone ringer.

For much of his career, there were two young boys growing up in Dad's home. Curious youngsters and their friends coursed through Captain Martin's modest Sparr Heights residence with great regularity. It was a good place not to have a gun, even if you were a cop.

"OK," was about all I could muster as I emerged from my beer-assisted, daytime slumber.

"You know your father never keeps a gun in the house."

"Yeah, I know Mom, there's another serial killer out there, he just killed the old couple in Glendale. Dad must have seen something that bothered him."

"Well, he didn't say anything to me about it."

He rarely did, I knew that, and so did she.

"Mom, his picture was in the *LA Times.*"

"That was a press conference," she offered and then continued, 'It wasn't so much a press conference as a conversation with neighbors about the murders of their friends."

"There just aren't many double murders in Glendale, that's why you live there, Mom."

"Why didn't your father say something?"

"I think the *Times* photo covered that, Mom. Keep your doors and windows closed, I'm going back to bed 'cuz I gotta work tonight. Bye Mom."

I had to terminate the conversation. I had made it through without divulging the change that came to my own room in the Walnut house.

One of my shotguns had a new home, sandwiched between the box spring and the mattress. It complemented the .38 under my pillow. Neither got used on the Night Stalker, but the shotgun was pressed into service, albeit briefly.

It must have been a day off because both my roommate and I were home. It was well into the wee hours of the morning and I was in a deep sleep. So deep that it wasn't the opening of one of my windows from the outside that startled me, it was the warm breeze that was invading my bedroom.

I saw the window shades moving.

I pulled the shotgun from its hiding place and shouldered the weapon. No need to chamber a round, or remove the safety. I knew if the riot gun was needed, there wasn't time for the extraneous. No one was entering, so I quietly moved into my doorway to reduce the amount of body exposure. If someone was going to take a shot, there just wasn't much of me presented. The tense seconds halted when I noticed a black high heel and the feminine form of a lower leg stepping into the room. The rest of her pushed the shade away with a liquored-up giggle.

I lowered the shotgun upon realizing it was a suitor looking for the other cop, friend and partner with whom I resided in that view home in Walnut.

I stepped back into the room, concealing the shotgun behind my right leg. I directed her to the bedroom she was truly seeking, closed my door, stowed the shotgun and pondered the tragedy that was almost visited on an unwitting twenty-something whose name I barely knew.

So, this is the type of social impact that cases like the Night Stalker, Hillside Strangler, Manson and others brought to many restful and unsuspecting communities. While this will never compare to the losses suffered by the victims' families, these ancillary consequences typically don't receive the attention they are due.

An entire region—millions of people—were terrified, left sleepless and took on behaviors outside their norm. Explanations and safety advisories delivered by a high-ranking cop on a crowded cul-de-sac likely did little to assuage the fears of the law-abiding and fearful. Dad took a gun home, perhaps for the first time in his 27-year police career. He had witnessed death before, but not this manner of death. The swipes of a machete delivered blood in high volume.

I had a gauge for Dad's behavior, and like it or not, so did Mom. The taciturn Chief of Detectives for their city saw murderous ugliness inflicted on a couple living not far from his front door. It was a brand of murder uncommon to these parts, a threat to everyone. Precautions needed to be taken, whether popular with Mom or not. This tidbit might have been all that needed to be said by Captain Martin at the community meeting. Had the crowd realized how unusual this was for my Dad, little else would need to be said. "Protect yourselves at all costs" isn't something a ranking cop can tell people. There was no better messenger than his own actions.

He was at the murder scene on July 20, 1985. Detective Jon Perkins was charged with the investigation. Dad was in charge of all of Glendale's detectives and he reported directly to the Chief of Police. All of the reports from this horrific day, and all of the gruesome crime scene photos came across Dad's desk. He had the inside scoop on the murders of the Kneidings. He wasn't sharing it. Not with Mom and not with me.

The deadly reality was both husband and wife were nearly decapitated. The length and depth of the throat lacerations left precious little flesh connecting their heads to their torsos. The bodies were laid across each other nearly gaping wound to gaping wound. The oft-used murder descriptor, "senseless," definitely applied to what went on in a home often visited by the grown children and grandchildren of the victims.

Mom was worried that it could have been her house. Dad must have been, too; he was carrying a gun. Not something typically found beneath his Brooks Brothers suit coat.

It was one of those strange ways that murder touched lives: those of my parents.

For me it didn't stop there.

I'm still advocating for the family of a murder victim.

He was killed the second summer after the Night Stalker was captured.

He lived down the hall from me.
In an adjoining bedroom.
Of the view home in Walnut.
That was once visited by the twenty-something in black high heels.

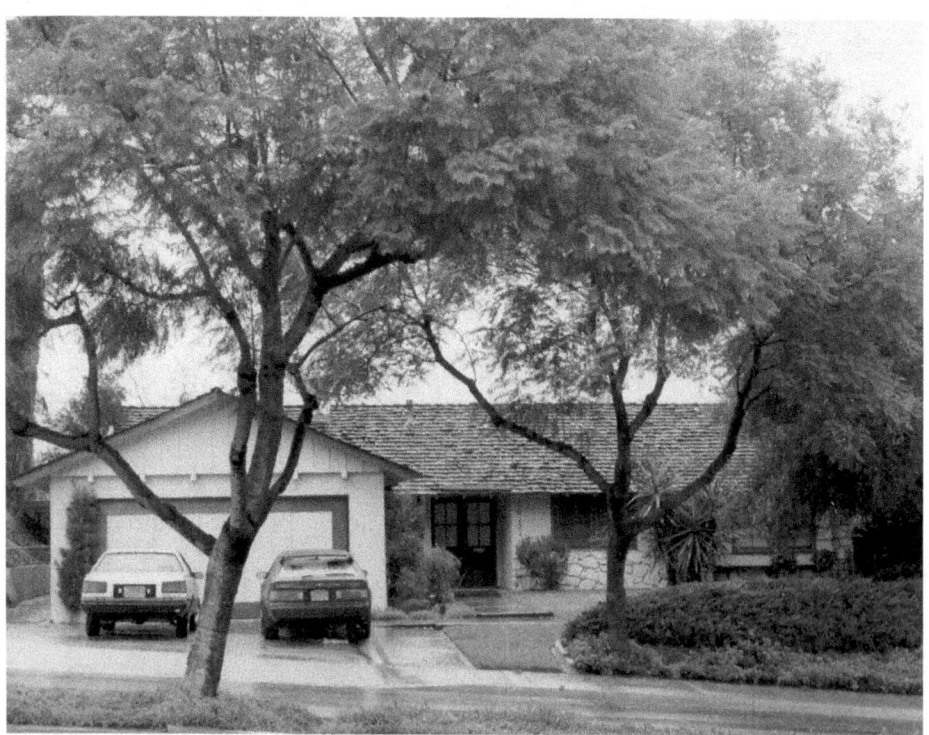

The Walnut house. (Author's collection)

THE BOTTOM LINE WAS PRETTY SIMPLE. ALL COPS WERE ON ALERT AND A SPECIAL TASK FORCE, LED BY FRANK SALERNO AND GIL CARRILLO, WAS WORKING DILIGENTLY TO COORDINATE MULTIPLE INVESTIGATIONS AND CAPTURE A SERIAL KILLER OR KILLERS.

IN THE TIME OF THE NIGHT STALKER

By Glen Creason

I should have been able to fall asleep standing up but instead I was lying awake, in a sweat with a crease between my eyes that you could have fitted a quarter in with ease. It was a typically warm August in 1985 and I had spent the last week packing my entire life into cardboard boxes and moving literally two domiciles across LA to my "dream house" in Los Feliz. Life was almost perfect in a sociological, statistical way. I had a great job, a pretty young wife and an adorable daughter entering toddlerhood sleeping just down the hall. We even had a white dog and a black cat in the lush new pad that was so nice when my old pals came over they asked, "So...when are your parents coming home?"

It was our second night in the new home and the master bedroom seemed as big as the Grand Canyon, especially compared to the submarine-like dimensions of my bachelor pad of a couple of years prior. Ironically the whole family thing started when I impressed a cute researcher from Fox Television with my encyclopedic knowledge of serial killers and my love of the Dodgers. The bard said "love reasons without reason" and we got married five months later. Now, two years later with the help of the deep pockets of my beloved father-in-law, we were moving into Los Feliz where our neighbors were on TV or taught the Classics at local universities. Most of my furniture was from Value Village in Lynwood and what it lacked in modern style it made up for in 1950s weight. Even in the bloom of youth the physical demands of moving the belongings of two packrats was Homeric, ending with the kind of fatigue you get when your actual young bones ache. It was a happy tired since we made the journey excited about a new life in a neighborhood famous for happy families.

We looked forward to watching our favorite TV show *Cheers* in our spacious front room where a deluxe Sony Trinitron TV with a whopping 27-inch screen awaited to envelope us in adventure while actual forced air would cool the entire house when activated. Technology seemed limitless, evidenced by the new two-deck $400 cassette dubbing machine we had purchased and an electric portable typewriter that I was going to write my blockbuster novel on soon. I had spent the week before the move bouncing back and forth between my job at Central Library as a reference librarian in the History Department and transporting essentials to the Dream House. This included boxes and boxes of vinyl records, cinderblock bookcases, bales of *Rolling Stone* hard copy magazines and other hernia-inducing weighty objects, including my wife's impressive shoe collection. I even hastily hung pictures on the wall before our phone lines were connected to make it as homey as our "dump house" was way across town. We were setting sail on the *Love Boat* and I never noticed those lifesavers emblazoned with *S.S. Titanic* scattered on the deck. As Paul Harvey used to say, we were "on our way to forever together."

In the real world the news had been filled with terrible stories about a sadistic serial killer loose in Southern California and since his m.o. involved the murder of men and rape and murder of their spouses, our Dream House bedroom window at waist high level from the back patio troubled me greatly. This monster had recently been given the title the "Night Stalker" after the equally chilling "Walk-in Killer." The entire city was on edge since there seemed to be no rhyme or reason to his horrendous crime spree which ranged from Glassell Park to Glendale, Burbank, the San Gabriel Valley and even Pomona. No one seemed to know where he would strike next and doors and windows were locked shut all across the basin despite the heat of summer turning bedrooms into saunas.

The Monday after we moved, Channel 2 featured a terrifying special program on the now connected murders that were terrifying LA and baffling the police. It really was like a classic horror film—but for real— and we were the characters waiting for the worst. President Reagan's tax plan, unrest in South Africa, and Hurricane Elena faded before the hysteria of a sadistic killer on the loose. Every news stand blared headlines about the Night Stalker and police sketches portrayed a scruffy everyman who could be anyone, anywhere. There was no place to hide and the victims were just like me and my wife. Even hippy radio like KPFK joined in the hunt for the killer who was exceptionally vicious, torturing mercilessly before killing.

California had more than its share of monsters with the Tool Box Killers, Randy Kraft, the Zodiac Killer, the Hillside Strangler, the Freeway Killer, Juan Corona, Edmund Kemper and even Charles Manson; but this one was stalking and killing close to home. Most of the murders were within an hour's drive from our new neighborhood. Everyone in LA was locking up tight and looking over their shoulders, including my parents, siblings, friends and workmates. On our second night in our hermetically-sealed new house right in the heart of this paranoia one of the old framed photos I had tacked on the wall of the Dream House gave way to gravity and crashed to the floor in the wee hours of the morning. After levitating in bed I realized I was the man of the big house and to protect my wife and daughter I had to investigate while the dog barked furiously at the picture frame in the next room. We even turned off the A/C because it masked sounds in the house which also made the bedroom heat up like an oven. I sat up fretting and wishing with an entire city that the cops would catch this depraved monster who was on the prowl. Thus, my insomnia was based on real fear. It got worse from there.

In the mid-1980s the reference desks at the old library in downtown were busy enough to work up a tennis match style sweat and you dealt with many strange characters from off the mean streets of downtown. None of us behind the desks thought much about their reasons for asking the weird questions we would hear daily. Some of it was funny and absurd but there were moments that made the hair rise up on the back of your neck. One man in particular that myself and my boss Frank helped one hot afternoon during this nervous time was creepy enough to cut through the masses of strange folks. He was scruffy looking, with yellowing teeth and dead eyes that made you feel more than uneasy. He wanted books on horoscopes and torture, which luckily were in another department, the next room over from History. He was wearing a black dirty T-shirt with Jack Daniels printed on the chest and he smelled bad, but many do in the unwashed world of downtown. We sent him off to the Social Science Department where his books might be on the shelves and he did not return, which was fine with us.

Truthfully, feeling trouble radiating off some patrons was not unusual since thousands of mental patients had been dumped onto the big urban centers in an attempt to end the warehousing of the mentally ill in institutions so the numbers and severity of disturbed patrons was steadily increasing. One more creepy guy with the aura of a growling dog did not cause me to think twice about him. However, a couple of mornings later, I opened the *Herald-Examiner* newspaper while having breakfast with my colleagues at the Yorkshire Grill to see that guy's mugshot staring at me. Richard Ramirez was his name and he was living at the Cecil Hotel over near Sixth and Main, just five blocks away. I had looked into the evil eyes of the Night Stalker just days before and now my body temperature just sort of lowered several degrees. He had killed fourteen innocent people and ruined the lives of other victims without having a grain of regret.

One of the residual effects of having a baby in the house and witnessing the innocence of a precious part of yourself was that I no longer read any true crime books. After such a life-affirming event, I no longer wished to think about pure evil or the reasons why people mistreat each other so viciously. My pondering of the mind of sociopaths who murder and rape without remorse was now pushed out of my mind. Like most normal people, like everyone I know, we can watch a guy get blown to pieces on a movie screen or witness horrendous stuff on TV but if a fight breaks out in the stands at a sporting event it turns our stomachs.

Real violence is repulsive and it was truly justice when the following day some plain neighborhood folks in Boyle Heights caught this Night Stalker rat as he scrambled to escape, and righteously beat him within an inch of his sorry life. The same regular citizens whom he had terrorized cut him down to size and sent him off to a jail cell where he rotted for 28 years until cancer ended his life. Ramirez sat in a jail cell at last and we could open the windows, exhale and jump back into the good life. The *Love Boat* and my life was ready to set sail, at least for six months when an iceberg known as the Central Library fire was waiting in the deep water.

NIGHT STALKER TIMELINE

Once the similarities in murders and attendant evidence were linked, a multi-jurisdiction task force was formed. Many crimes occurred in the City of Los Angeles, but still more occurred in areas served by the Sheriff. Investigators from the Sheriff's homicide bureau took charge. The collaborative effort included law enforcement agencies who believed Ramirez had capered in their city.

JUNE 28, 1984

At the time of Los Angeles resident Jennie Vincow's 1984 murder, there wasn't a hint of the greater problem. Ramirez's previous crime of magnitude was committed in San Francisco and no linkage to the Los Angeles killing had been made.

MARCH 17, 1985

Nearly a year passed when Ramirez debuted his late-night variety show of violent felonies. It was of all days, St. Patrick 's Day 1985, when Ramirez shot three innocents, killing two of them.

Maria Hernandez was shot by Richard Ramirez at the front door to the condominium she shared with Dayle Okazaki. Hernandez instinctually raised her hand in defense of Ramirez's attempt to shoot her in the head. Hernandez fell to the floor briefly and then fled, only to encounter Ramirez again outside of the building.

During the interceding moments, Ramirez shot and killed Okazaki inside the condo.

Hernandez later identified Ramirez during court proceedings.

After fleeing the attacks on Hernandez and Okazaki, Ramirez found Tsai Lan "Veronica" Yu of Monterey Park seated in her car. Ramirez dragged the 30-year-old woman from her car and fatally shot her multiple times.

The attacks of these women rightly elevated media interest. The news coverage concurrently spurred attention to personal safety and served to increase fear in the region. Sadly, this was but the beginning of a crime epidemic that would scare scores of southlanders before, during and after the summer of 1985.

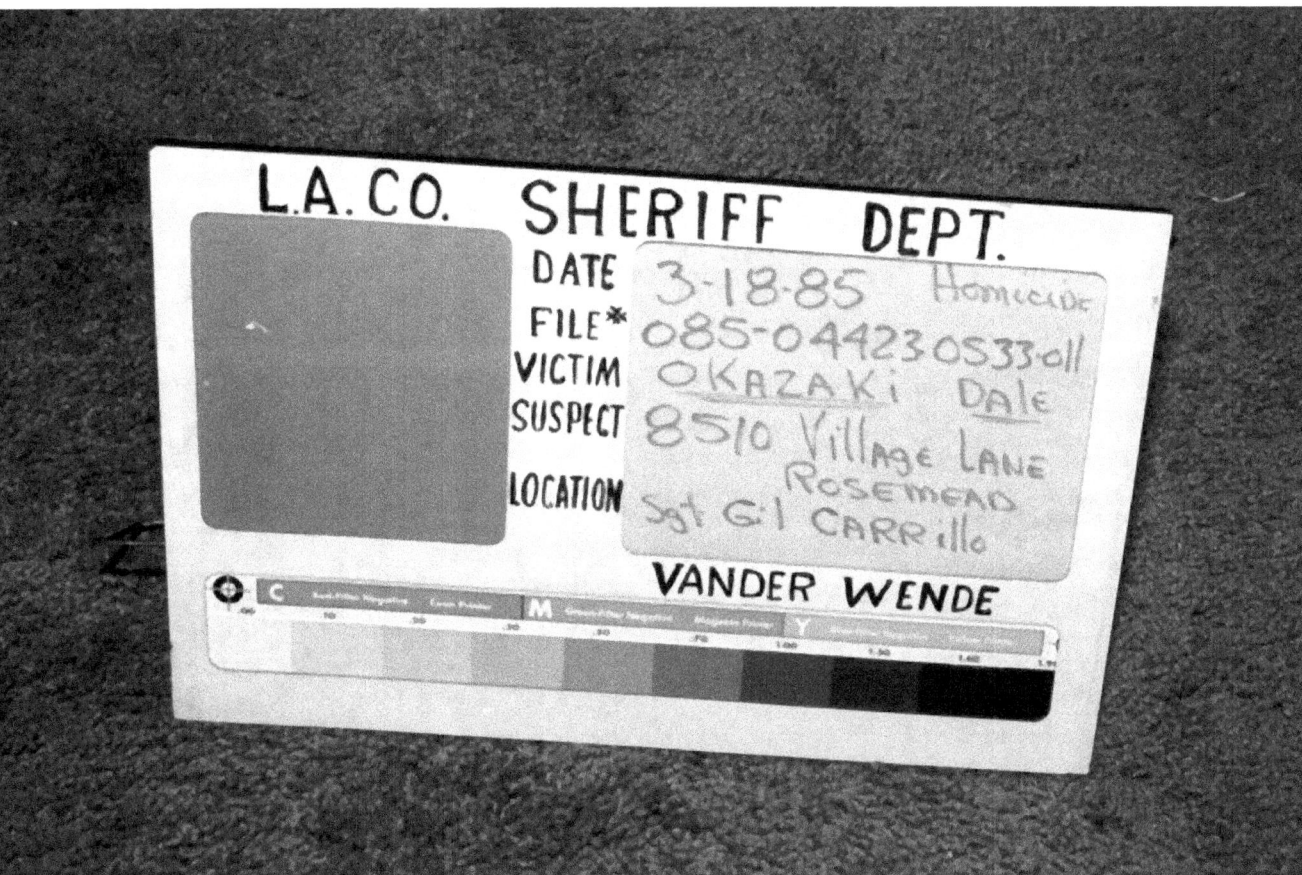

Sheriff's Detective Sergeant Gil Carrillo was called to investigate the brutal attack of Maria Hernandez and Dayle Okazaki at their Rosemead condominium. (Los Angeles Sheriff's Department)

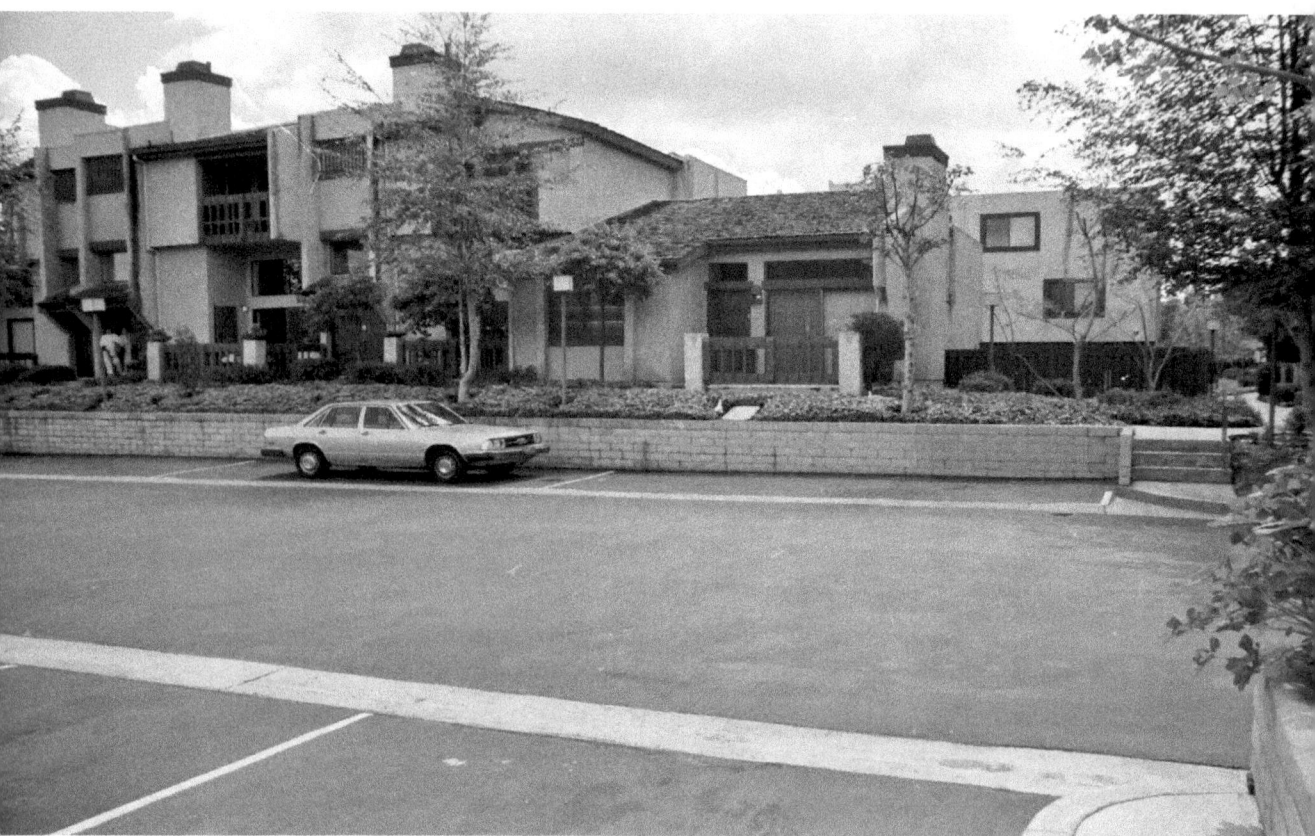

Rosemead was an otherwise quiet suburb of Los Angeles located in the center of the San Gabriel Valley. Dayle Okazaki and Maria Hernandez resided in this condominium complex in the summer of 1985. (Los Angeles Sheriff's Department)

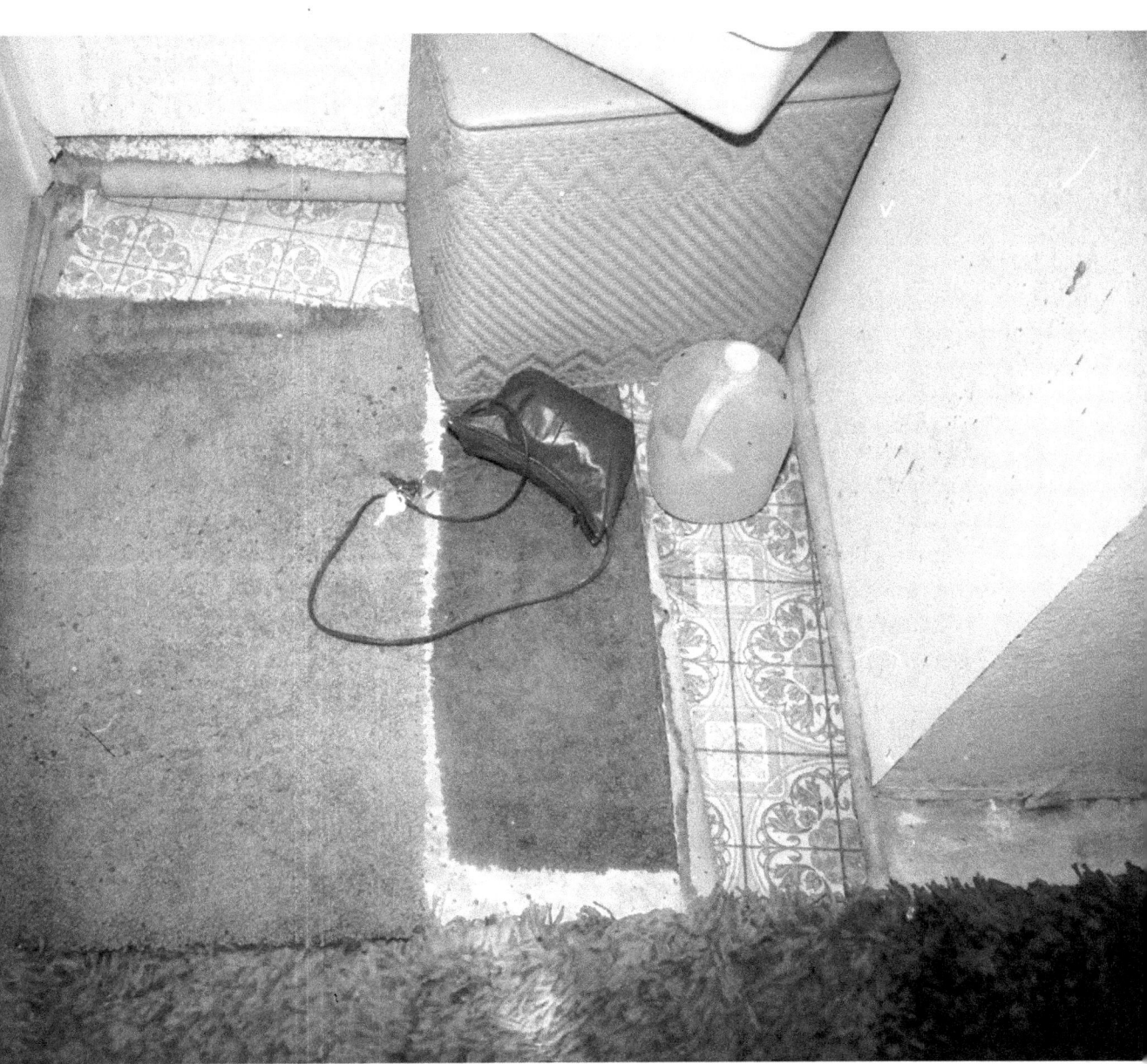

Maria Hernandez's car keys and purse as they were discovered immediately following the attack. (Los Angeles Sheriff's Department)

MARCH 27, 1985

Vincent Zazzara's lifeless body was found on a sofa inside his Whittier home. A business associate made the horrific discovery the morning after a visit to Zazzara's home where he found the front door ajar. After finding the door in the same condition the following morning, entry into the home and discovery of Zazzara was made. The Sheriff's department was notified. Their search revealed that Zazzara's wife had also been murdered and mutilated.

Order for forensic investigation at the Zazzara residence. (Los Angeles Sheriff's Department)

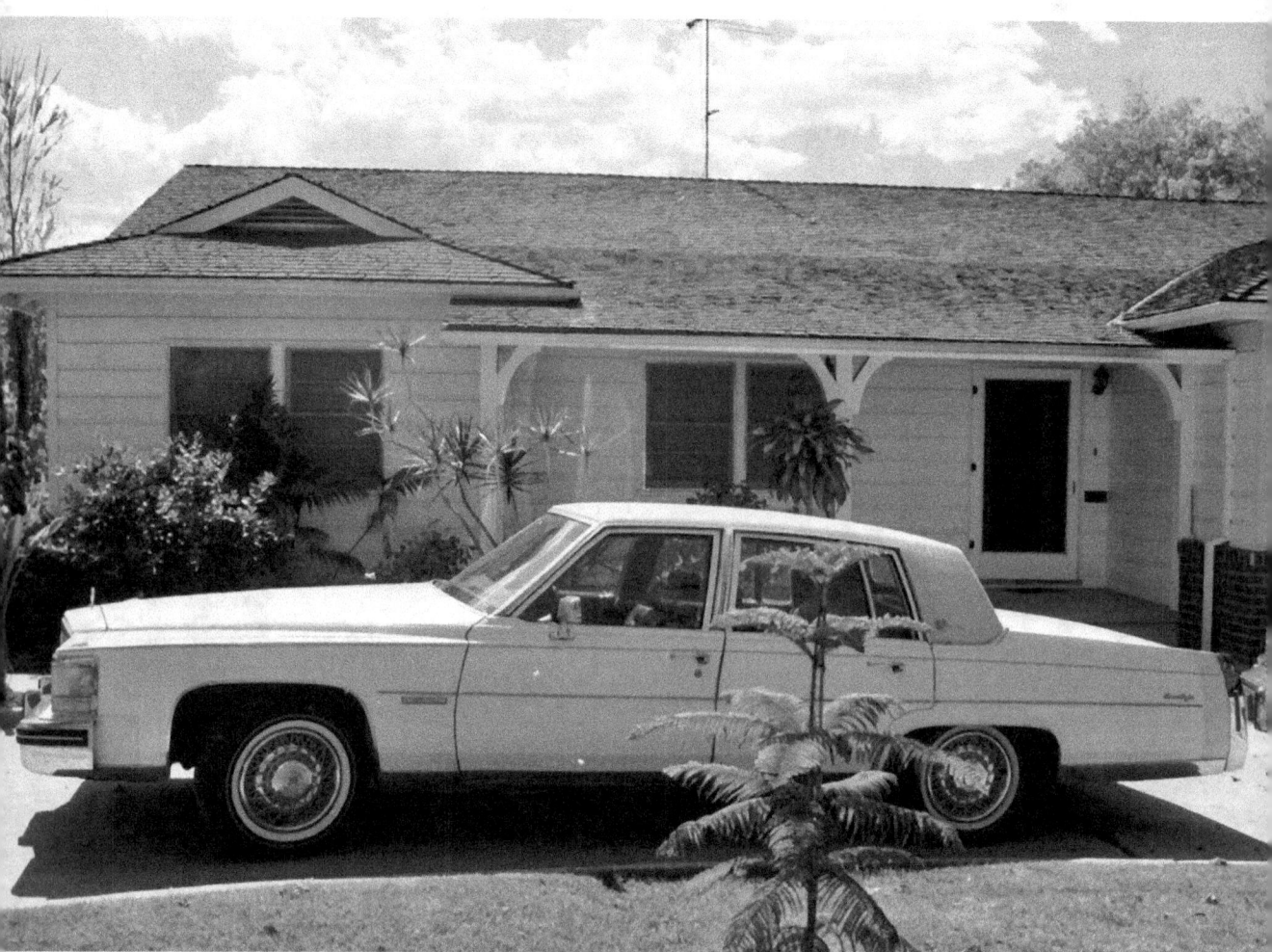

The Zazzara home, located in yet another quiet Los Angeles suburb, the
city of Whittier. (Los Angeles Sheriff's Department)

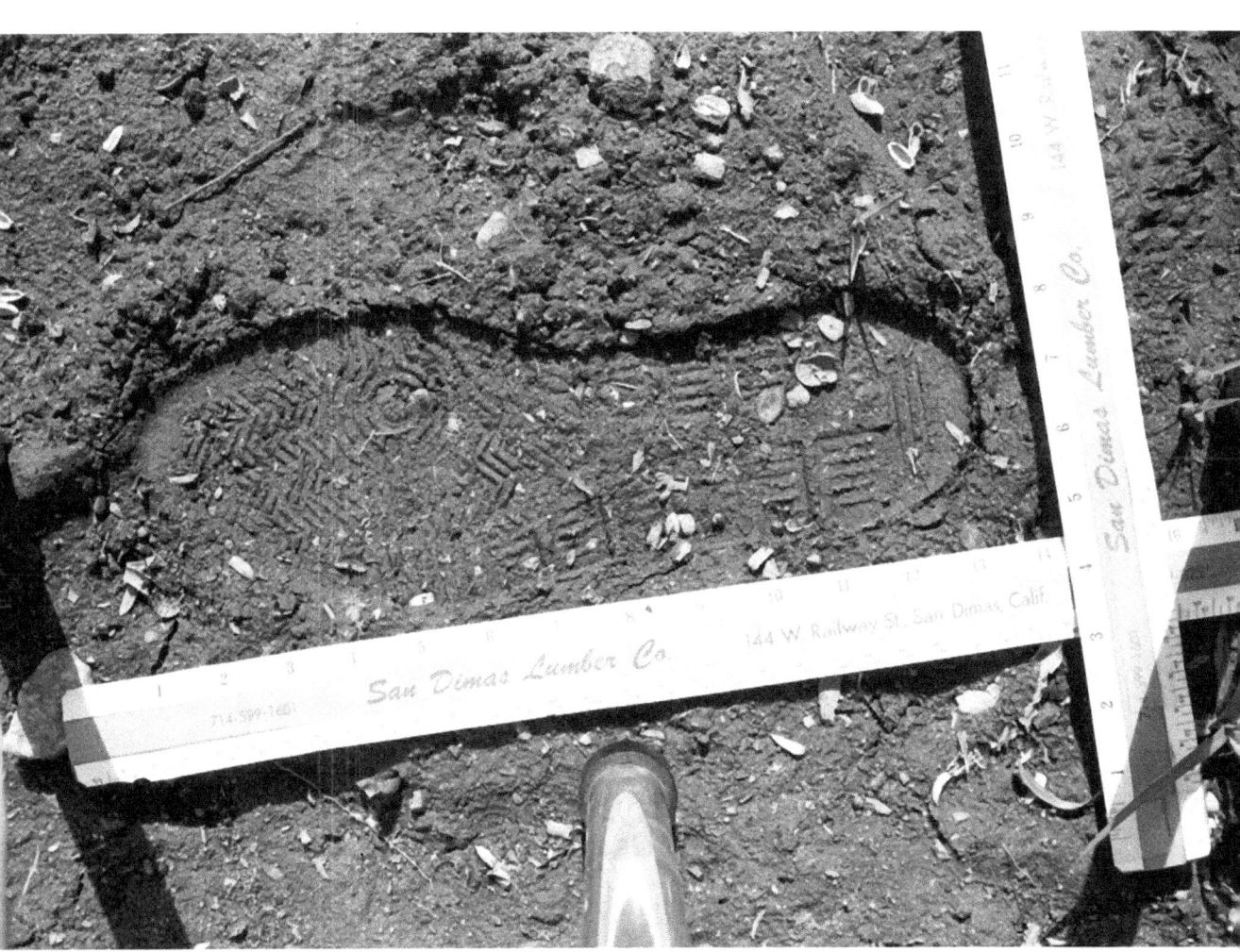

A shoeprint was found during the investigation of the Zazzara case.
(Los Angeles Sheriff's Department)

MAY 14, 1985

Six weeks would pass before more crimes were successfully ascribed to Ramirez. Lillian and Bill Doi were attacked in their Monterey Park home on May 14, 1985. Mr. Doi did not survive.

Believing he had done the devil's work, the killer scrawled a red pentagram (the sign of Satan) using red lipstick found in the home. A pentagram was also drawn on the leg of one of the victims.

For investigators, the circled star opened up another avenue of investigation. An examination of the local satanic scene might give context to the killings, or better yet, provide the identity of the killer.

For the general public, the revelation of satanic influence meant more and greater worries. The fact that elderly women were victimized frighteningly stirred women of all ages.

MAY 29, 1985

In Monrovia, 83-year-old Mabel "Ma" Bell resided with her disabled sister, 81-year-old Florence Lang. They lived nearly a half mile from their nearest neighbor. They were beaten, and it was four days before they were found. Bell died July 15.

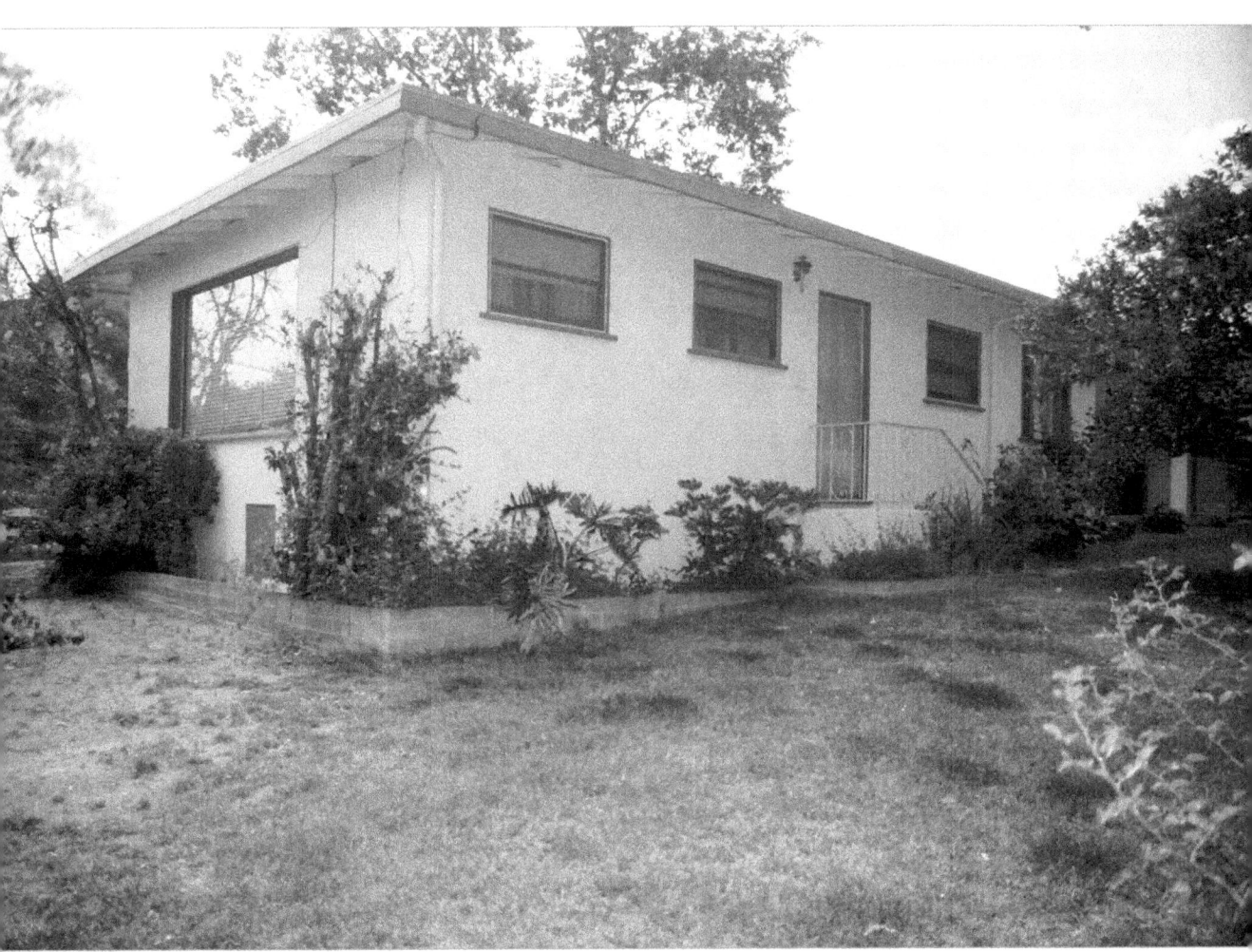

**The Monrovia home where Mabel "Ma" Bell and her disabled sister
Florence Lang lived. (Los Angeles Sheriff's Department)**

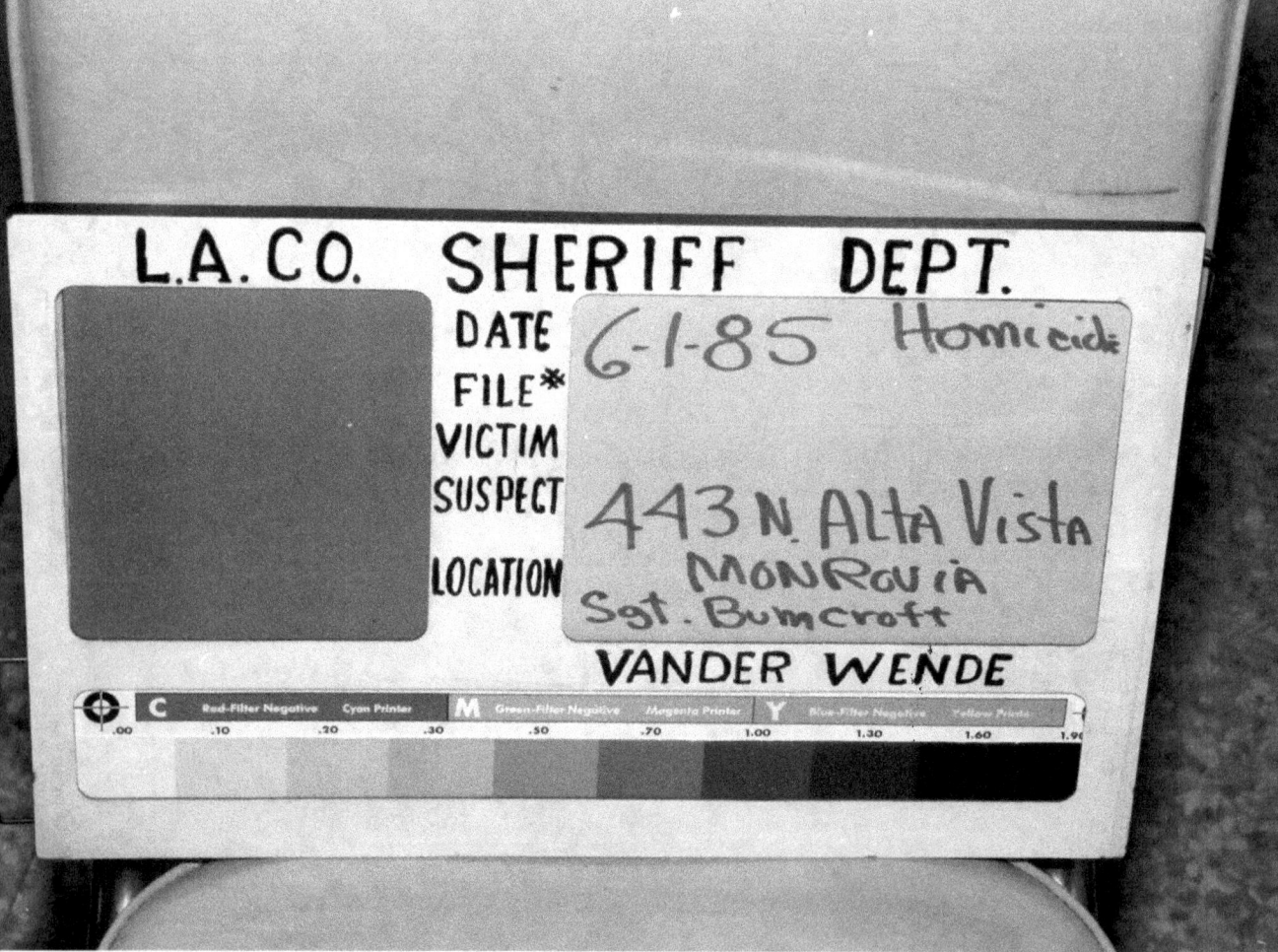

Crime scene identification slate. (Los Angeles Sheriff's Department)

Opposite Top: Tape and an electrical cord ripped from a clock were used to bind the victims. • Bottom: The hammer used to beat both Bell and Lang was discarded at the scene. (Los Angeles Sheriff's Department)

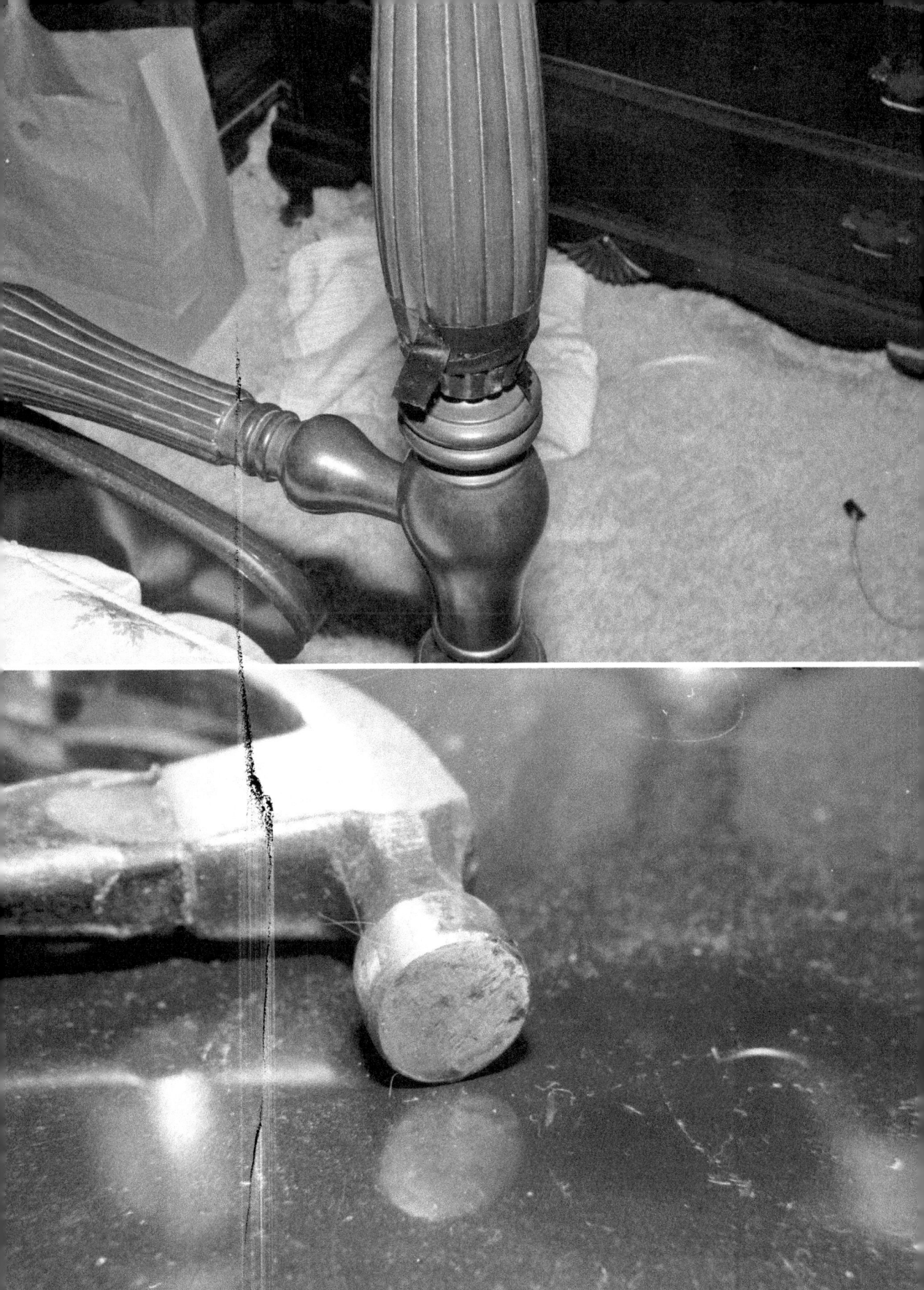

BELIEVING HE HAD DONE THE
DEVIL'S WORK, THE KILLER SCRAWLED
A RED PENTAGRAM (THE SIGN OF
SATAN) USING RED LIPSTICK
FOUND IN THE HOME. A PENTAGRAM
WAS ALSO DRAWN ON THE LEG
OF ONE OF THE VICTIMS.

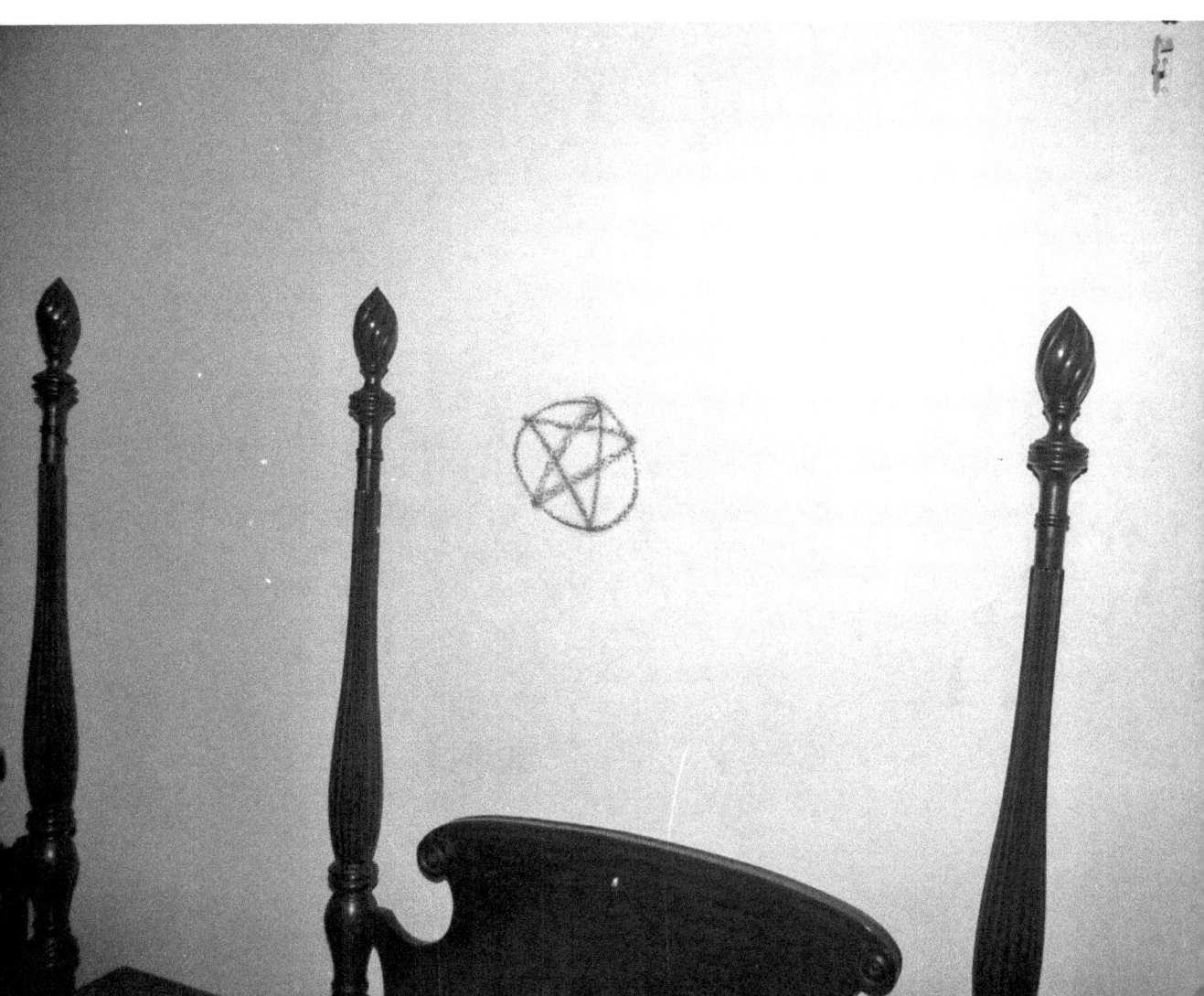

The encircled star, commonly referenced as a pentagram, as it appeared in the home of Mabel Bell and Florence Lang. (Los Angeles Sheriff's Department)

MAY 30, 1985

The night following the terrible attacks on the octogenarian sisters in Monrovia, Ramirez drove the same stolen car to Burbank and selected a home occupied by a widow and her eleven-year-old son. Ramirez used these handcuffs (opposite) to restrain the two while he ransacked the home and sexually assaulted the mother.

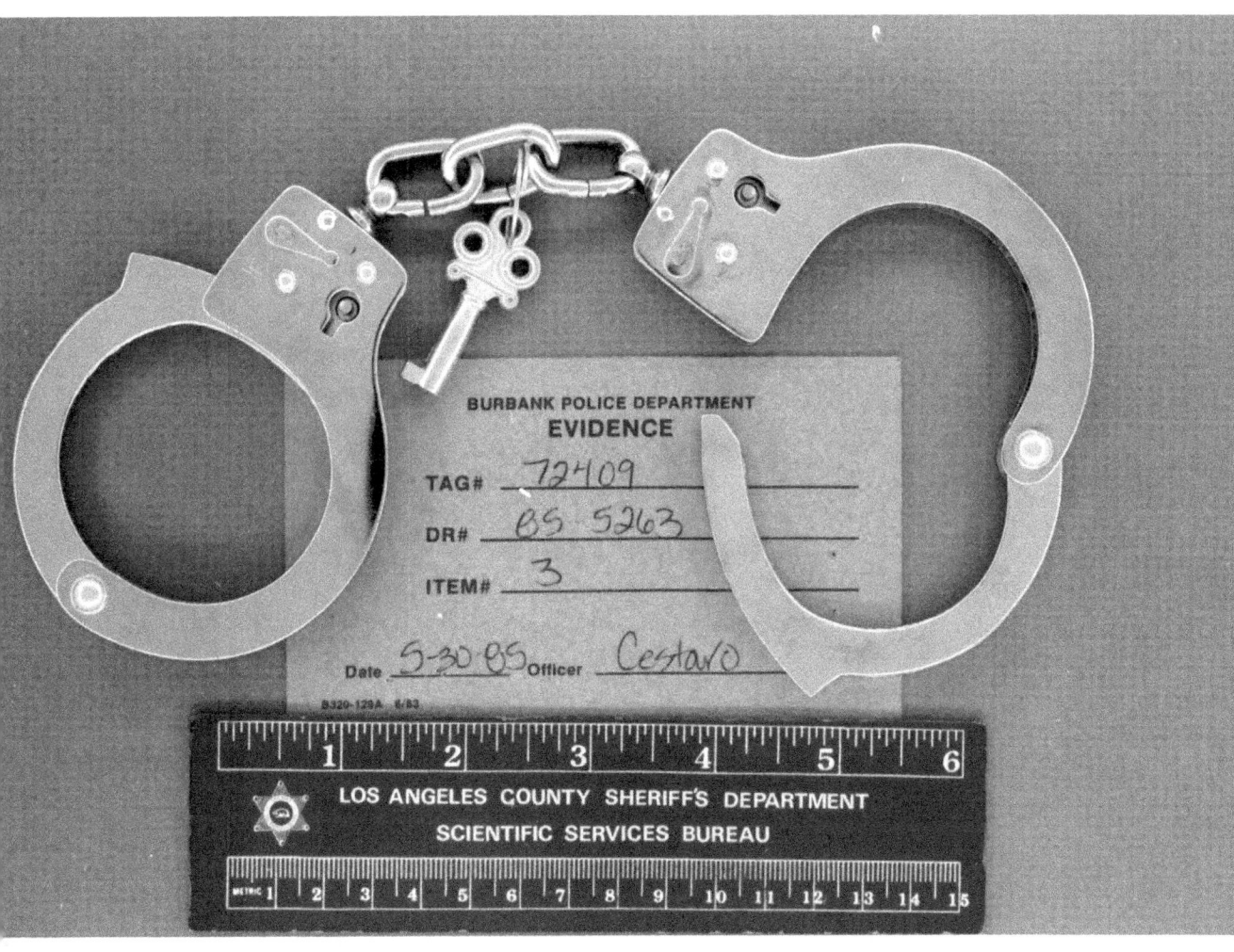

Handcuffs used in the Burbank assault. (Los Angeles Sheriff's Department)

JUNE 27, 1985

Special Education teacher Patty Higgins was alone when Richard Ramirez entered her Arcadia residence on June 27, 1985. Ramirez assaulted Higgins, stole her belongings, and slashed her throat. Higgins died of her injuries.

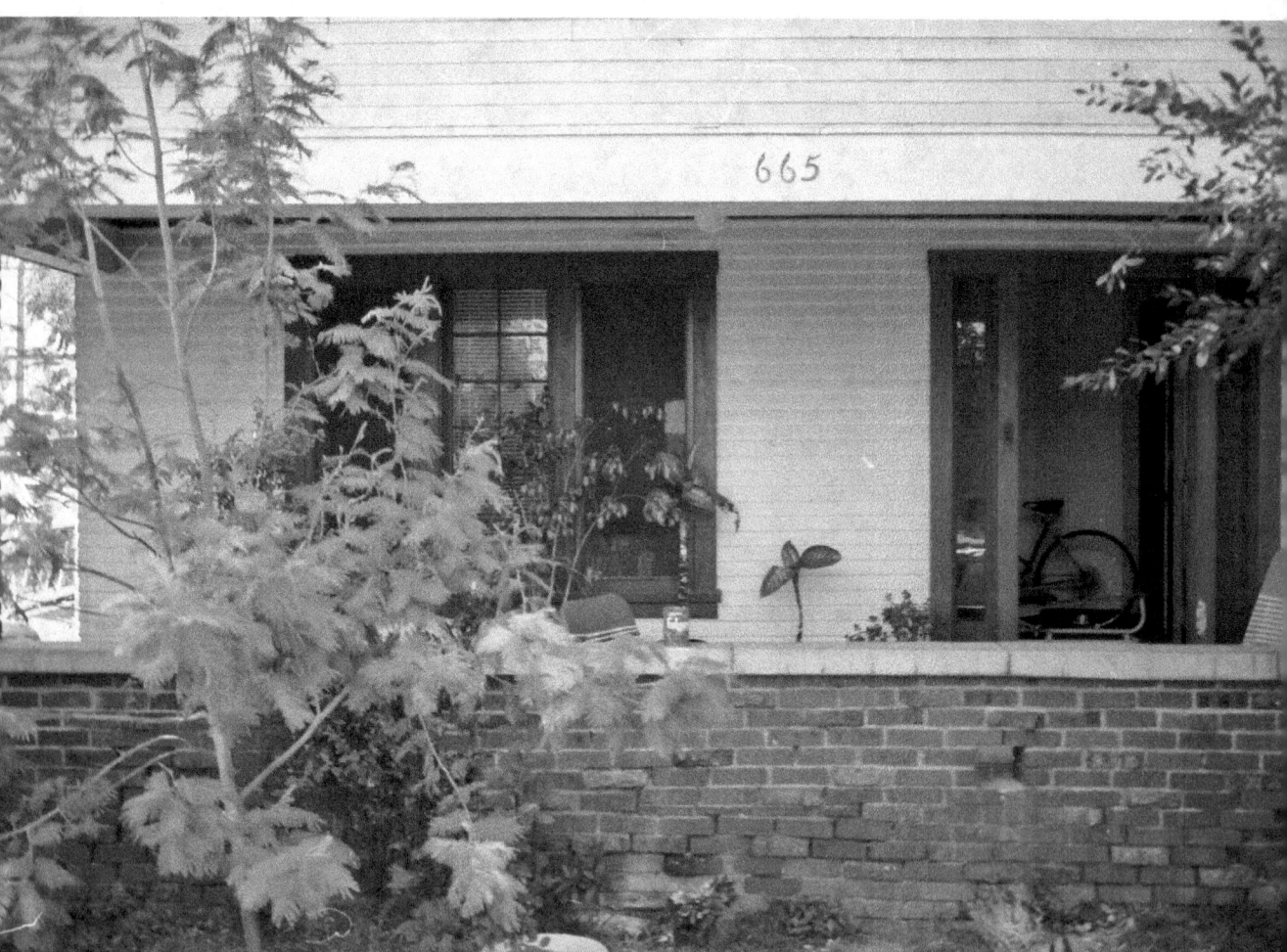

Patty Higgins's Arcadia home. (Los Angeles Sheriff's Department)

Crime scene identification slate. (Los Angeles Sheriff's Department)

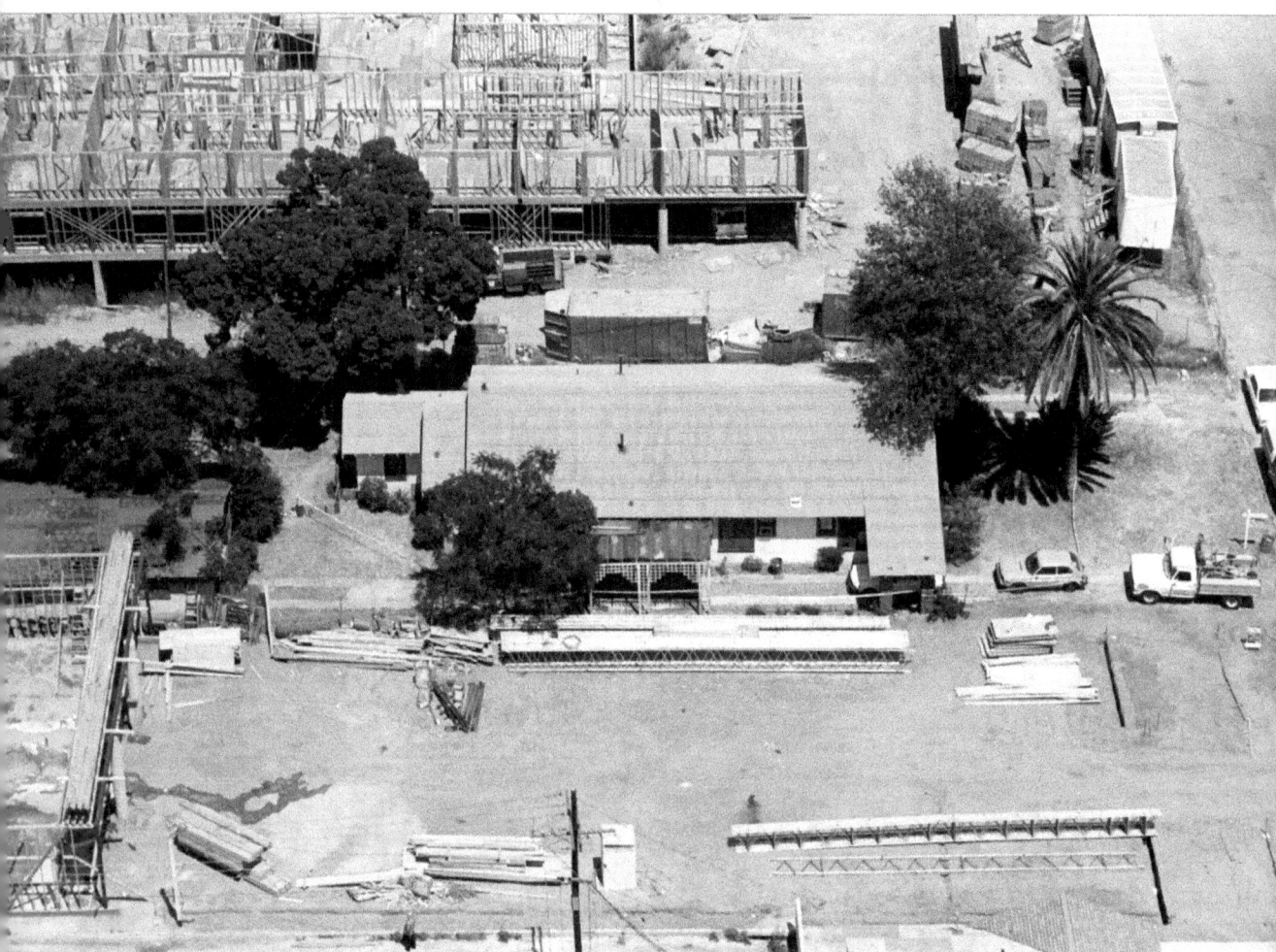

Aerial photograph of the location of the home in which Patty Higgins was murdered. (Los Angeles Sheriff's Department)

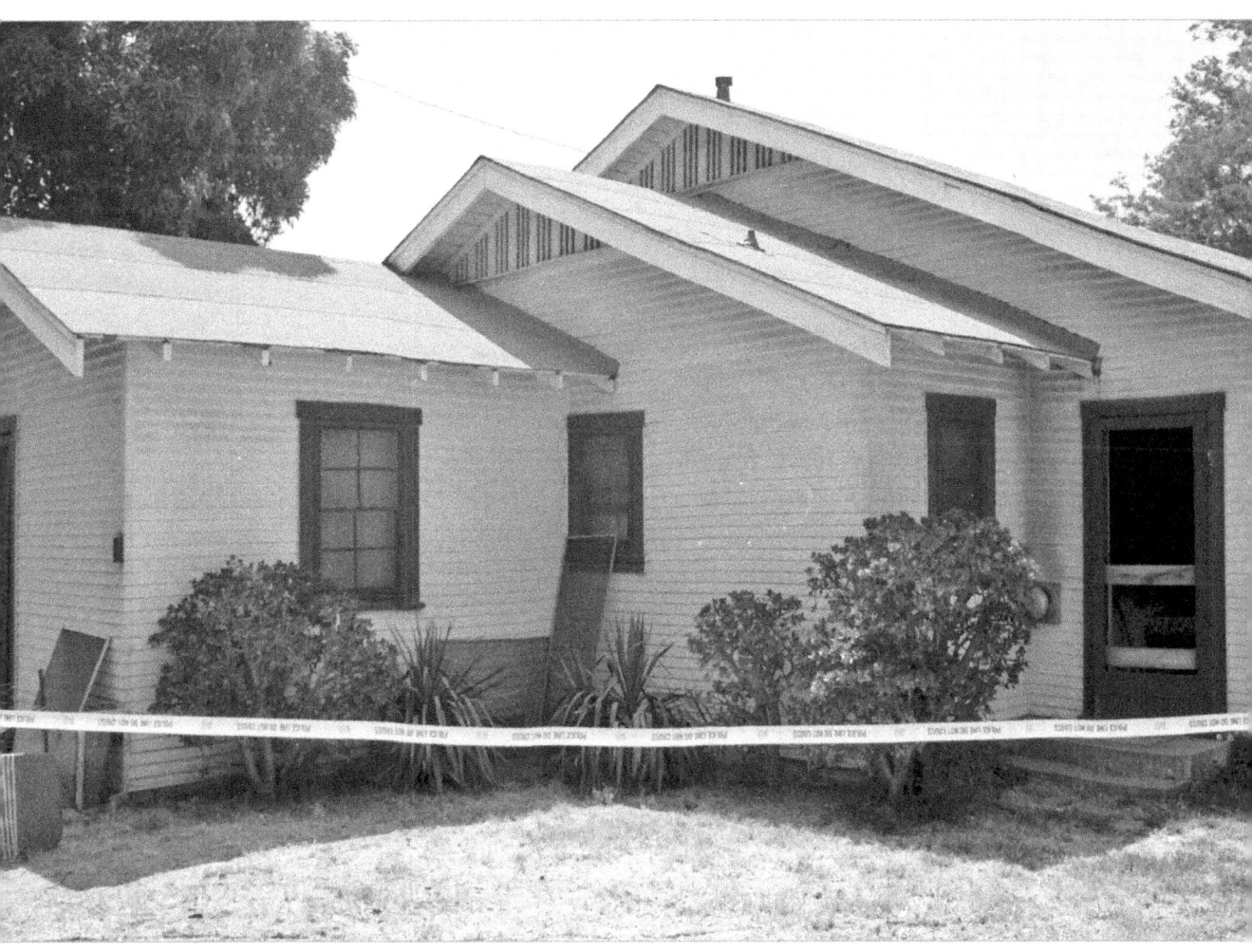

Ground level view of the Higgins crime scene; note window screens on ground. (Los Angeles Sheriff's Department)

MY CHILDHOOD SUMMER OF FEAR

By Christina Rice

The summer of 1985 was when the real-life Boogie Man came into our lives. He's never completely left mine.

I was eleven-years old in 1985 and living in the San Gabriel Valley when Richard Ramirez's reign of terror began. I remember seeing something on the news about murders in Northern California being linked to some down here. I only half paid attention, but my brother, who is five years older than me, sensed that something truly sinister was at play and that we were all vulnerable.

As the murders and press coverage increased, my mom and stepdad made no attempt to hide these incidents from us. How could they? This news was all over the place and they themselves were terrified. There was no way to mask this real-life horror story. My stepdad started sleeping with a shotgun next to him and on those nights when he was out of town on business, my brother curled up under my mom's bed, barely sleeping while clutching a butterfly knife with a six-inch blade.

As for me, I endured many restless nights sleeping with a twirling baton which had been all the rage at Cullen Elementary during the school year. In retrospect it sounds ridiculous, but the baton was the closest thing to a weapon I possessed. If the Night Stalker came though my window, I was ready to use it. My bedroom faced the street and my bed was directly under a window, so I always felt extremely exposed. Crawling into bed with my mom and stepdad had never been an option before and I assumed it wouldn't be now, so I powered through the anxiety of those hot summer nights with only my cat Snookie to provide comfort.

The heat. That's one of the first things that comes to mind when I think about the summer of the Night Stalker. It was so damn hot. In those days, I don't even think I knew what central air was. Sleeping with doors or windows unlocked, much less open, became unthinkable. I would repeatedly check every lock in the house before retreating to my bedroom for the night. Despite the stifling heat of the San Gabriel Valley, I would still crawl under my covers because I irrationally felt they provided an extra layer of protection between me and the Boogie Man. We invested in multiple electric fans that summer.

As the supposed patterns began to emerge of the locations the Stalker was targeting, my anxiety increased ten-fold. Yellow houses? Yes, our house was yellow, albeit faded because it hadn't been painted in years. Near a freeway? Yes, the freeway was close enough that in the dead of night I could hear police on their car speakers ordering people to pull over. Homes without dogs? We had a dog! A fierce miniature dachshund named Reggie provided me with a small amount of solace during those drawn-out months.

Finally, the Boogie Man's day of reckoning came. My brother had a television in his room and when he started screaming, "THEY CAUGHT HIM! THEY CAUGHT HIM!" I feared this was one of his frequent practical jokes designed to torment me. But even he dared not make light of the Night Stalker. I ran into his room, and we both jumped up and down, whooping, hollering, and crying as we watch the endless stream of interviews with those glorious civilians in East Los Angeles who has chased him down. Hell, we may have even hugged each other. It now makes me sad to recall that at the time I thought it one of the happiest days of my young life.

The summer of fear was over, but the effects have never diminished completely. In the three decades since these horrific events, I have never slept in a house with the windows open. I never will. My husband, who grew up in Pittsburgh, does not understand why I insist on closing the bathroom windows which a cat could barely fit through. He also gets upset that whenever he goes to work in the detached office, I lock him out of the house. It's not personal, I tell him. It's not even conscious. It's just that whenever I'm home, I instinctively lock every door and have done so since 1985. When we were house hunting a few years back, I wanted to find a place without any bedrooms facing the street. I had to concede defeat on that one. If you didn't live in Southern California that summer, you just wouldn't understand.

I've sometimes wondered if this deep-set, lifelong paranoia is due to being so young and impressionable at the time. But, no. People much older than me understand. We all have central air, deadbolts, and window sills dusty from a lack of use.

Deep down, we're all still afraid of the Boogie Man.

JULY 5, 1985

Ramirez's crimes typically began with his quiet night-time entry via a window. Some required the removal of a screen, like the one seen here discarded outside the Sierra Madre residence of a 16-year-old girl. Following a brutal physical assault on the teenager, Ramirez's bloody shoeprints were left behind, and discovered by Sheriffs' investigators. The victim survived the July 5, 1985 attack.

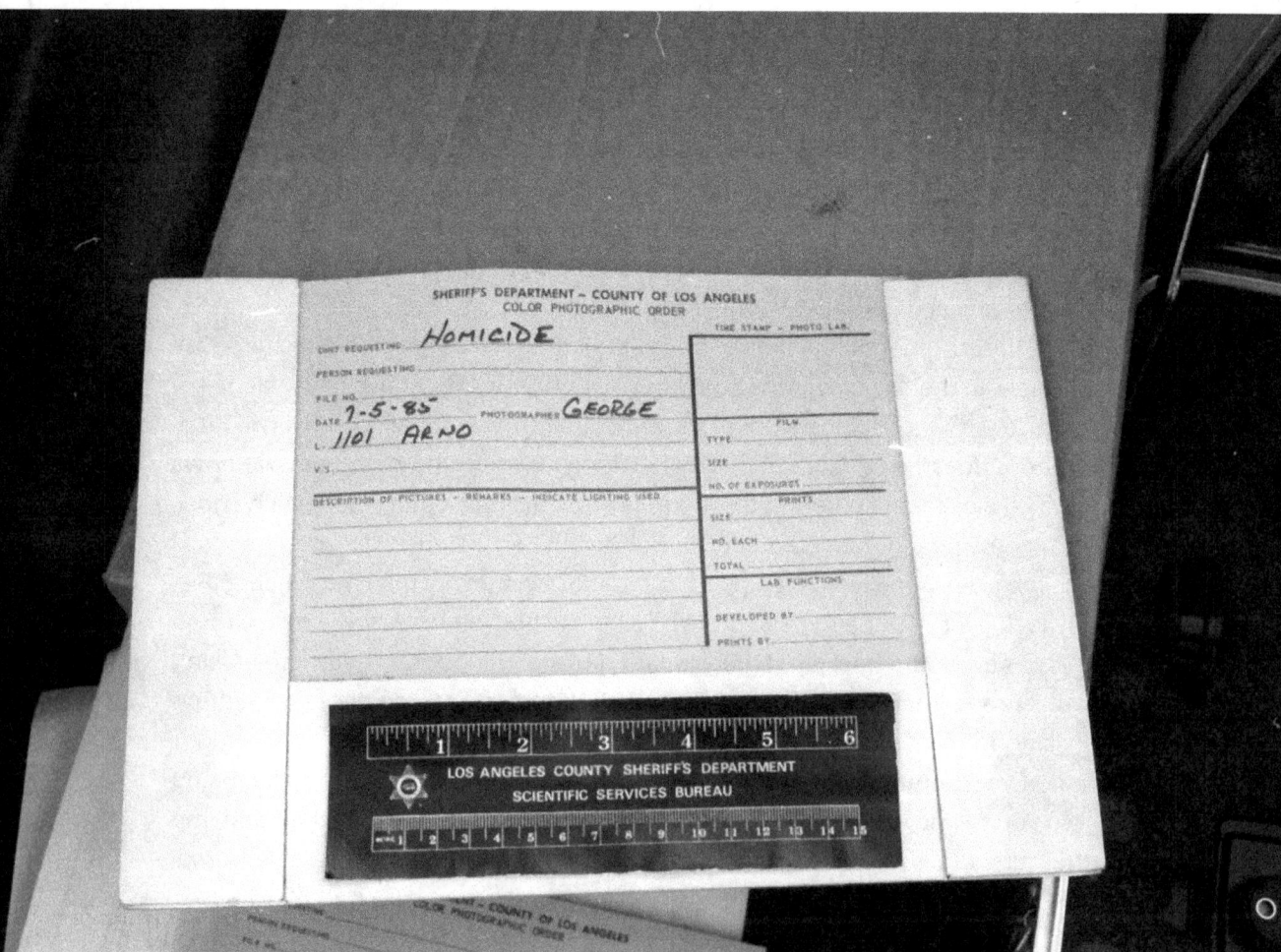

(Los Angeles Sheriff's Department)

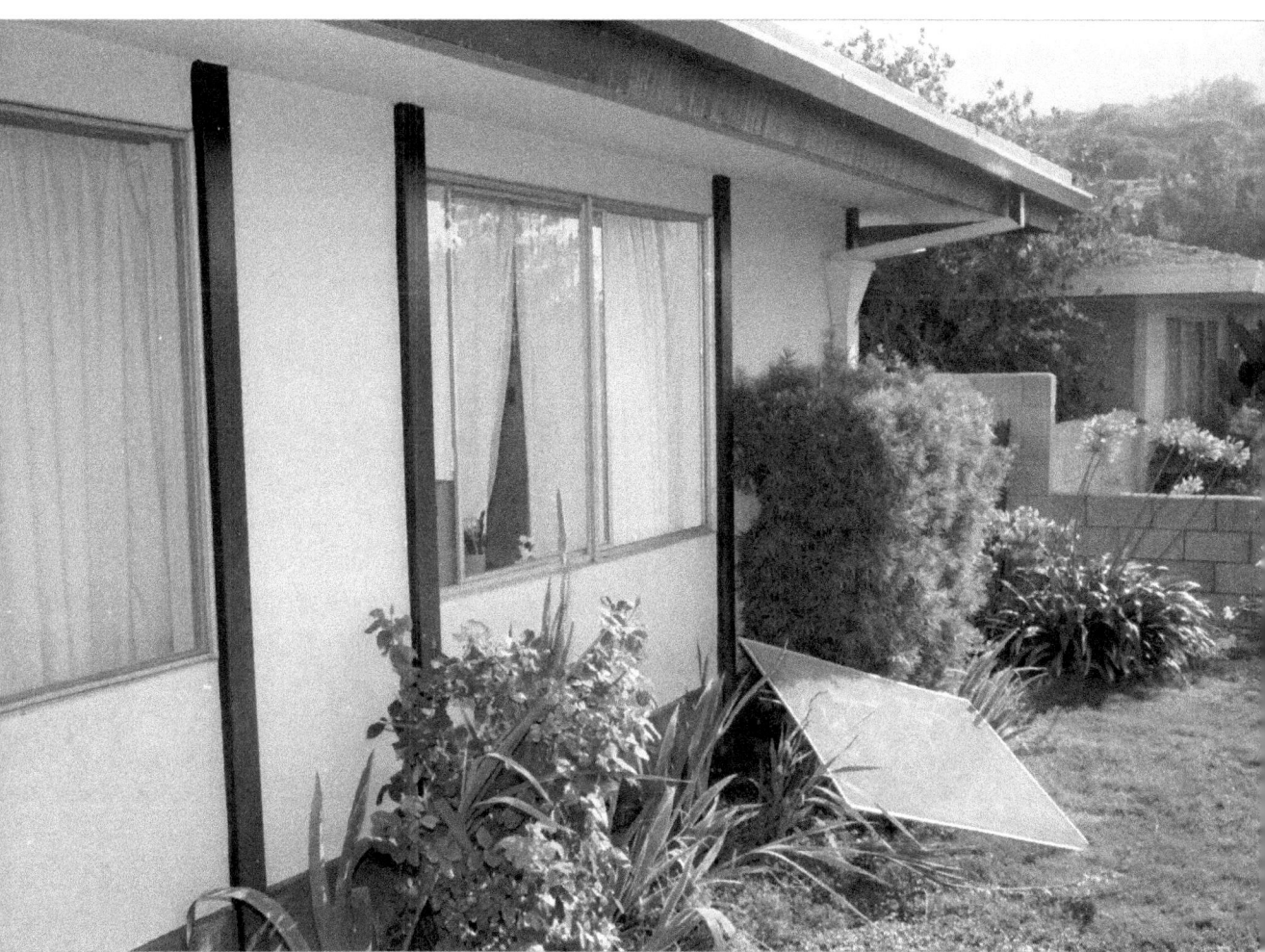

The point of entry was typically a window. (Los Angeles Sheriff's Department)

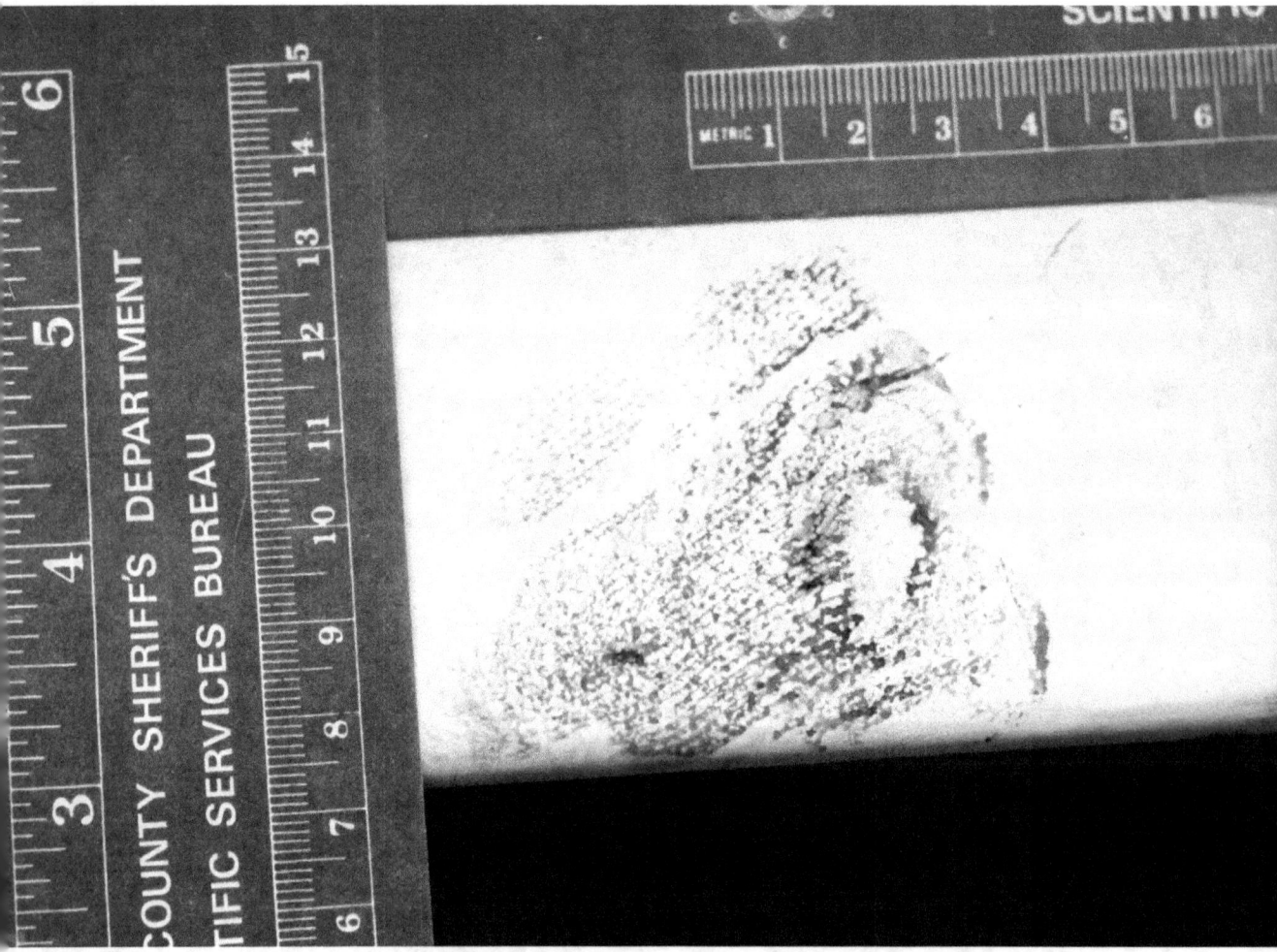

Image of a bloody shoeprint. (Los Angeles Sheriff's Department)

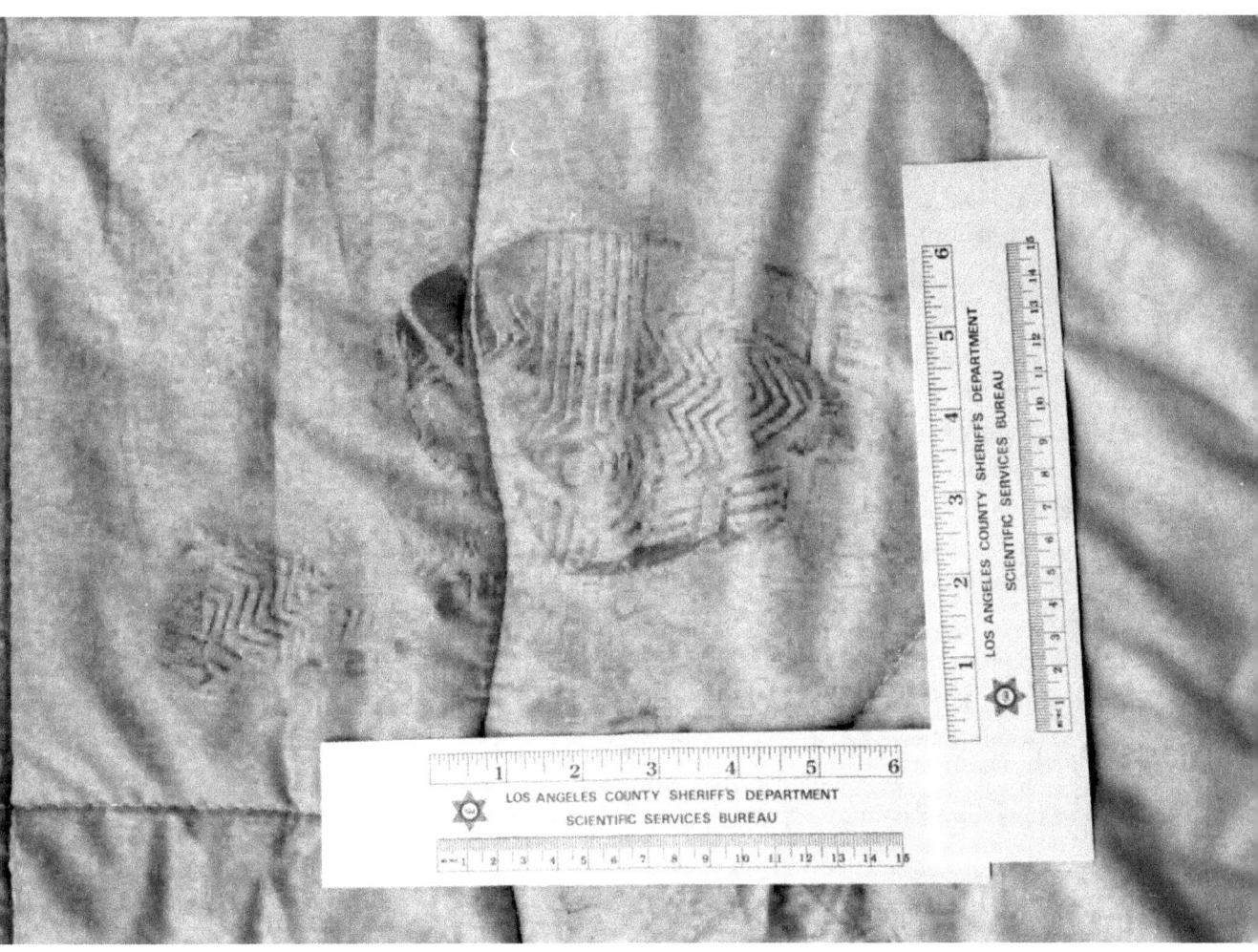

**A bloody shoeprint was discovered on the bedding of the young victim.
(Los Angeles Sheriff's Department)**

JULY 7, 1985

Yet another distinct shoeprint was found outside the home of Joyce Nelson on July 7, 1985. Nelson, who lived alone in her Monterey Park home, was beaten to death.

More than 600 worried and terrified residents crowd into a local neighborhood watch meeting. Law enforcement officials revealed that they were still unable to attribute the numerous killings to a single suspect.

If there was an occasion during the Night Stalker's crime spree that speaks to the magnitude of the social impact, it occured about this time. Given the time Gil Carrillo was committed to identifying and arresting the serial killer, his family was without their husband and father. Like so many other families, Carrillo's was fearful for their safety and temporarily re-located them to the home of Carrillo's in-laws.

Carrillo's partner, Frank Salerno, too, began taking additional safety precautions at his home. He devised an early alert system for his backyard.

Adding these measures to my father's concerns should fully elucidate the level of terror spreading throughout the region. Three very tenured cops were taking unprecedented steps to protect themselves and their families.

Opposite Top & Bottom: Crime scene identification slate. (Los Angeles Sheriff's Department)

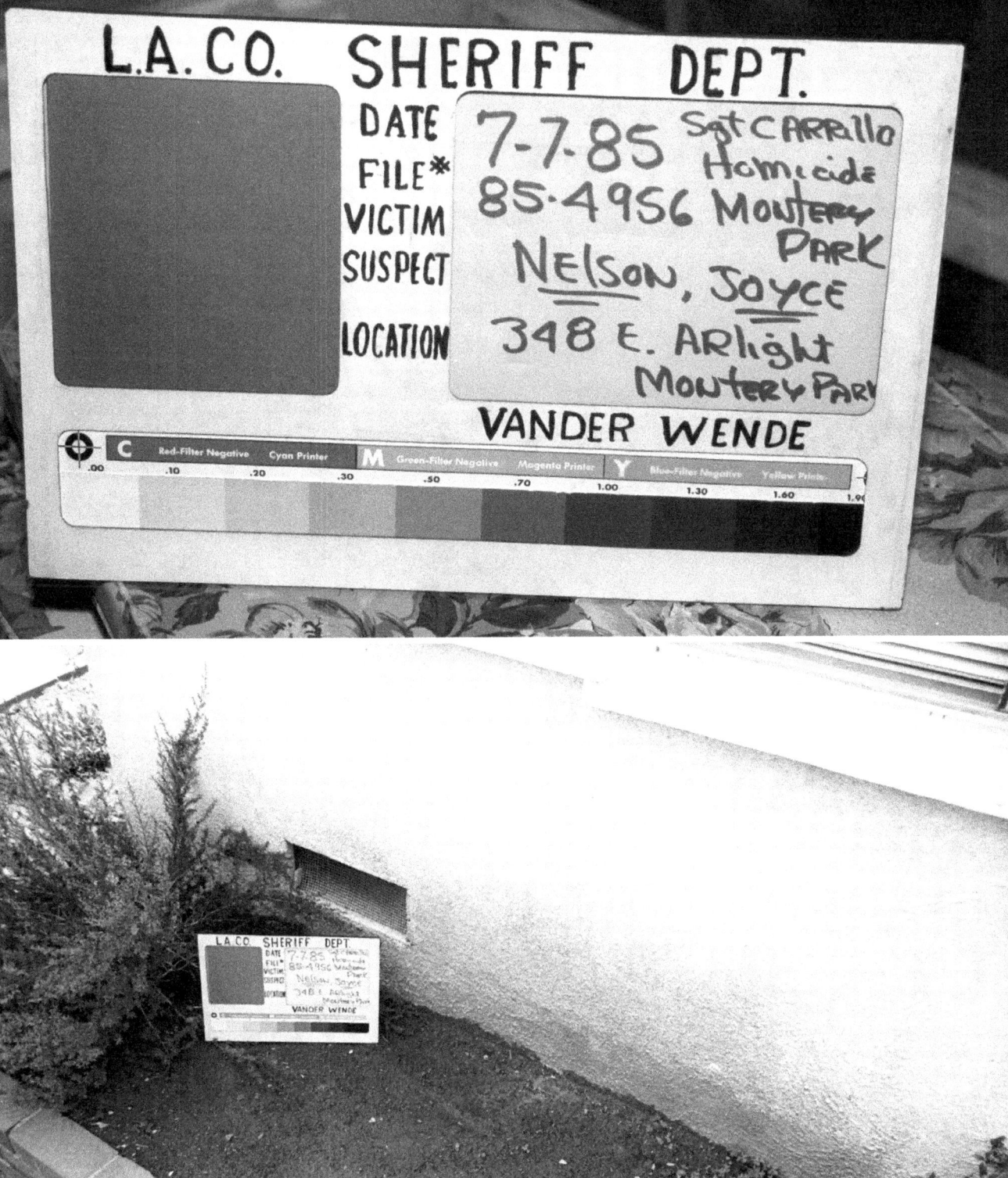

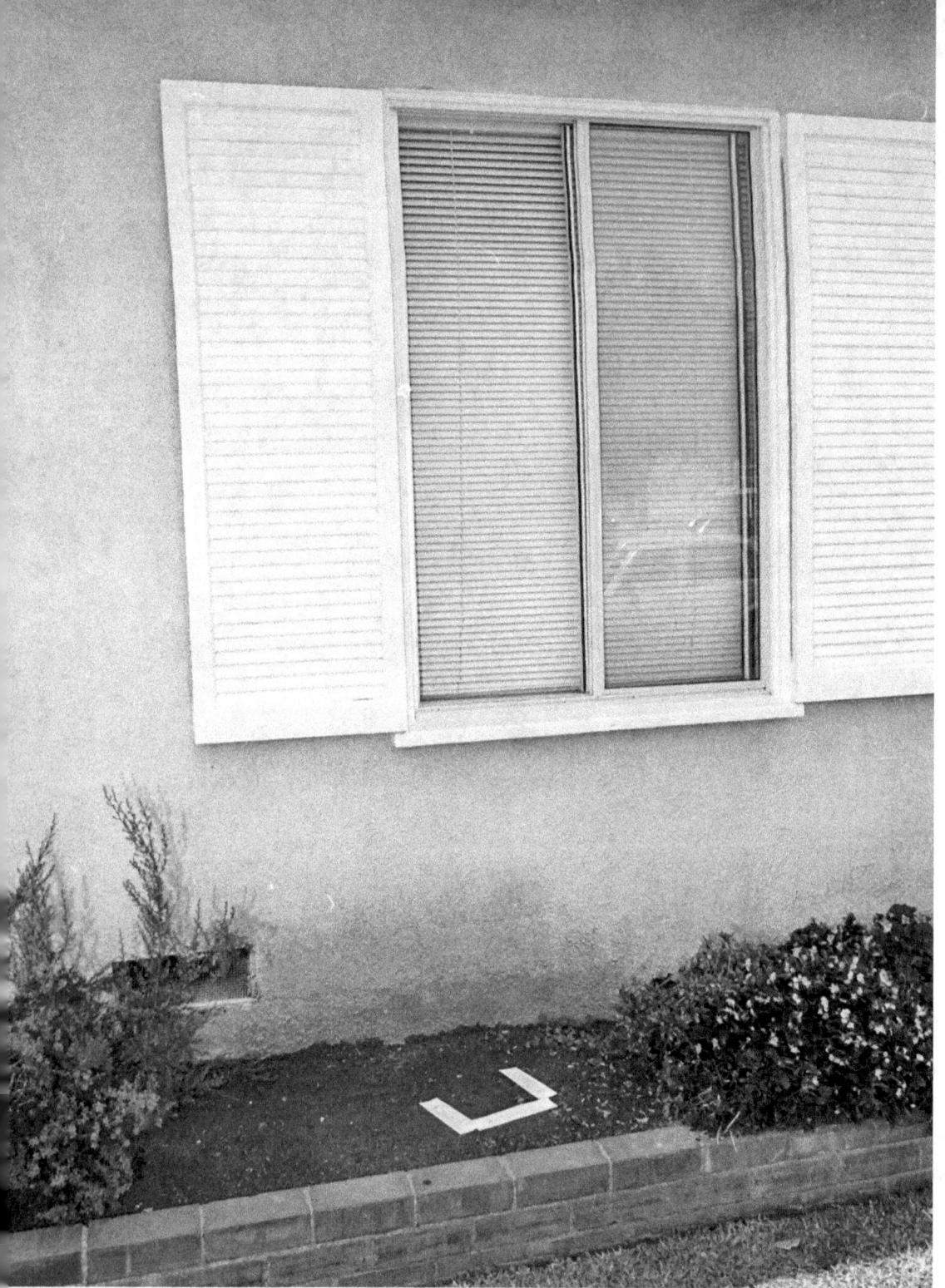

Rulers were used to bracket the area in which a shoeprint was discovered. (Los Angeles Sheriff's Department)

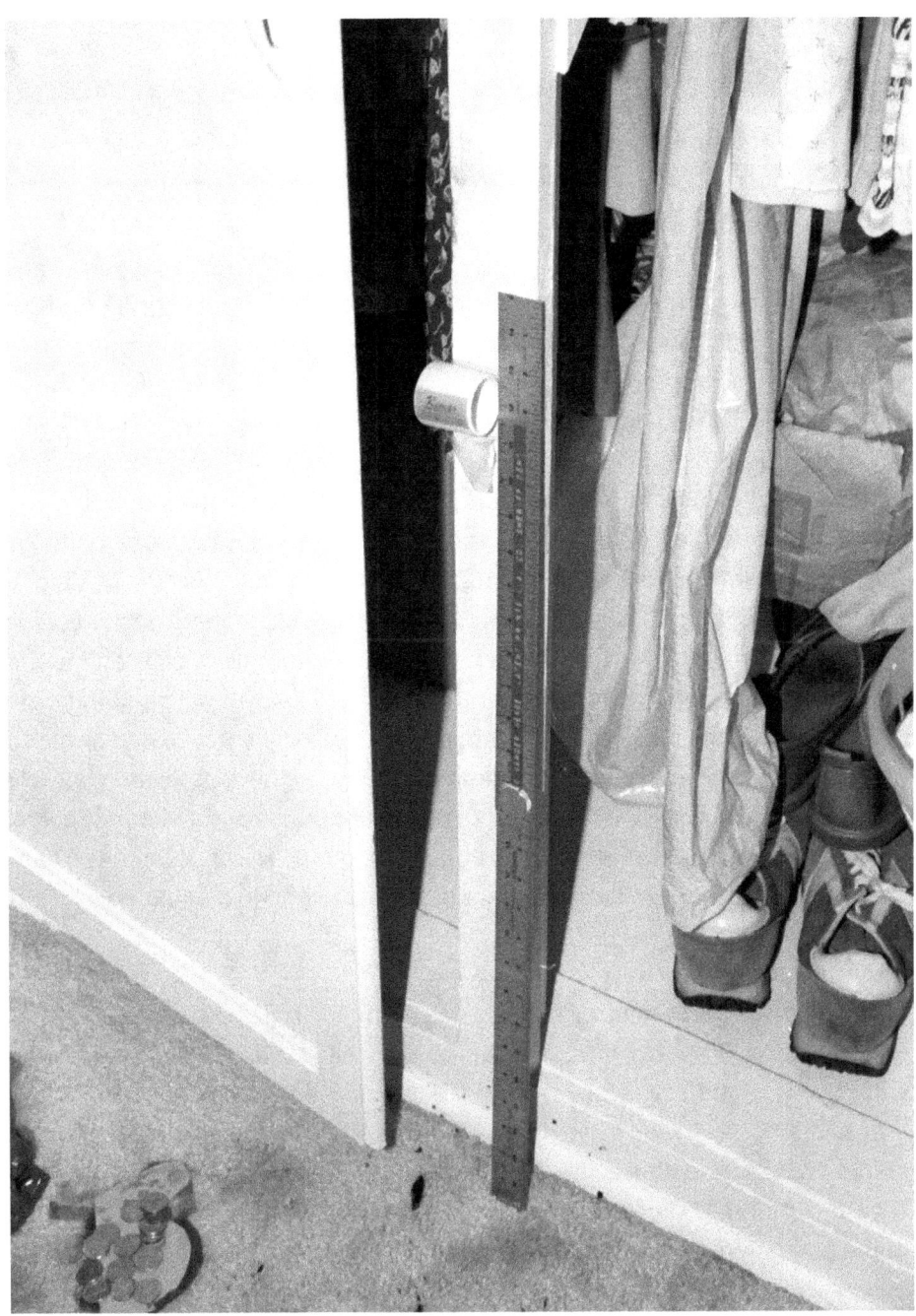

A yardstick shows the distance from the floor to the point at which a fingerprint was lifted. (Los Angeles Sheriff's Department)

CLOSE ENCOUNTERS WITH THE NIGHT STALKER

by Ester Petschar

Encounter #1

It was early evening, almost too late for me to feel comfortable grocery shopping by myself. But I decided to stop at El Rancho Market on Huntington Drive, which was on my route home from work. I was waiting in the checkout line, standing behind a skinny, very distinctive-looking guy with black hair and a very unpleasant vibe. He yelled, "This is a holdup!!" He was waving a black .22 gun in the air. He was wearing a white shirt and a baseball cap, and had a devil tattoo on his left hand. I remember I was wearing a pair of my favorite alexandrite earrings and I thought, "There's no way this guy is going to get my earrings," and I ran up the nearby stairs. I knocked on the locked office door and the manager inside refused to open the door for me. Then I found the upstairs bathroom, and with another lady and her young daughter who had also run up the stairs, we hid there until we heard the police had arrived. I remember overhearing another customer describing the robber and was able to tell the police about the devil tattoo, which another witness denied seeing. The robber was Richard Ramirez. I remembered his face and when the case broke, realized who he was. I never shopped at El Rancho ever again.

Encounter #2

I worked down the street from a Salvation Army Thrift Store that was in a mall on Valley Blvd. & Santa Anita. I was in the store almost daily. I stopped in after work one day and saw a guy buying a black baseball cap with white letters that said "AC/DC." I didn't know what that stood for. Even though his hair was longer, I recognized him as the very same guy who held up the El Rancho Market a few months before. After leaving the store, I was on the freeway going home and I saw him in my rearview mirror driving closely behind me. Then he pulled alongside and stared intensely at me with a big, really nasty smile. He had hardly any teeth. He really scared me, and then he took off. As I eventually came to learn, it was Ramirez.

Encounter #3

One day, my husband and I were clearing weeds from Forest Park St. in El Sereno, near our home, when a guy drove up from Commodore St. and turned left on Rising Dr. His license plate had the letters ULF—I remembered that because it's the same name as a relative of my husband's who had visited from Sweden. Someone up the hill sold drugs, so traffic was always going up the hill. I recognized him as the same guy I had seen twice before—Ramirez. At that time I was housesitting for my in-laws and my husband was working nights, so I spent a few weeks alone at night in a house isolated on a hillside in that neighborhood. Most of that time I was scared and nervous and didn't sleep much.

Also This...

One of the victims, Joyce Lucille Nelson, worked at Coast Envelope Co. in Commerce. My mother and aunt worked there full time and both my sister and I worked there on summer breaks, so we were all friends with Joyce.

My husband often played the videogame Centipede on his lunch breaks at the liquor store on Evergreen near 8th. He worked nearby. That's where Ramirez was spotted by someone when his photo appeared on a newspaper. He was chased to East LA by some people who had recognized him where he was finally apprehended.

When I think about my three chance encounters with the Night Stalker, plus knowing one of his victims, I can't believe I was that close to such a vicious killer. Sometimes when a killer is caught, people say they can't believe it because the suspect seemed so normal or seemed like a nice quiet neighbor. When Ramirez was caught, it was pretty clear to me he was guilty of his crimes, he had such a sinister presence.

JULY 20, 1985

Another residence in the San Fernando Valley of the City of Los Angeles was the scene of a murderous attack on July 20, 1985. Chainarong Khovananth fell victim to the killer in the Avia athletic shoes. Shoeprints were found both inside and outside the murder victim's home. Sheriff's investigators revisited the scene and took these photographs following the initial investigation by LAPD homicide detectives.

A second lethal attack was made by Ramirez on July 20, 1985. Maxson and Lela Kneiding were robbed and murdered in their Glendale home. Their bodies were found after fellow churchgoers noticed neither had attended a regularly scheduled service at the nearby Seventh-day Adventist Church.

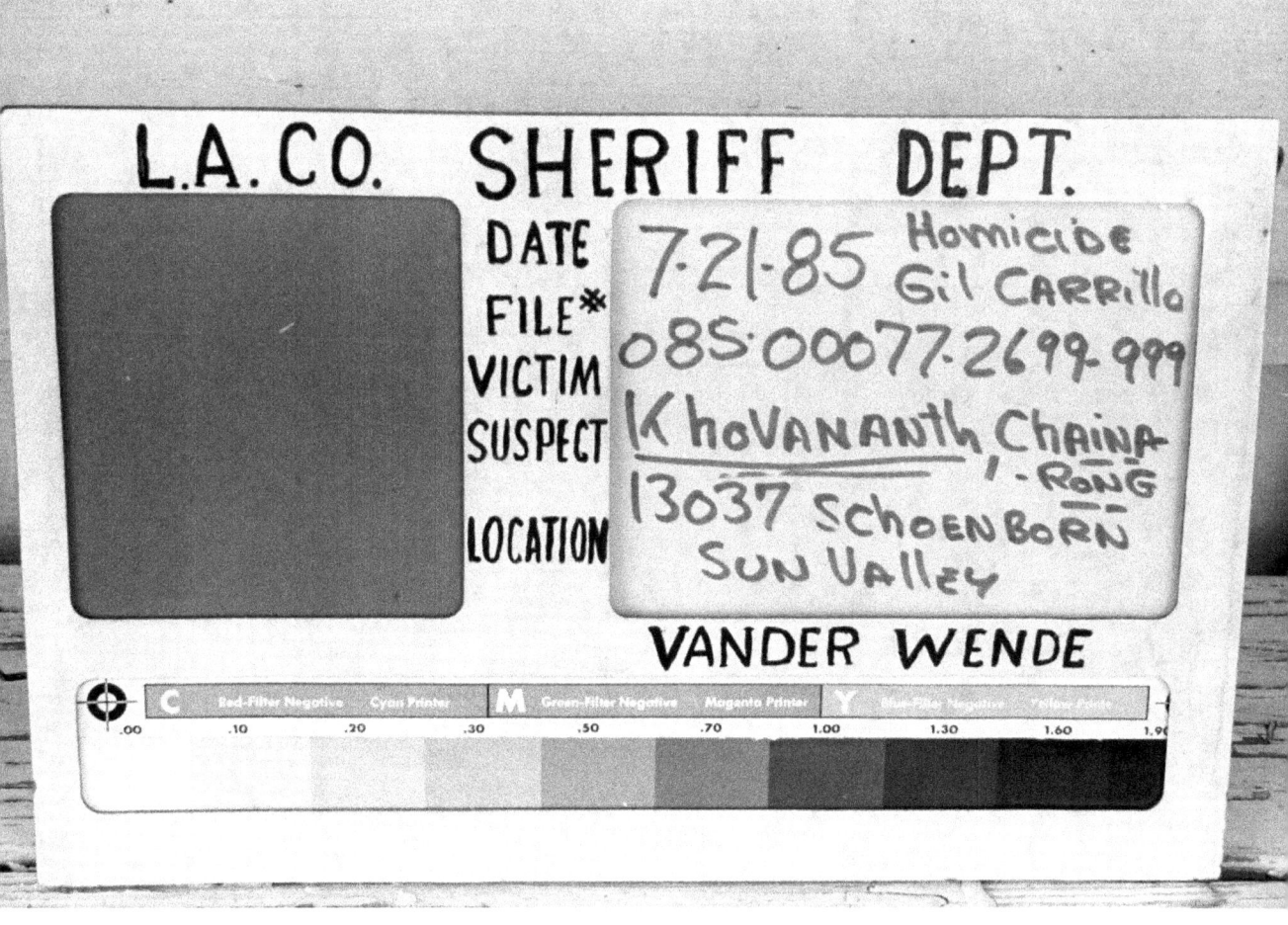

Crime scene identification slate. (Los Angeles Sheriff's Department)

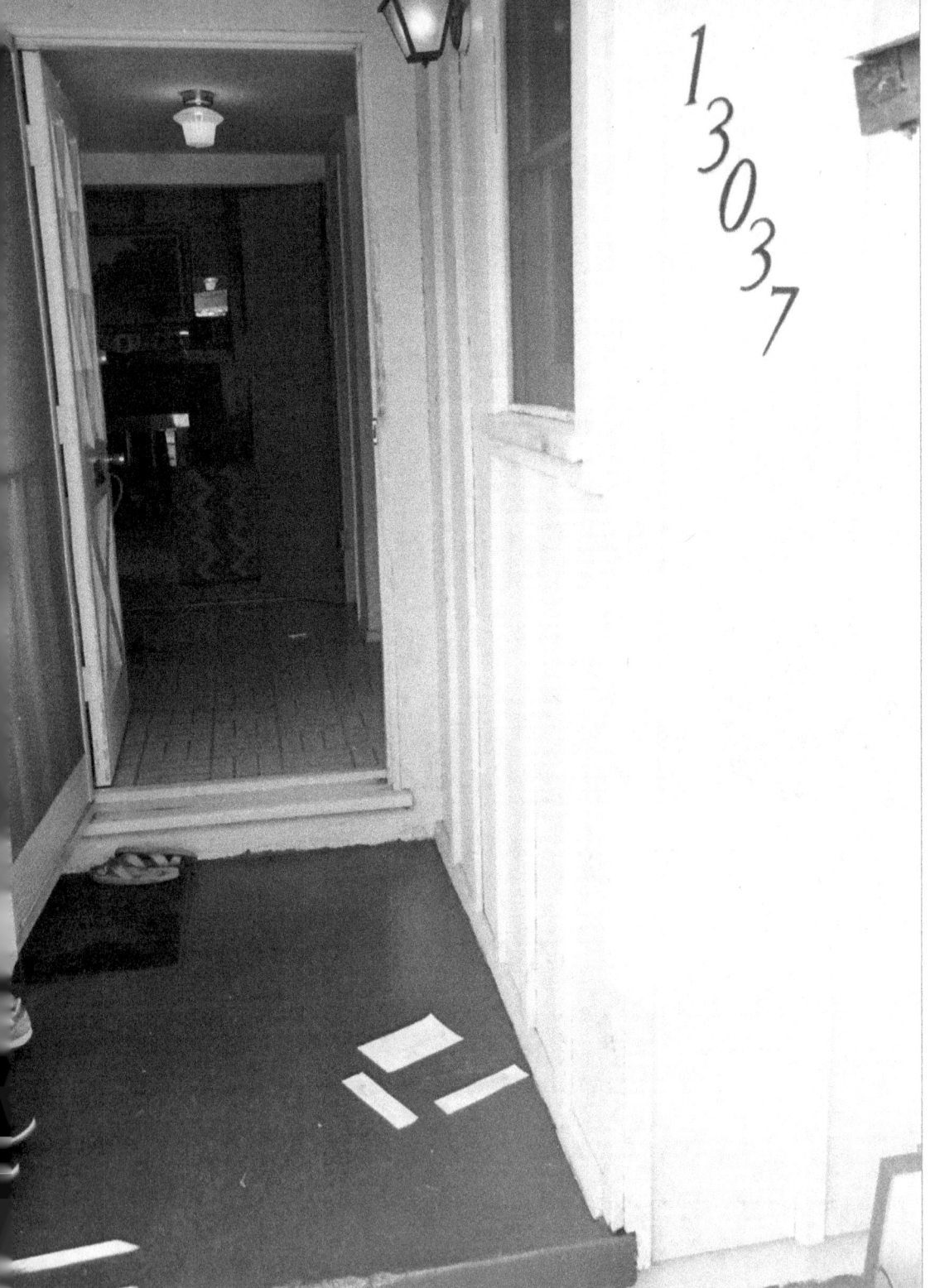

The entryway of the Khovananth home where rulers form a border around possible evidence. (Los Angeles Sheriff's Department)

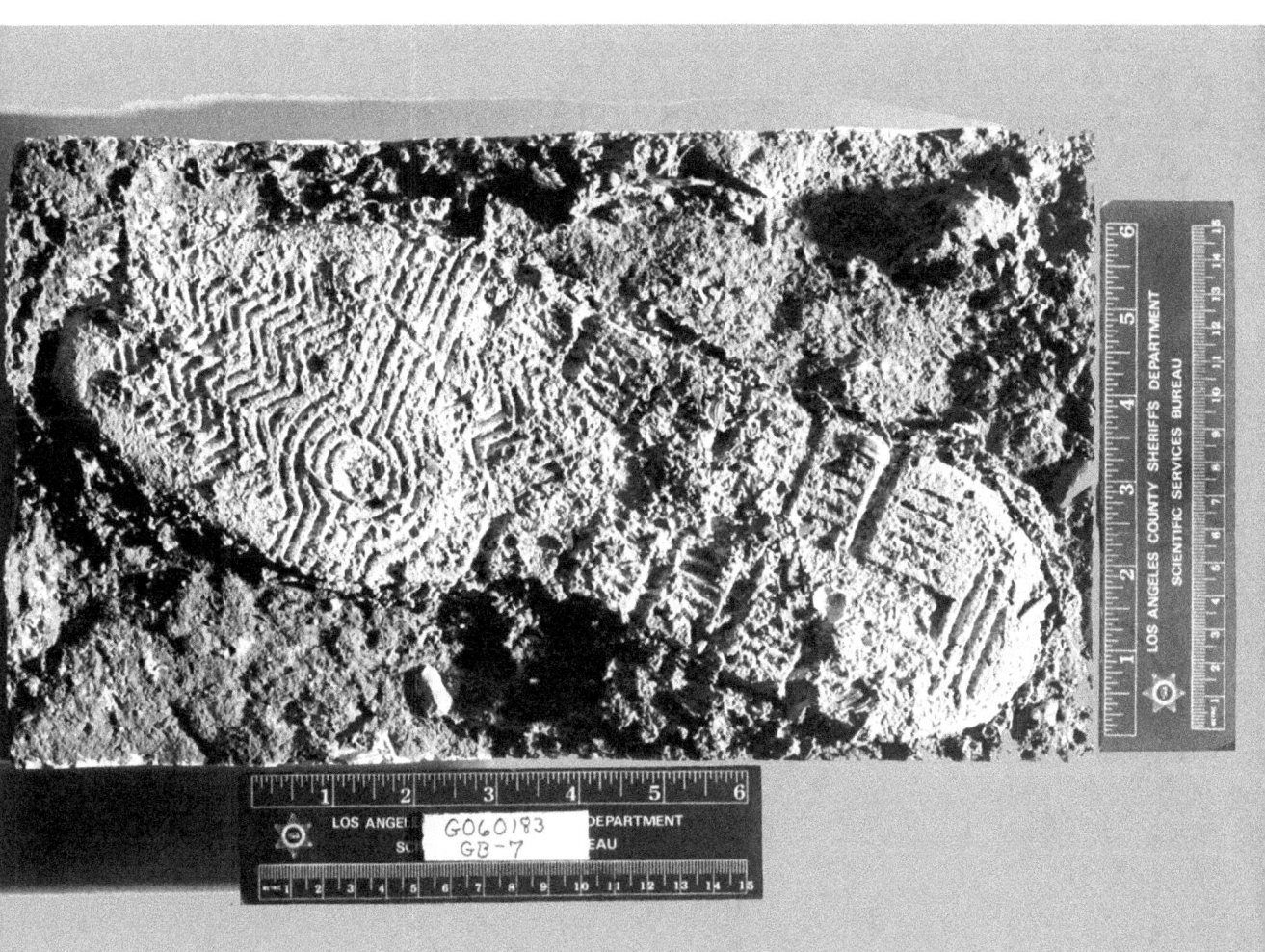

A plaster cast of the shoeprint found outside the Khovananth home was made for evidentiary reasons. (Los Angeles Sheriff's Department)

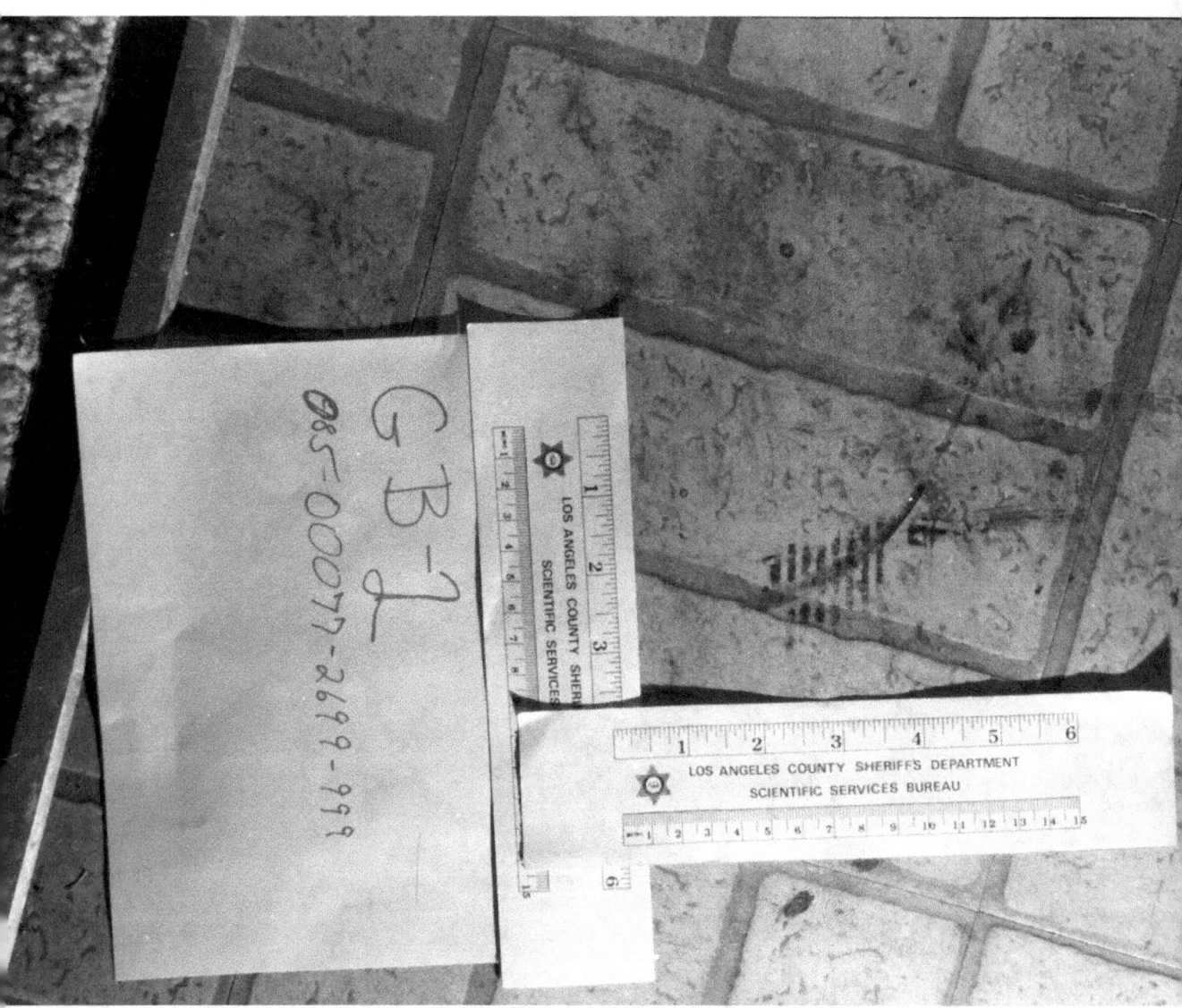

A partial bloody shoeprint was also located within the home. (Los Angeles Sheriff's Department)

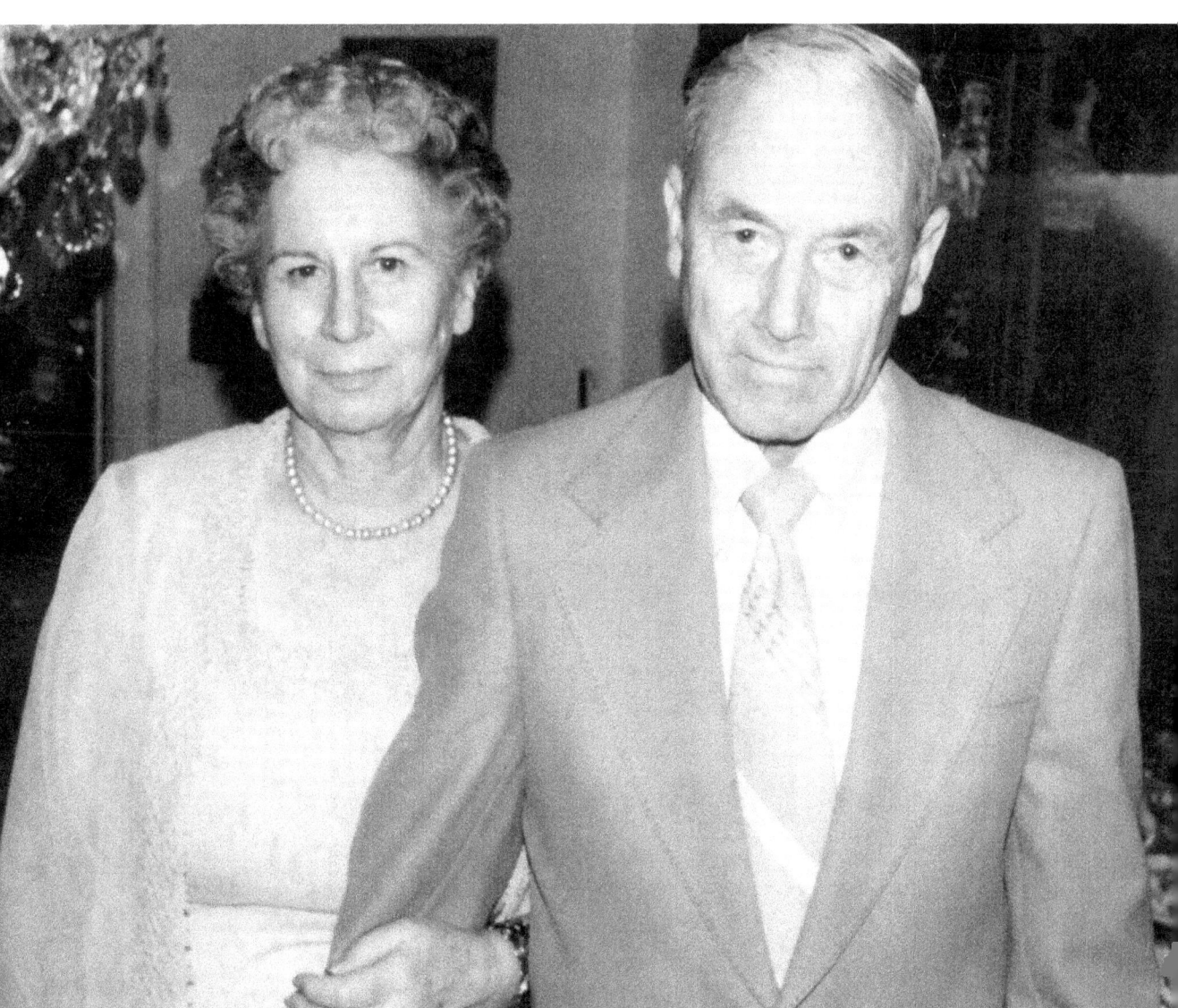

Lela and Maxson Kneiding. (Herald Examiner Collection)

MANY OF THOSE WHO LIVED IN THE OTHERWISE QUIET GLENDALE NEIGHBORHOOD CROWDED INTO ZERR COURT FOR A MEETING WITH GLENDALE POLICE OFFICIALS. CAPTAIN GLYNN MARTIN, HIMSELF A LOCAL RESIDENT, ADDRESSED THE FRIENDS AND NEIGHBORS REGARDING THE MURDERS OF THE KNEIDINGS. WHILE MEETINGS OF THIS SORT WERE INFORMATIVE, BY THIS TIME, FEARS WERE NOT EASILY CALMED.

Opposite: Following the murders of Lela and Max Kneiding, the Glendale Police Department addressed concerned neighbors about the terrible crime. Captain Glynn Martin (author's father) addresses the many interested neighbors on Zerr Court. (John McCoy/Los Angeles Times)

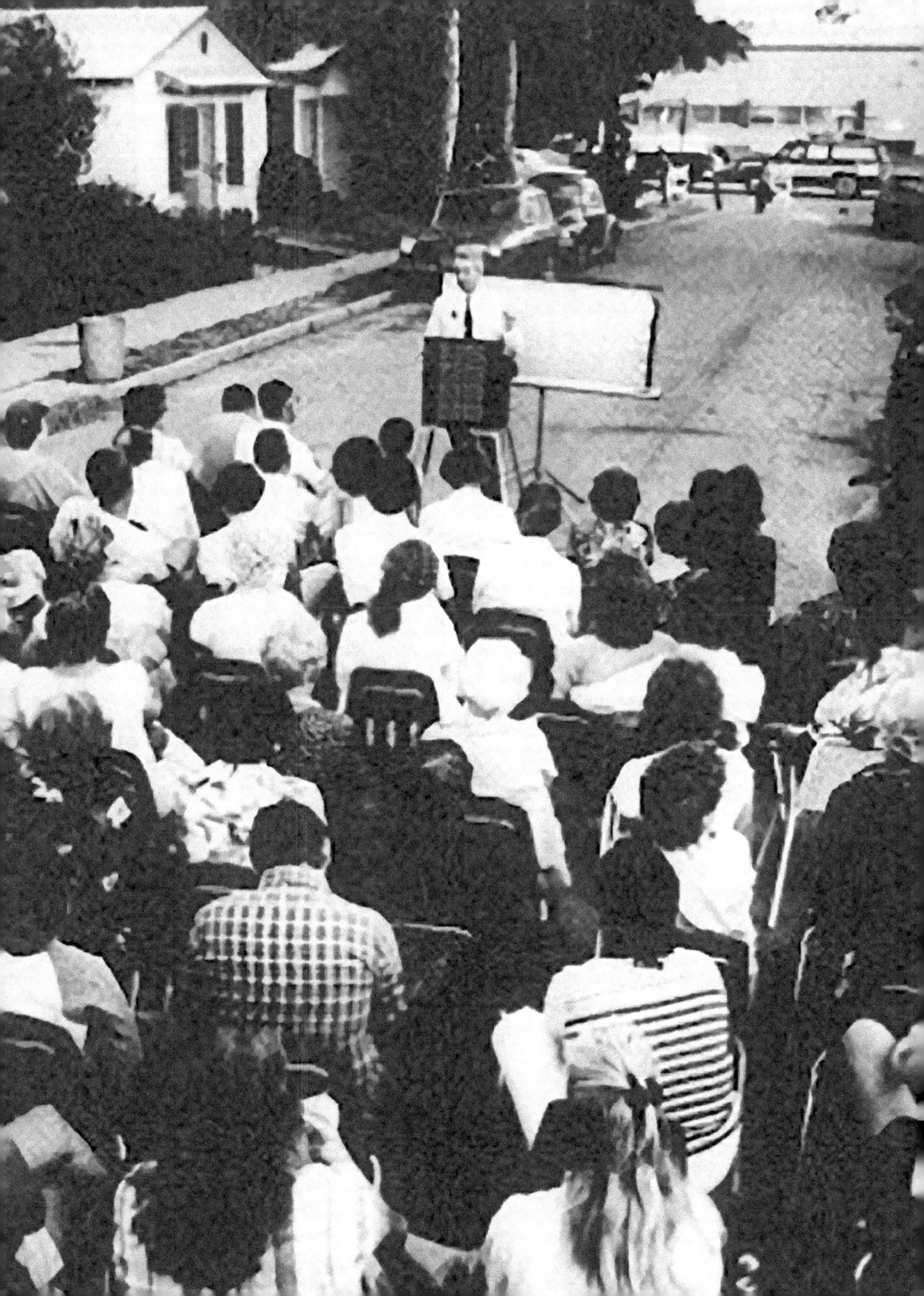

AUGUST 8, 1985

On August 8, 1985, sometime after 2:30 am, Ramirez entered the home of Elyas and Sakina Abowath. Ramirez cut the cords to the couple's telephones, and shot and killed Sakina's husband, Elyas, while their 3-year-old son slept in an adjacent bedroom. Ramirez brutally assaulted Sakina, ordering her to "swear on Satan." Ultimately Sakina's son awoke, only to be bound by Ramirez. The assault resumed.

In the hours following the attack in the Abowath home, Sheriff Sherman Block held a press conference, bluntly stating,

"There's definitely a killer out there."

Several crime scenes revealed that telephone wires had been severed. In cases where victims survived, this meant the victim had to seek aid outside the residence.

By now the many killings, including their demonic nature and brutality, had become worrisome to many. The Sheriff's remarks confirmed the fright that had set upon scores of Southland residents. The various protection measures perceived or employed continued, grew or advanced. And until the identification and capture of Richard Ramirez, the reports of his crimes would continue to adversely impact those that lived, worked and played in the Greater LA area. Of course, no one was impacted more personally than the many victims and their families.

Unbeknownst to Ramirez, the theft of Bill Gregory's Toyota Corolla station wagon would ultimately yield the evidence needed to make a positive identification. A sketch of Gregory's stolen car was circulated among law enforcement officers due to the belief that Ramirez was the car thief.

Indeed he was.

Ramirez, however, had ventured beyond the major valleys of Los Angeles and traveled to Mission Viejo where a teenager heard Ramirez creeping outside his home. Joseph Romero III observed the stolen Toyota station wagon passing by, and was able to see and recall several digits of the stolen Toyota's license number.

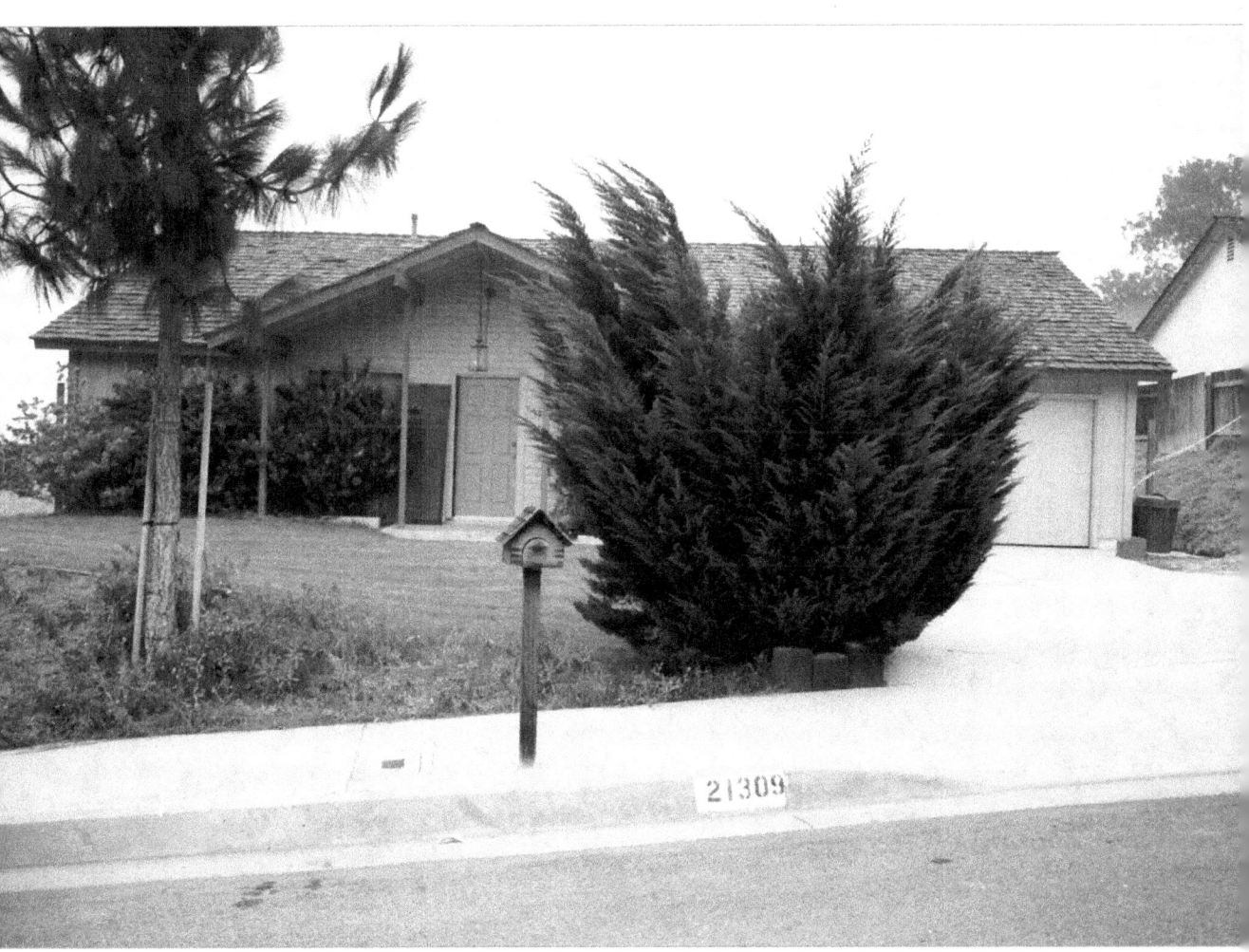

Home of Elyas and Sakina Abowath. Note crime scene tape to right of garage. (Los Angeles Sheriff's Department)

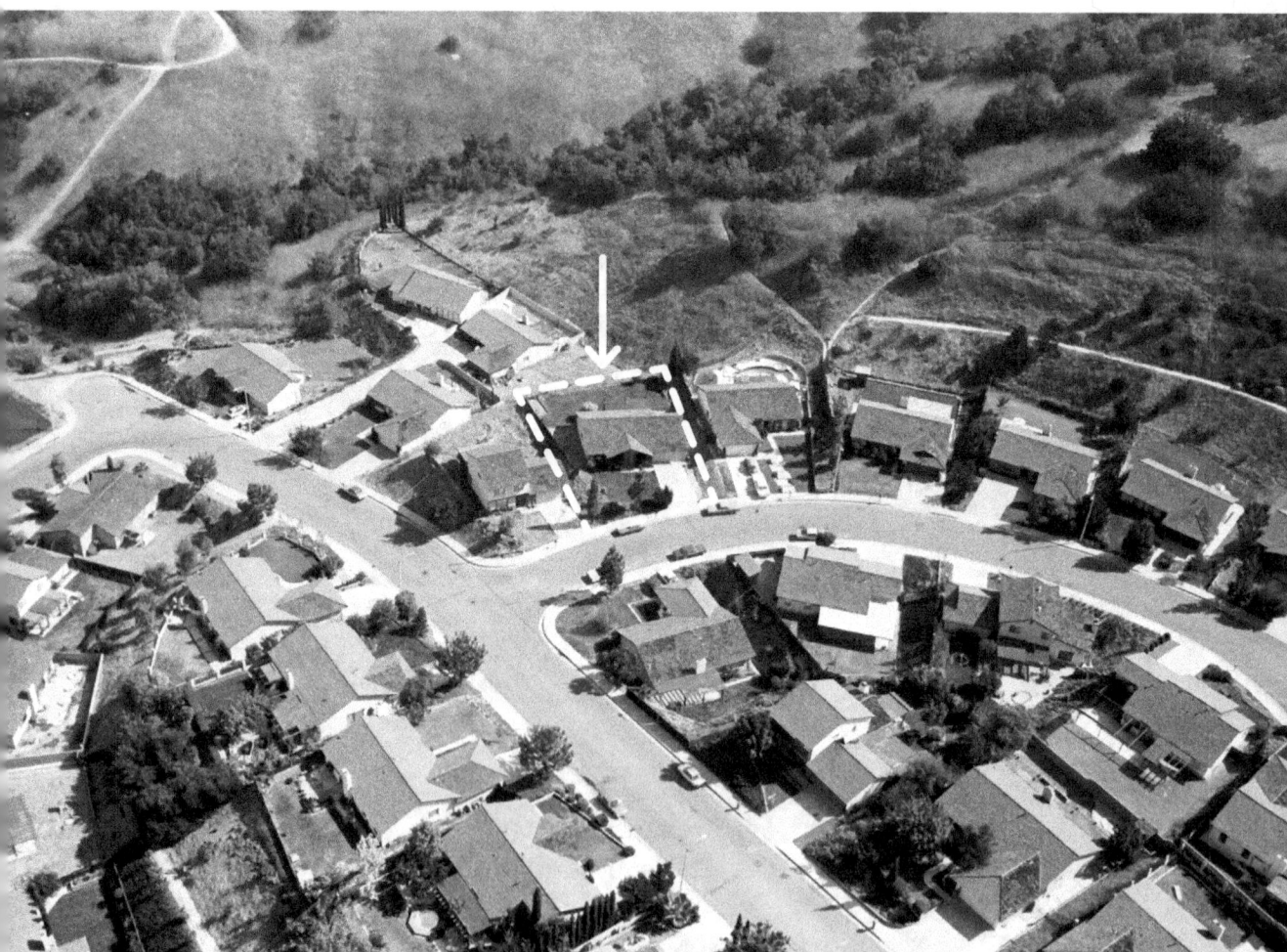

Aerial view of the Abowath residence. (Los Angeles Sheriff's Department)

Opposite Top & Bottom: Telephone wires were severed at several crime scenes. (Los Angeles Sheriff's Department)

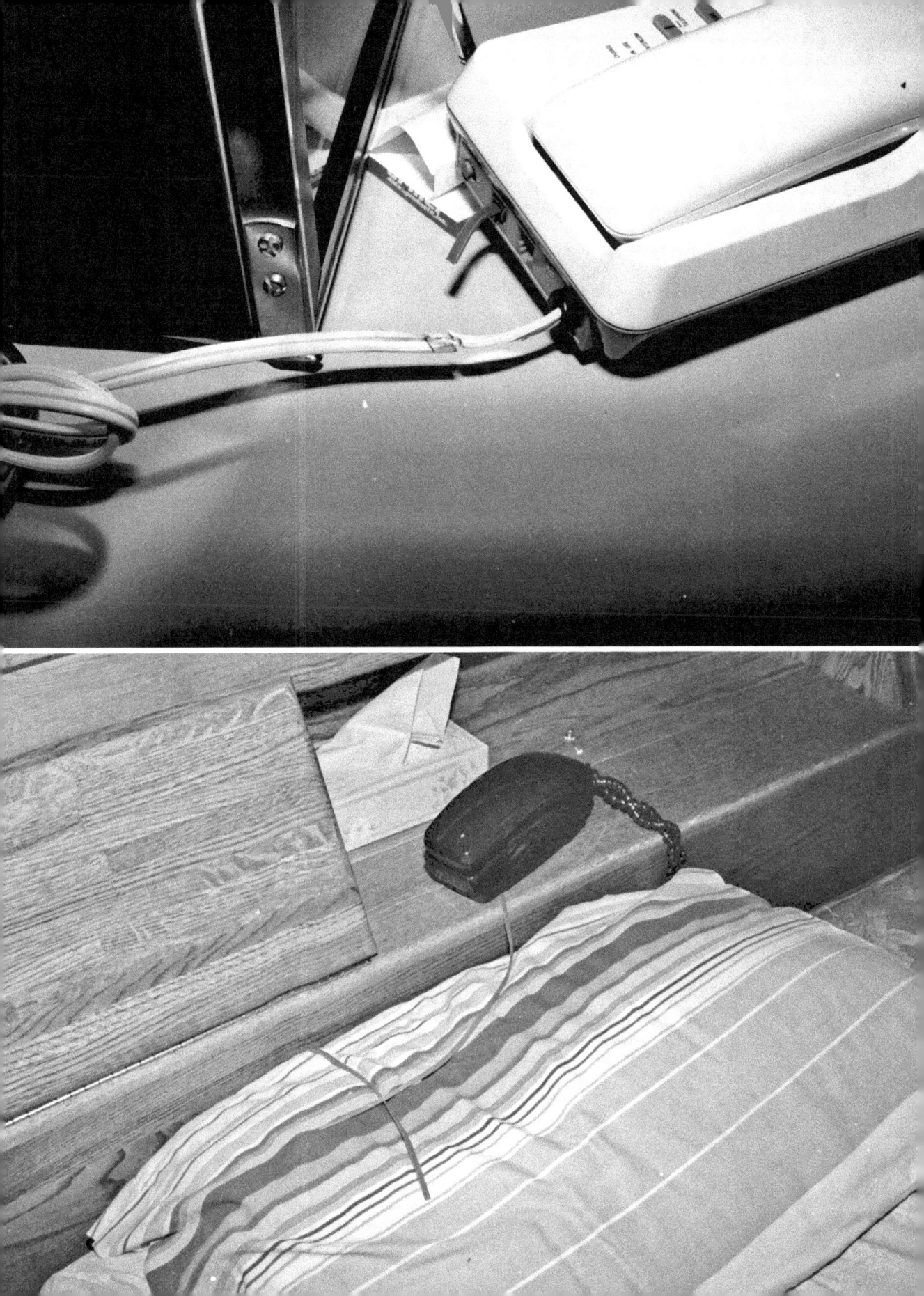

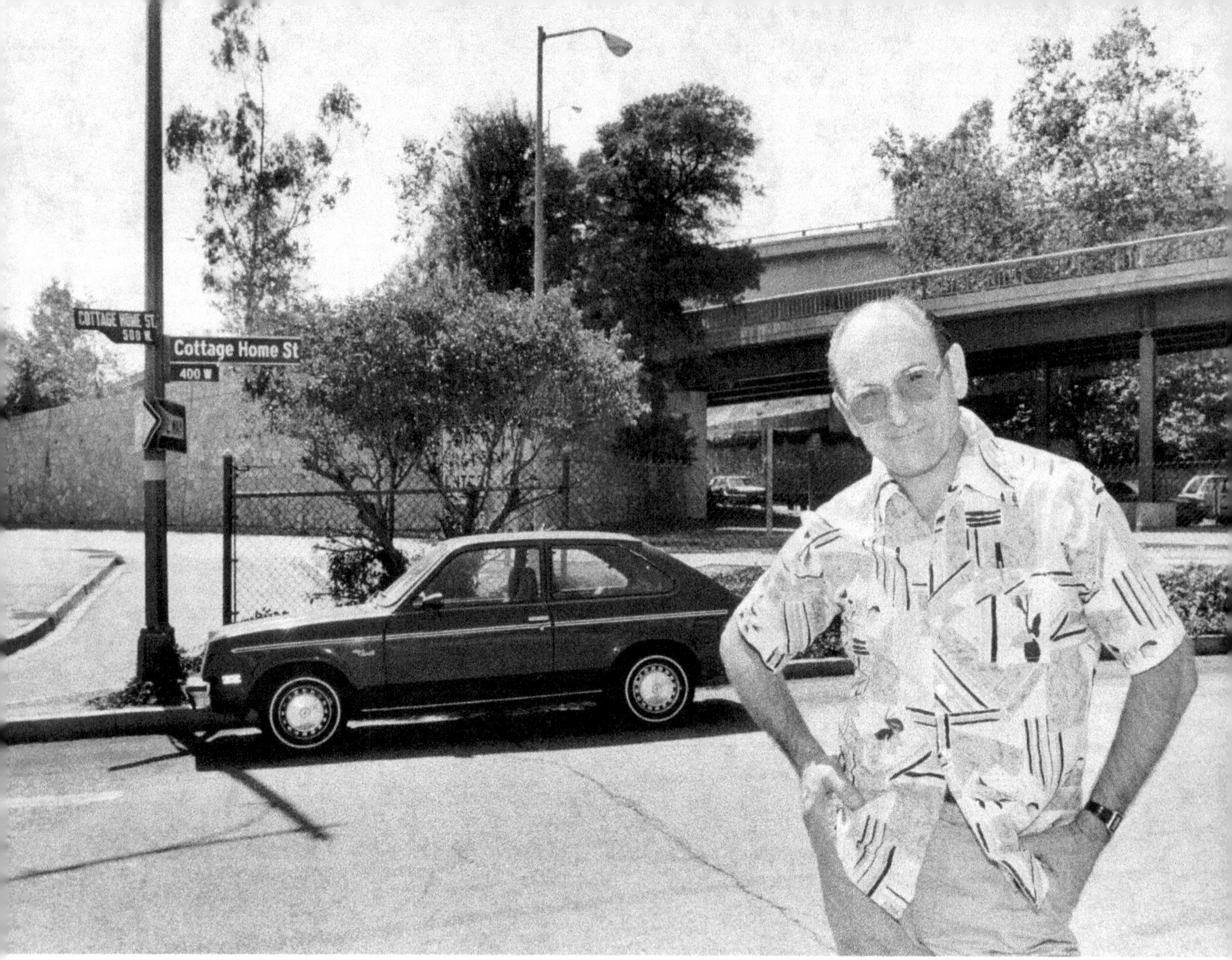

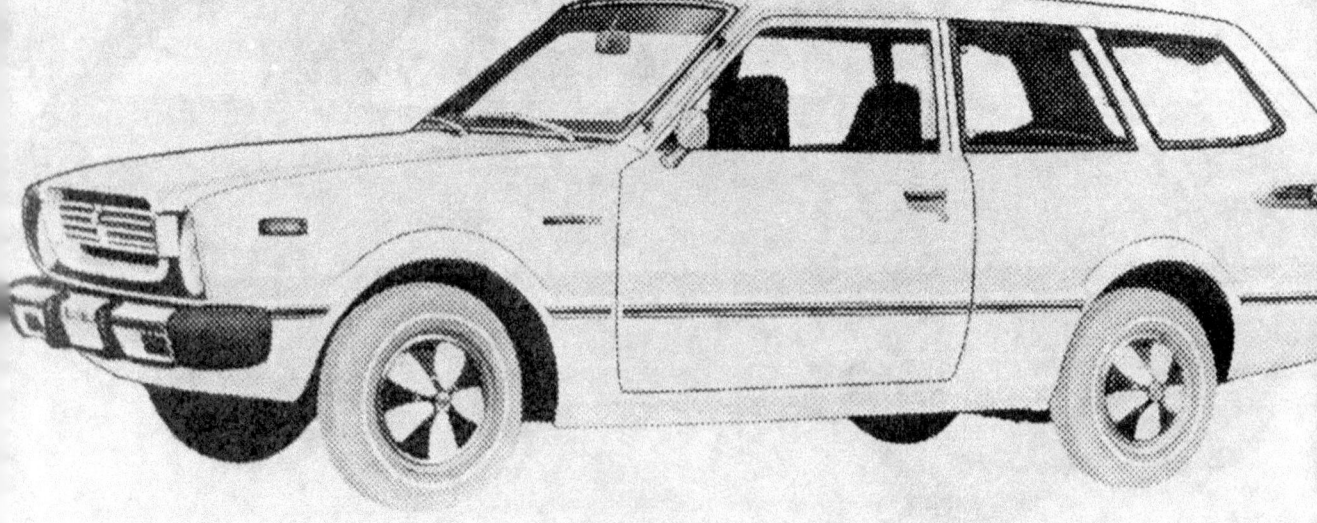

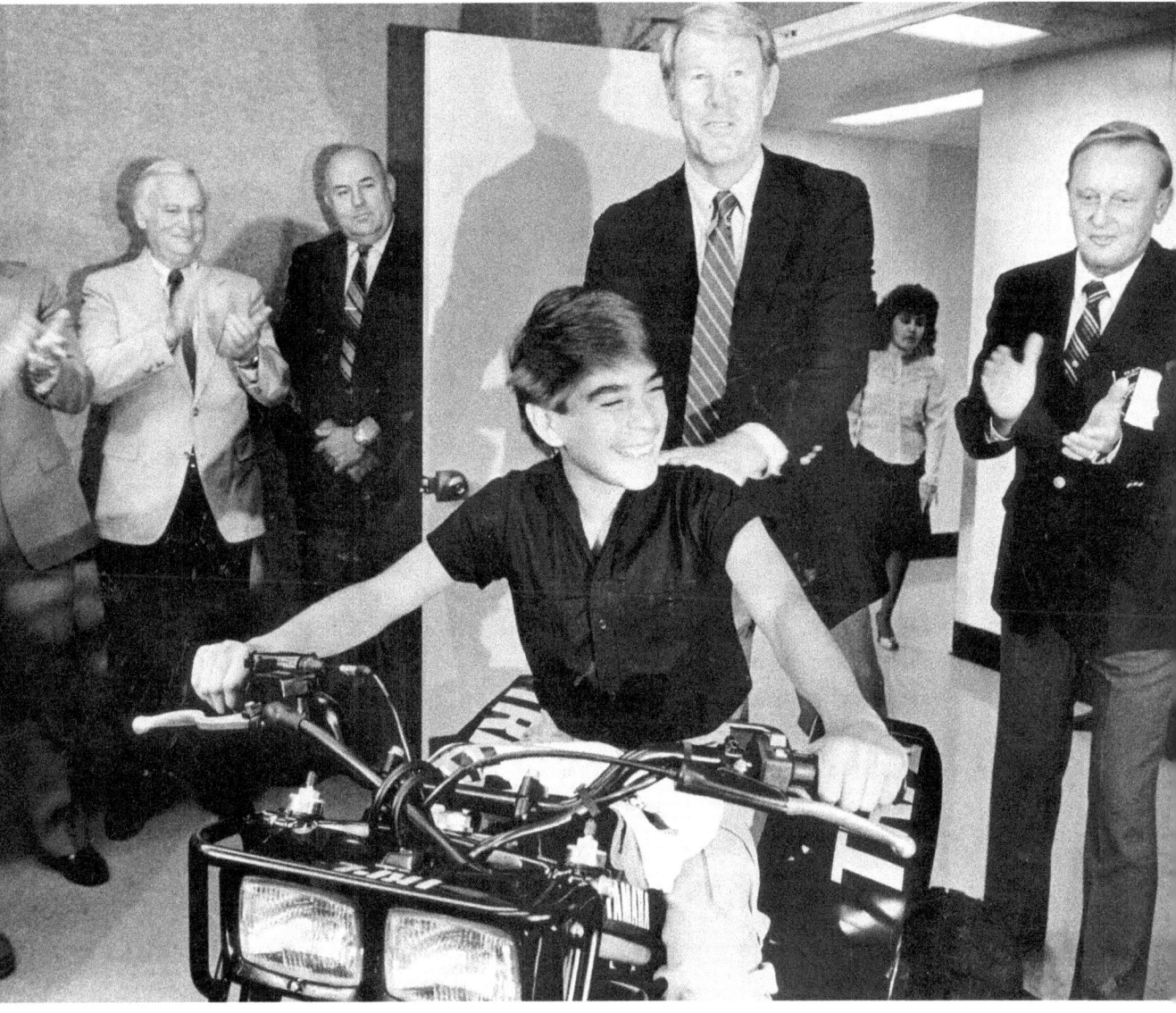

Joseph Romero III (seated on ATV) recalled several digits of the stolen Toyota's license plate. (Anne Knudsen/Herald Examiner Collection)

Opposite Top: Bill Gregory, owner of the Toyota Corolla station wagon, shown on Cottage Home Street in Chinatown, near where the car was stolen. (Anne Knudsen/Herald Examiner Collection) • Bottom: Sketch of the Toyota circulated to the public by police. (Herald Examiner Collection)

NO ONE WAS SAFE

by Kathy Kristof

The killings started when I was a newly-minted college graduate, and living alone for the first time. Like so many other things when you're young and seemingly invincible, I thought I could ignore them.

The first victim—at least the first that we heard about at the time—was a 79-year-old widow living in a sketchy part of the city. It seemed like an isolated incident. Maybe neighborhood thugs with a vendetta. Although the crime happened only five minutes from my little apartment, I felt like it was a world away.

That was the summer of 1984.

Within a few days, the Olympic Games opened in Los Angeles and life went on more or less uninterrupted. I was 24-years old, working nearly non-stop, trying to establish myself as a journalist and make enough of a living to pay rent and make the payments on my new red Fiero.

It was an inexpensive two-seater. A "sports" car that ended up having so many systemic mechanical defects that Pontiac discontinued it within five years of its launch. I'd go into my Mid-Wilshire office at 7 in the morning and often wouldn't return to my studio apartment in the Los Feliz area until well after dark. Mechanical breakdowns were an inconvenience—a reason to keep my auto club membership up to date—not a huge worry.

But shortly after my 25th birthday, there was another murder. And another. And another. They were random. Brutal. The killer would break in, usually at night, killing men, raping and killing women—sometimes as their children watched. News accounts revealed a satanic element to the killings.

A few of the victims survived the gunshot wounds, beatings and rapes. Their stories were terrifying. And the attacks were happening all around me. Monterey Park. Burbank. Sierra Madre. Glendale. Northridge. Victims were old, young, couples, singles, parents, grandparents. He used guns, knives, blunt objects, electrical cords.

There was no reason, no pattern, just attack after attack—usually in the dead of night.

In the spring and summer of 1985, the Night Stalker crept into my psyche and into the heads of everyone I knew.

He was all over the news, often striking again within days of a previous murder. He had taken to carving or drawing pentagrams on the bodies of his victims. Survivors said they were forced to "swear to Satan." He became the main topic of conversation that summer. It didn't matter whether you were in the office, at lunch, at dinner with family. You wanted to make sense of it. Find a pattern. A motive. Put some reason to the killings overwhelming the city.

It didn't matter how sweltering it might be in your apartment. You locked your doors and windows. You kept a weapon—even if it was nothing more than a dented Louisville Slugger—by the bed. All we really knew about the Night Stalker was that an evil phantom was robbing, killing and raping with a voraciousness that seemed impossible—certainly inhuman.

No one was safe.

Finally, in late August, a survivor was able to give authorities a description. They found a stolen car that the Night Stalker had used and police lifted a fingerprint. It led authorities to a drifter of my years. Richard Muñoz Ramirez had a lengthy rap sheet. They released his creepy mug shot and virtually every newspaper and television station in California published it to help the public identify this rapacious murderer.

A few days later, Ramirez attempted to hijack a car in East Los Angeles after being recognized by a group of elderly Mexican women on the street. Bystanders took chase and eventually caught him, beating him relentlessly until the police arrived.

Ramirez was eventually convicted and sent to death row where he filed an endless series of appeals. These sustained him until he finally succumbed to B-cell Lymphoma in 2013. I am not normally a vindictive person. But I hope he suffered.

I still sleep with a baseball bat by my bed.

AUGUST 24, 1985

The significance of Joseph Romero's observation escalated the following morning. The Orange County Sheriff's Department was investigating a rape and attempted murder of a couple just 1-1/2 miles from the Romero home. Billy Carns and his girlfriend had recently moved to Orange County from North Dakota. Just two days earlier, Carns's mother had cautioned Billy about the California serial killer on the loose. Carns was shot multiple times, suffered brain damage, but survived.

Ramirez ultimately abandoned the car in a parking lot near Beverly Books in LAPD's Rampart area. Through Rodney Shelton's office window, LAPD detectives awaited Ramirez's return to the vehicle. A day passed and the detectives rightly opted to impound Bill Gregory's stolen Toyota and search for evidence. A partial fingerprint was lifted.

Both the car and the fingerprint were sent to the Orange County Sheriff's Department. A computer matched the fingerprint lift to a Texas man—Ricardo Ramirez.

In short order an LAPD booking photo of Richard Ramirez from a December ,1984, arrest was located and widely circulated to Southern California law enforcement officers, and beyond. The booking photo compared favorably to the previous composite sketches drawn by LAPD's sketch artist, Fernando Ponce.

Some victims reported their attacker was wearing a black baseball cap, and previously a cap with the logo of the heavy metal band AC/DC had been found at a crime scene, so a black cap was added to the LAPD sketch.

The task force investigating the series of Ramirez's crimes decided to enlist the help of the general public and the news media. The booking photo was released to news outlets, and featured on the front page of one of LA's daily newspapers, the *Herald-Examiner*.

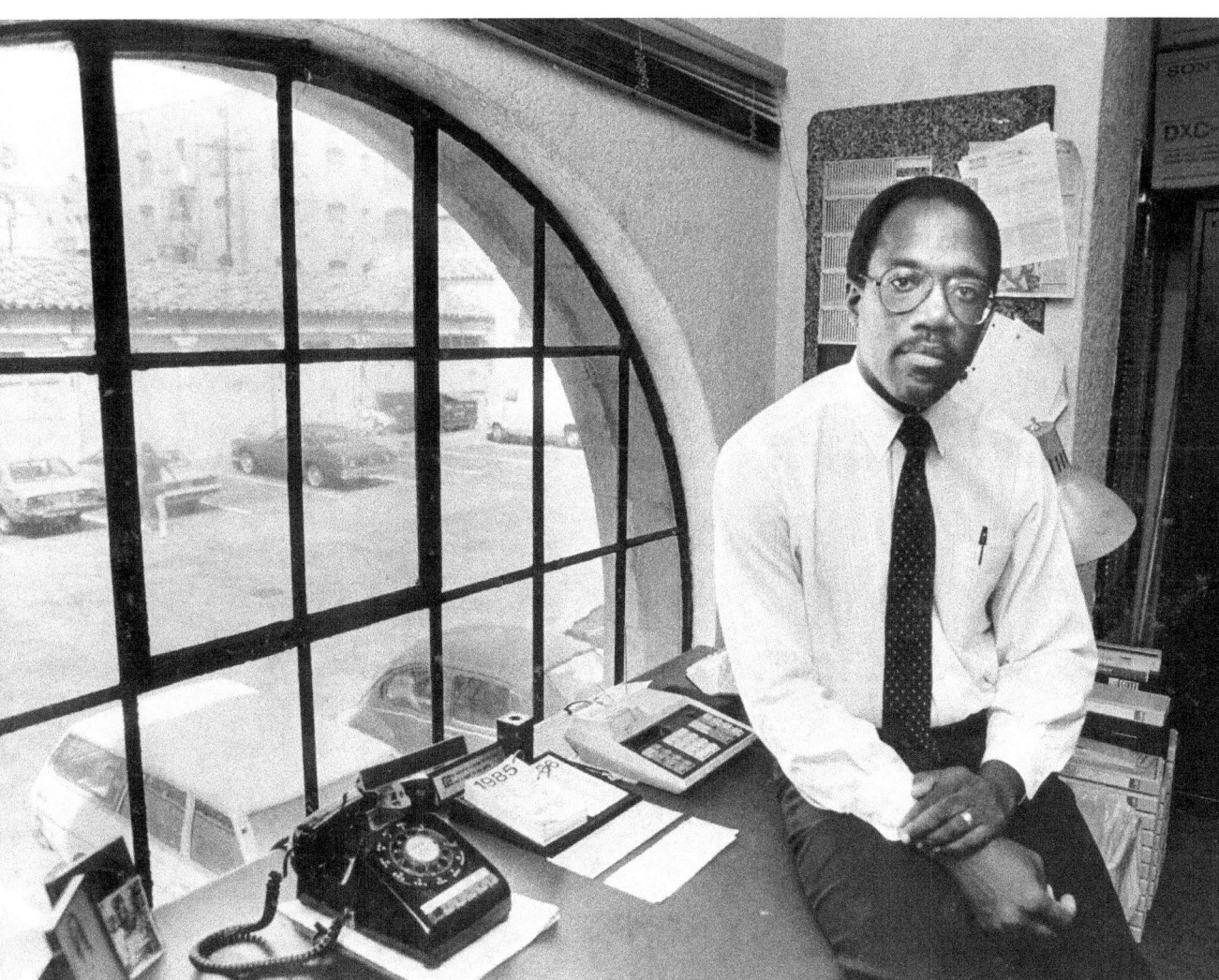

Rodney Shelton's office window where LAPD detectives awaited Ramirez's return to the stolen Toyota. (Paul Chinn/Herald Examiner Collection)

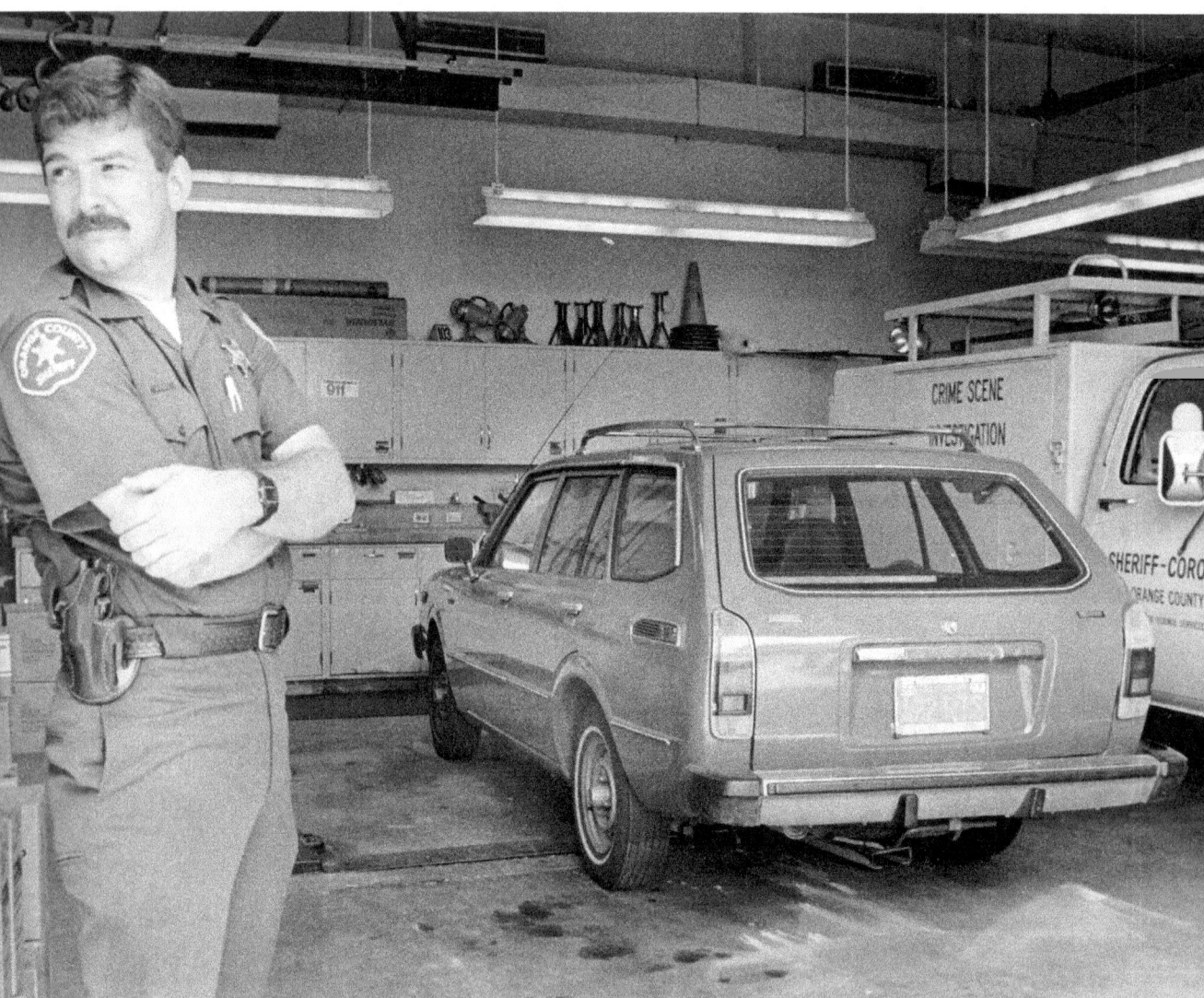

**Orange County Sheriff's Department found fingerprints in the Toyota.
(Paul Chinn/Herald Examiner Collection)**

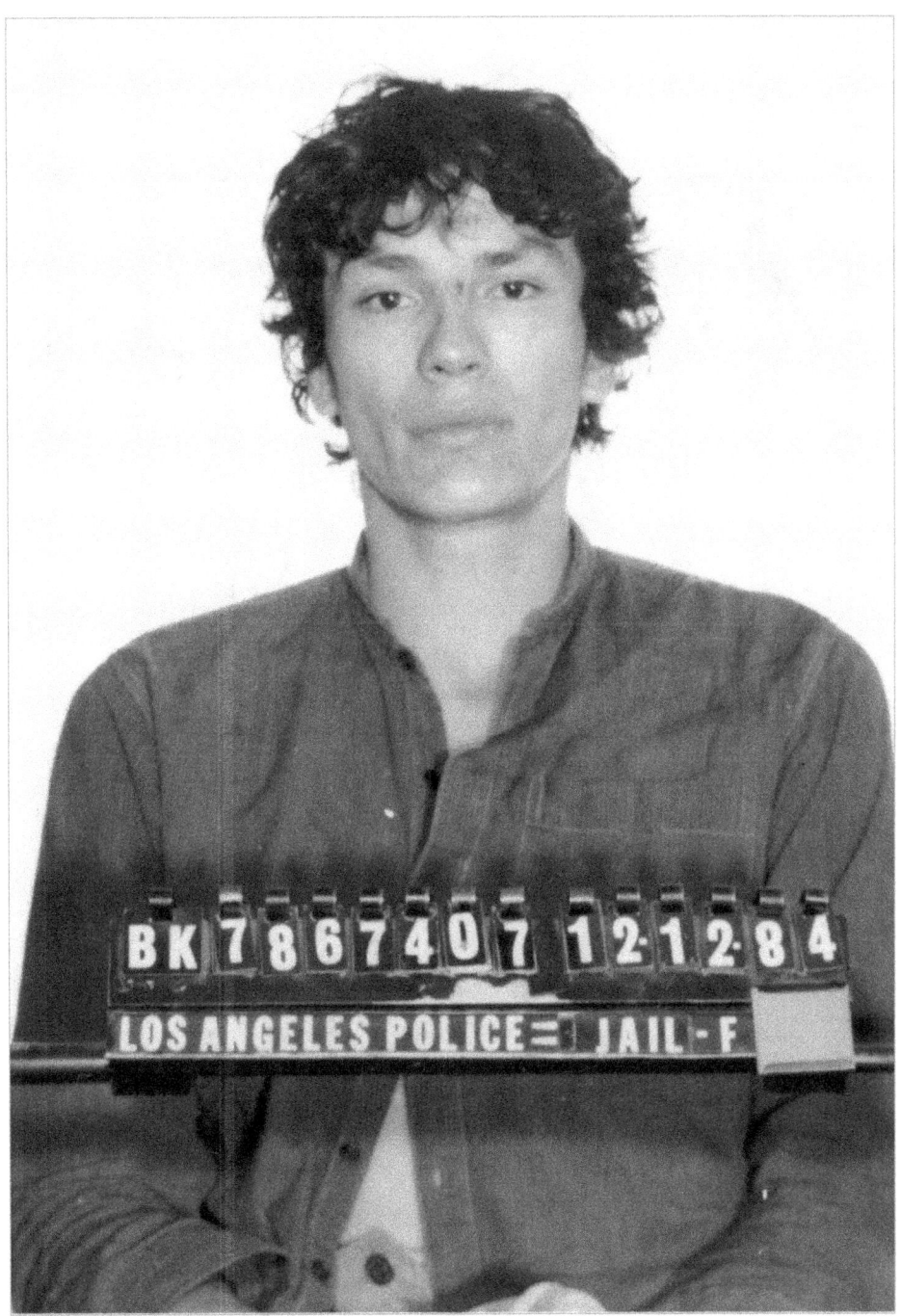

Richard Ramirez's booking photo. (Herald Examiner Collection)

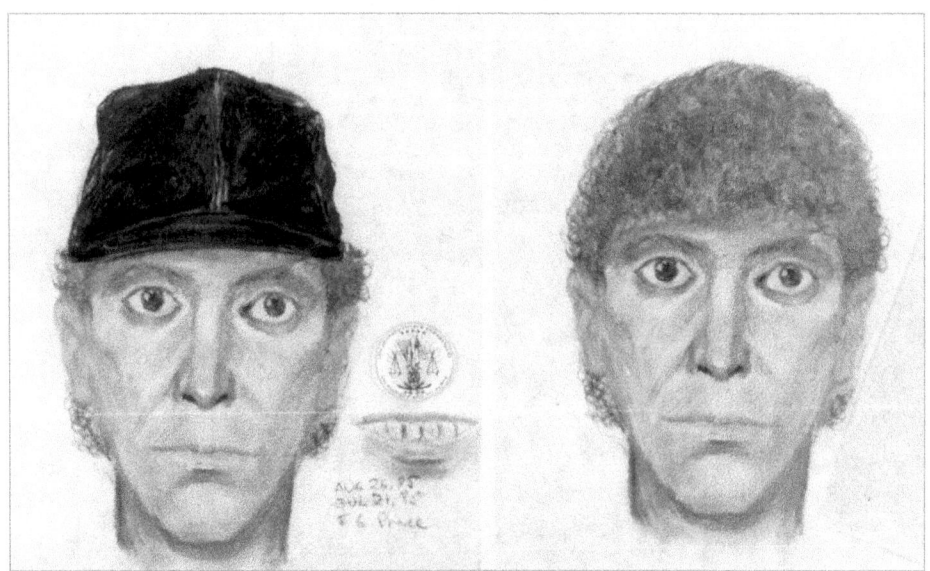

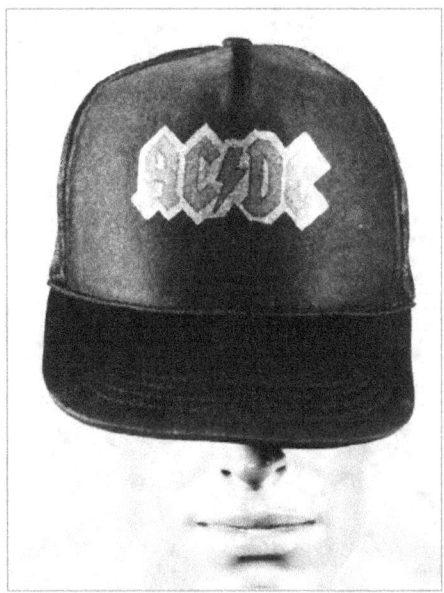

Top: A black cap was added to the LAPD sketch. (Herald Examiner Collection) • Bottom: (Los Angeles Sheriff's Department)

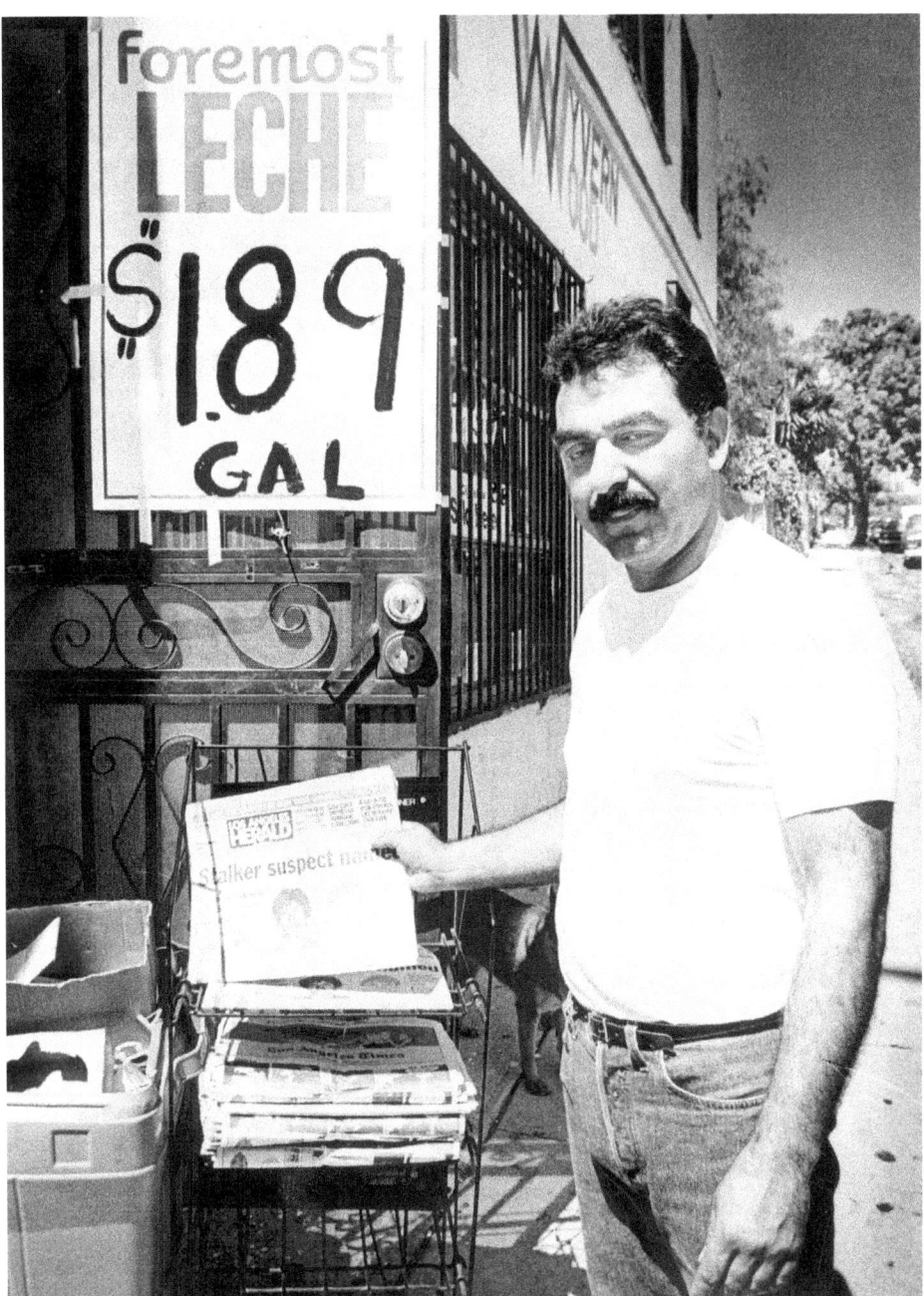

Armando Lojero holds the *Herald-Examiner* in front of East LA's Wyvernwood store at 8th and Evergreen where Ramirez saw his photo in the newspaper. (Leo Jarzomb/Herald Examiner Collection)

AUGUST 31, 1985

Ramirez made his way through the streets of East Los Angeles, pausing in an attempt to steal Arturo Benavidez's car from the front of his barbershop. Benavidez phoned the authorities, and the hunt for the Night Stalker was underway in earnest.

Ramirez fled from the barbershop, in search of a means to leave the area immediately. Ramirez happened into a yard on Hubbard Street and attempted to steal a Ford Mustang that Faustino Pinon had given his daughter. Ramirez tried to drive off with the running vehicle. Pinon reached inside the vehicle in an attempt to remove the keys. Ramirez threatened and fought with Pinon, meanwhile the car stalled.

Ramirez fled on foot, bounding over a five-foot fence and winding up in the street where there was plenty of activity.

Ramirez encountered Angelina De La Torre who was getting ready to enter the family car with her 4- year-old daughter, Amber. Ramirez demanded Angelina's keys. When she failed to comply, Ramirez punched Angelina in the stomach. She screamed. Ramirez entered the car and tried to get it started.

Neighbors came to her aid. Her husband brought a two-foot metal bar, with which he reached into the car and immediately pounded Ramirez's head. Ramirez took off running for a final time. Manuel De La Torre and his neighbors chased Ramirez down the center of Hubbard Street. From behind, Manuel successfully knocked Ramirez to the ground with another strike of the metal bar. Others helped hold Ramirez until Deputy Andres Ramirez (no relation) arrived and handcuffed Richard Ramirez.

LAPD officers who had stopped to retrieve the backpack Richard Ramirez had ditched during his flight through a nearby back yard, transported the handcuffed Ramirez to nearby Hollenbeck Station.

Mayor Tom Bradley, in the company of LAPD Assistant Chief Barry Wade, visited Hollenbeck station and spoke with members of the law enforcement task force and members of the community. "California can breathe a sigh of relief, a very dangerous man is off the street."

The arrest of Richard Ramirez on August 31, 1985, was far from the end of the Night Stalker's domination of the local news. Ramirez's arraignment in the courtroom of Judge Elva Soper occurred just four days later. In the coming years, a preliminary hearing, motions and a protracted trial would bring further attention to the serial killer.

As a result fears were validated, and continued.

Following his arraignment, Ramirez was returned to jail in the custody of the Los Angeles Sheriff's Department. Most prisoners travel to court via a Sheriff's bus with many others. Ramirez was transported alone in a specially barred van with a police motorcycle escort and a helicopter overhead as additional measures of security.

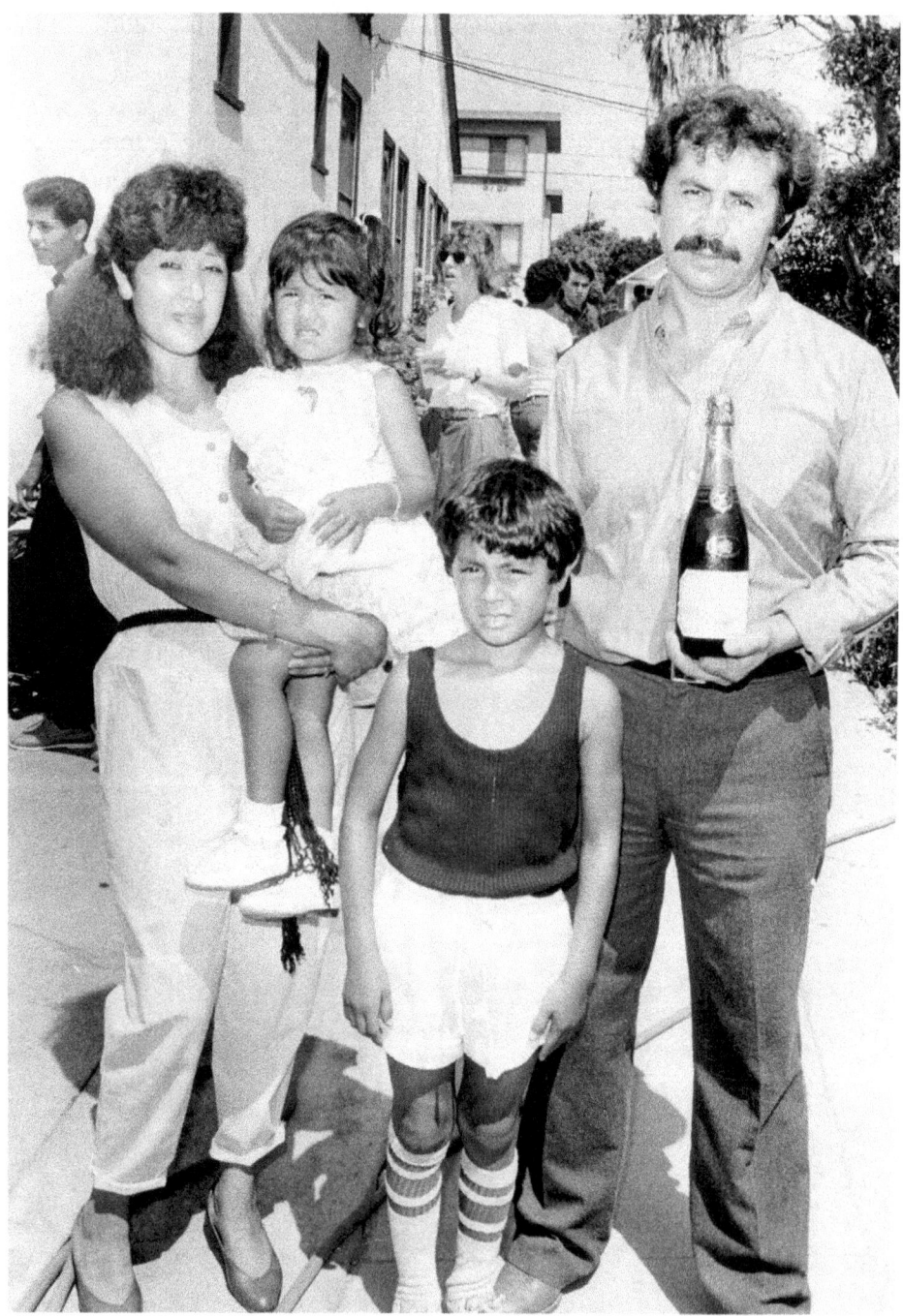

The De La Torre family. (Mike Sergieff/Herald Examiner Collection)

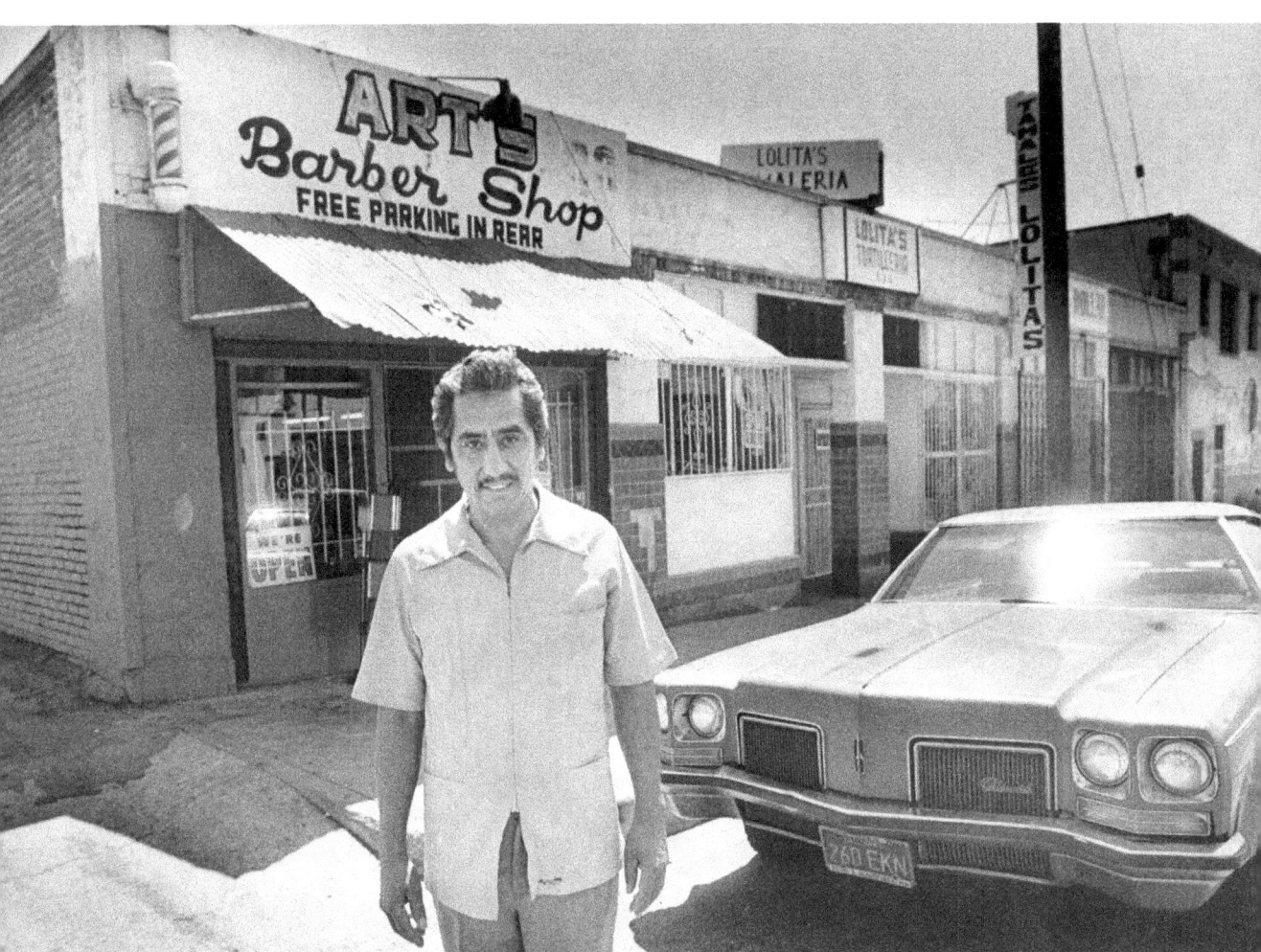

Arturo Benavidez in front of his barbershop. (Leo Jarzomb/Herald Examiner Collection)

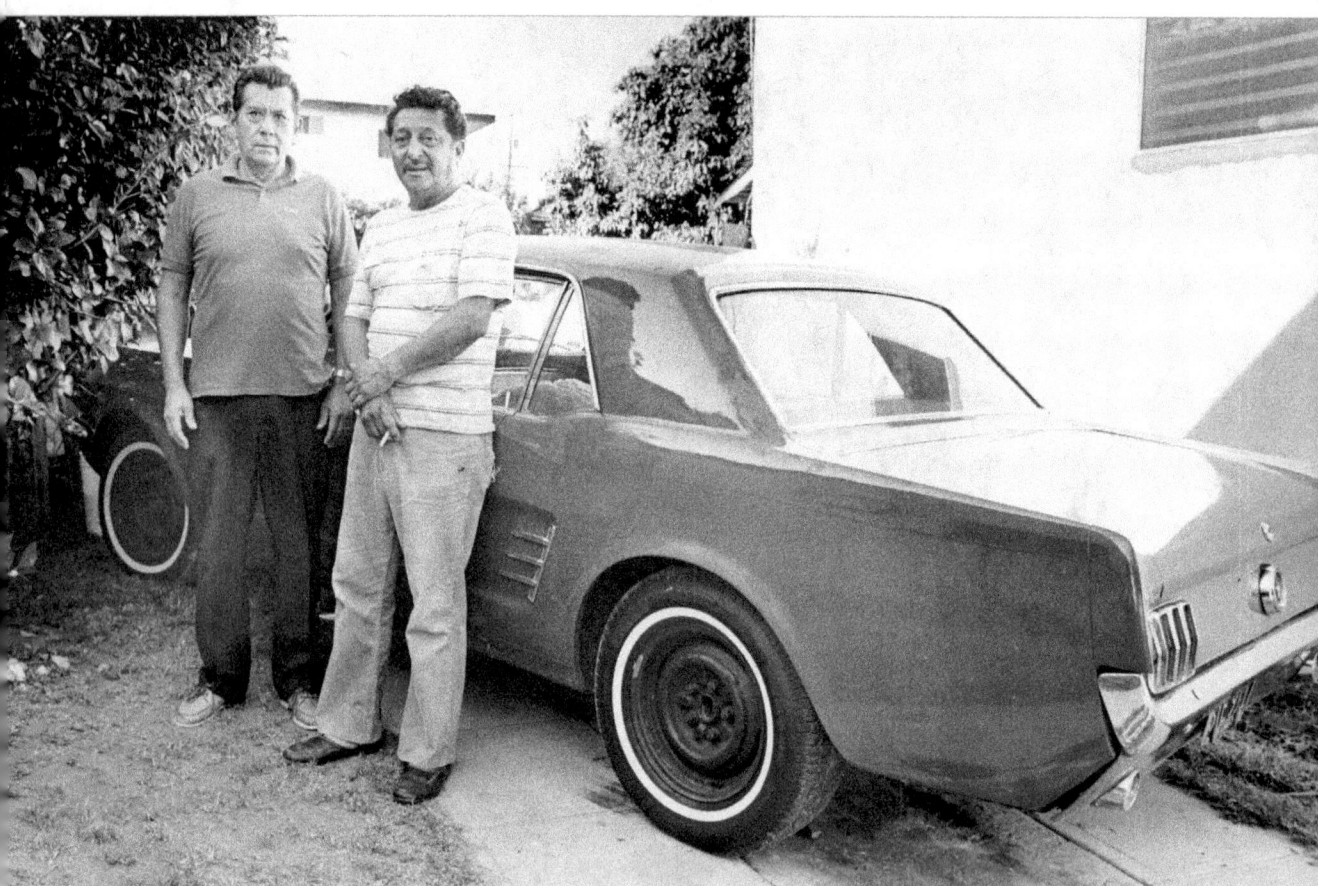

Ramirez attempted to steal this Ford Mustang that Faustino Pinon had given his daughter. (James Ruebsamen/Herald Examiner Collection)

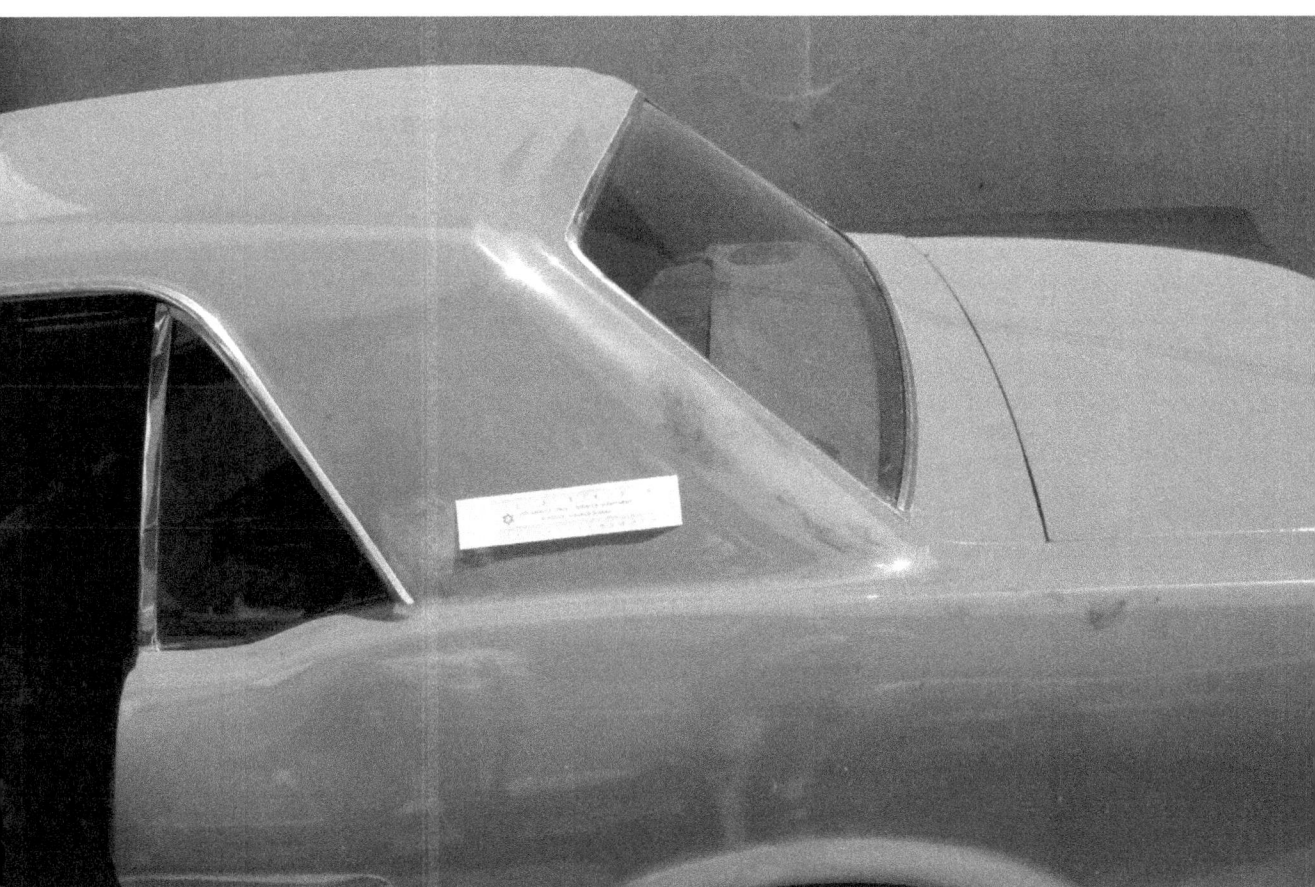

Pinon reached inside the vehicle in an attempt to remove the keys. Ramirez threatened and fought with Pinon, meanwhile the car stalled. (Los Angeles Sheriff's Department)

Sheriff's investigators made note of the address where Ramirez was being held by citizens. (Los Angeles Sheriff's Department)

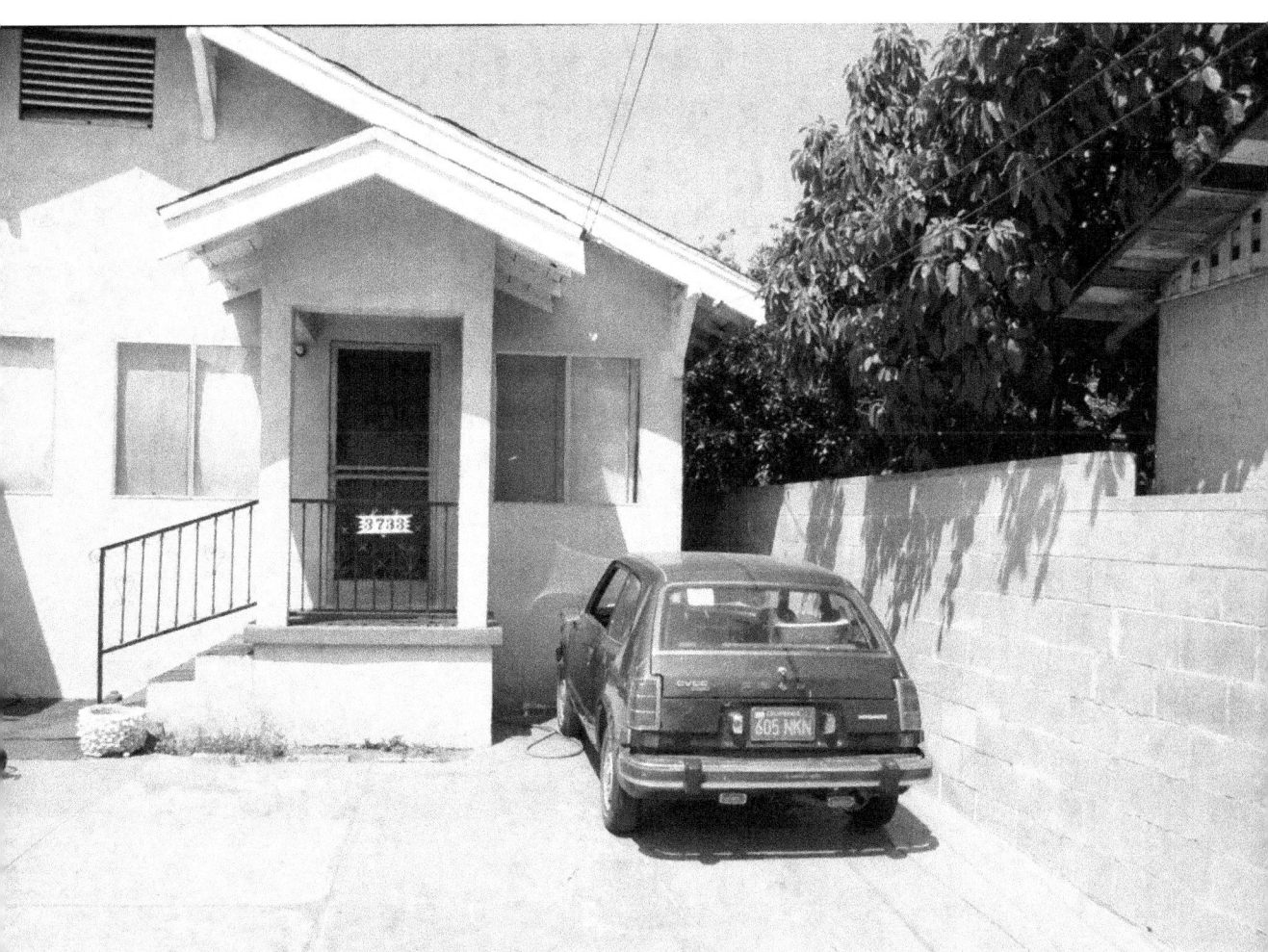

The struggle to gain control of Ramirez began in front of this East Los Angeles home. (Los Angeles Sheriff's Department)

RICHARD RAMIREZ WAS TRANSPORTED TO LAPD'S HOLLENBECK STATION WHERE A CROWD OF MORE THAN ONE THOUSAND GATHERED. THE CROWD'S ACTIVE DISDAIN FOR RAMIREZ INCLUDED THE CHANT, "GIVE HIM TO US, GIVE HIM TO US." LAPD ASSIGNED TWO DOZEN MORE OFFICERS TO CONTROL THE CROWD.

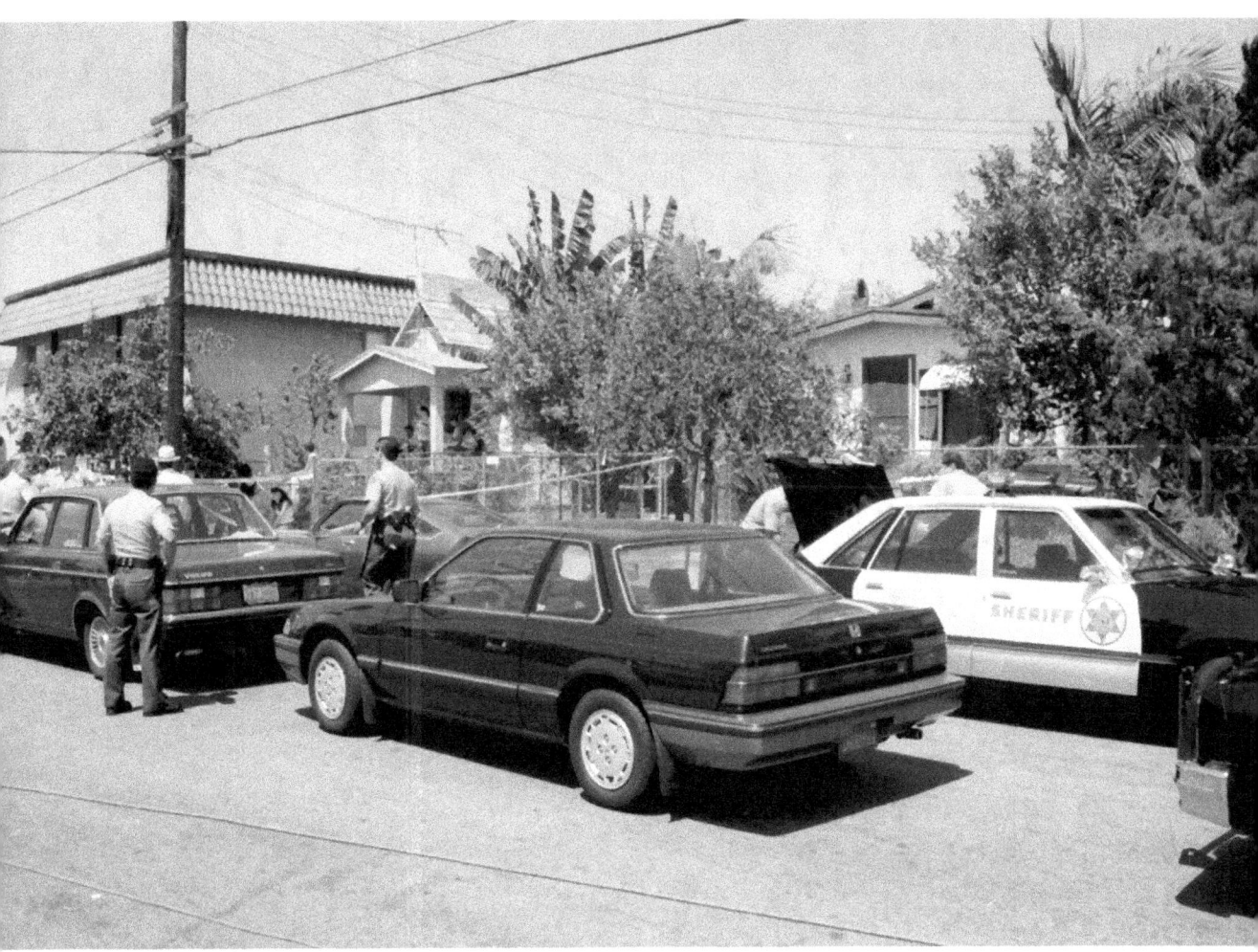

Sheriff's deputies and LAPD officers quickly responded to Hubbard Street where reports of the capture of Richard Ramirez were verified. Ramirez was transported from this neighborhood to LAPD's Hollenbeck Station where lead investigators Frank Salerno and Gil Carrillo had their first contact with Ramirez. Carrillo personally fingerprinted Ramirez. (Los Angeles Sheriff's Department).

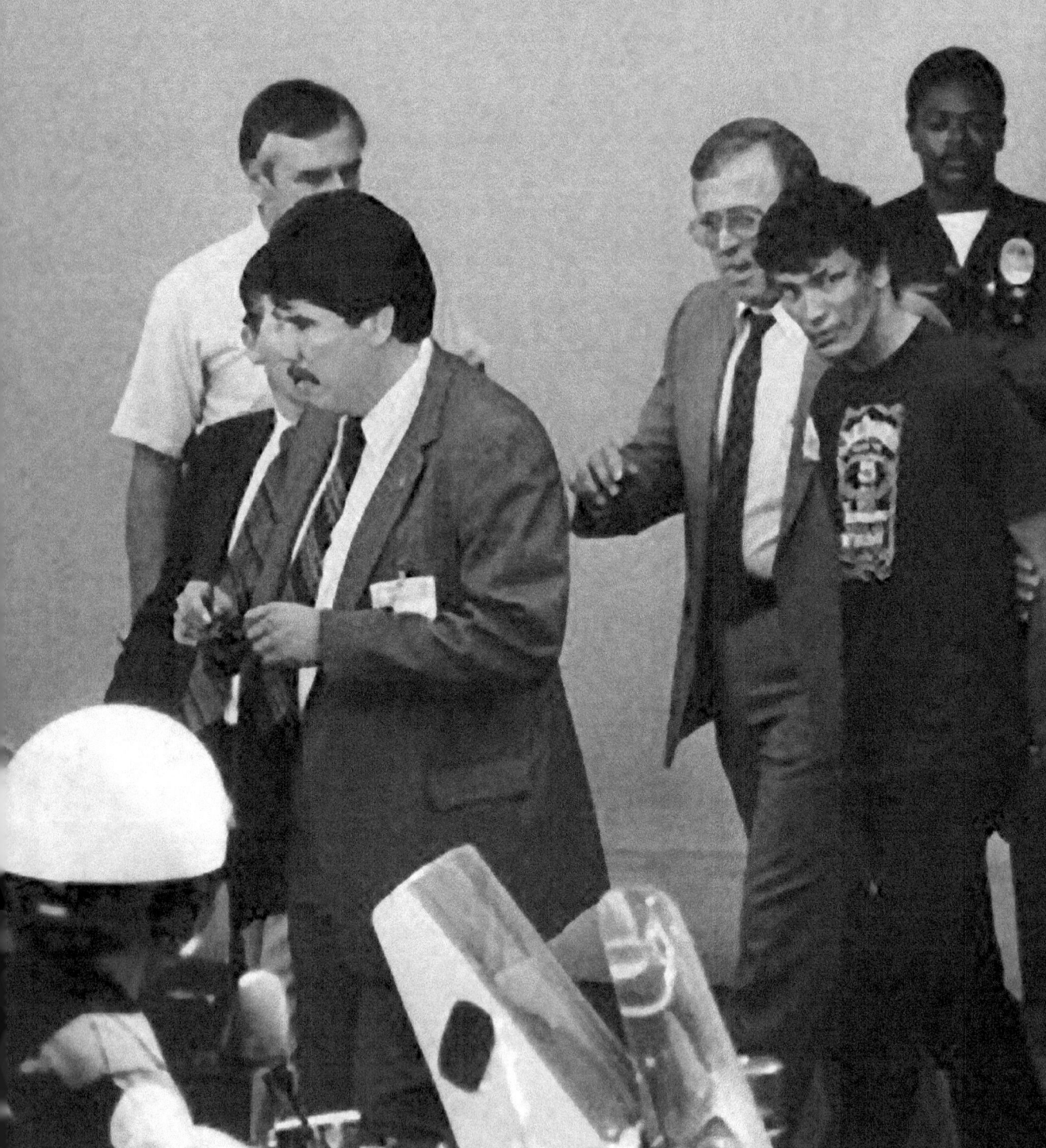

Lead Investigator Gil Carrillo of the Los Angeles Sheriff's Department clears a path for Richard Ramirez as they exit Hollenbeck police station following the capture of Ramirez by a group of East Los Angeles residents. Carrillo's partner, Frank Salerno, walks between Ramirez and the uniformed LAPD officer. (Bill Alkofer/Orange County Register)

"CALIFORNIA CAN BREATHE A SIGH OF RELIEF, A VERY DANGEROUS MAN IS OFF THE STREET."

—MAYOR TOM BRADLEY

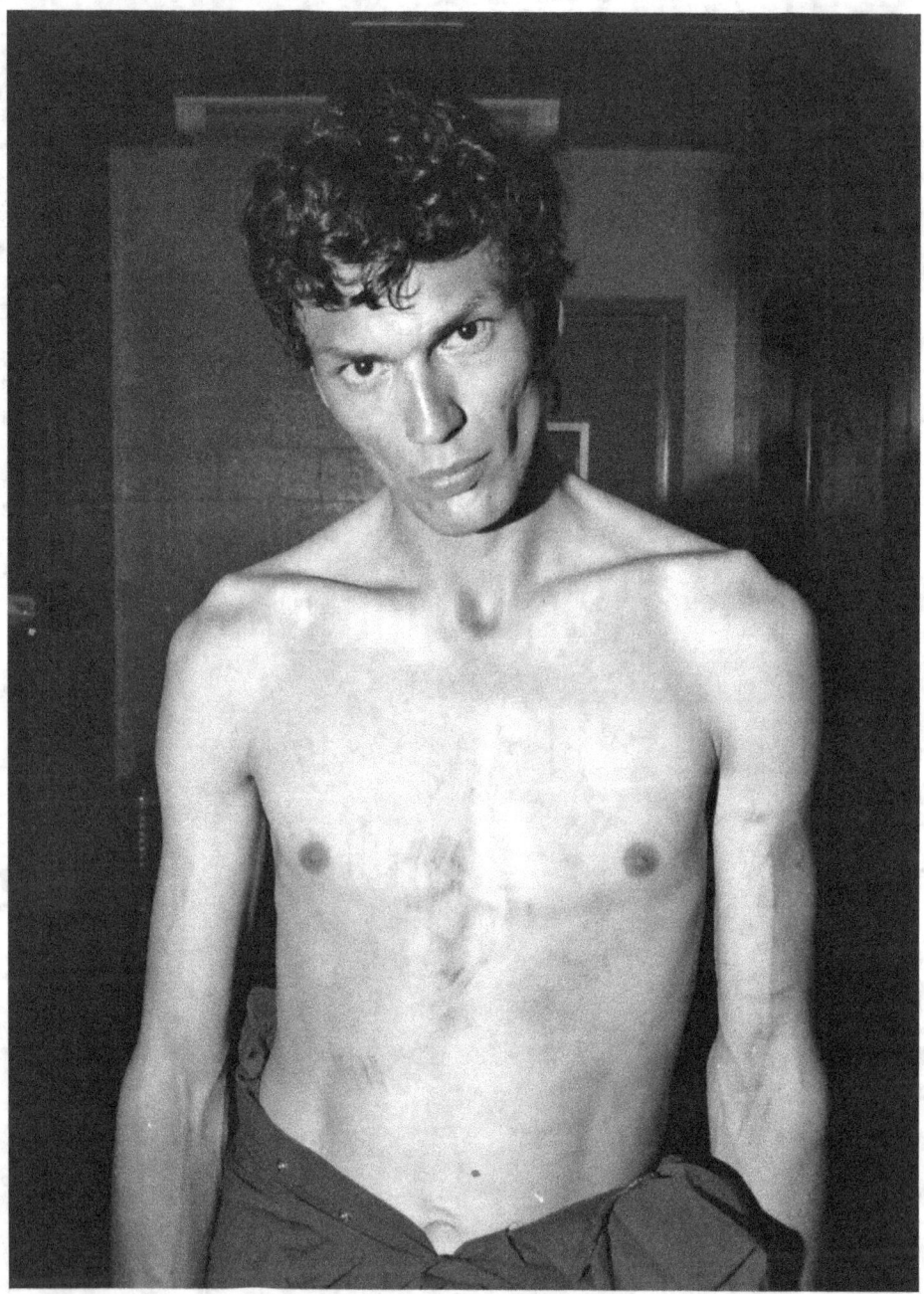

All of Ramirez's clothes were seized as evidence. Ramirez was given a blue jail jumpsuit in which he was photographed after his arrest.
(Los Angeles Sheriff's Department)

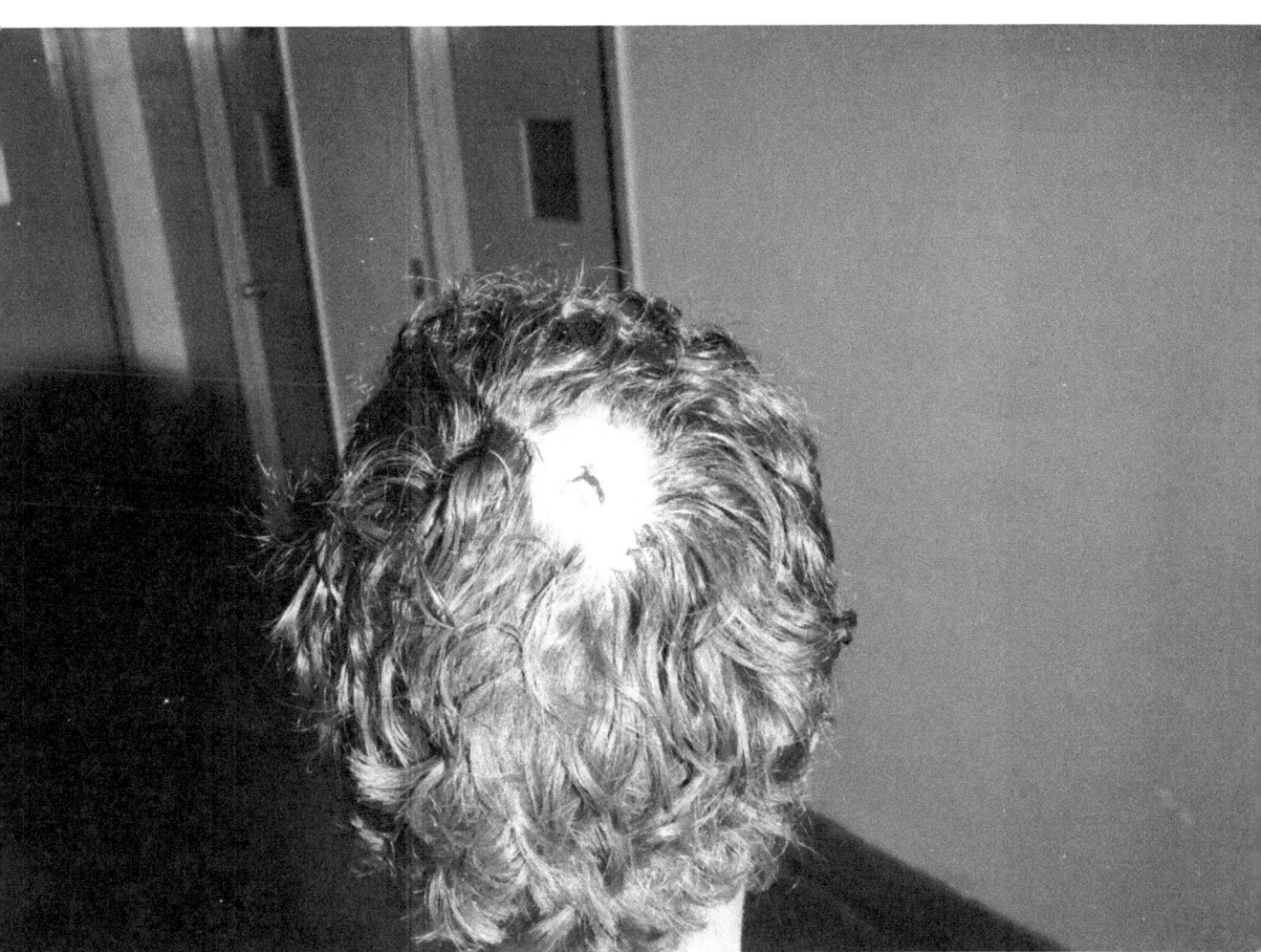

The wounds inflicted by Manuel De La Torre. (Los Angeles Sheriff's Department)

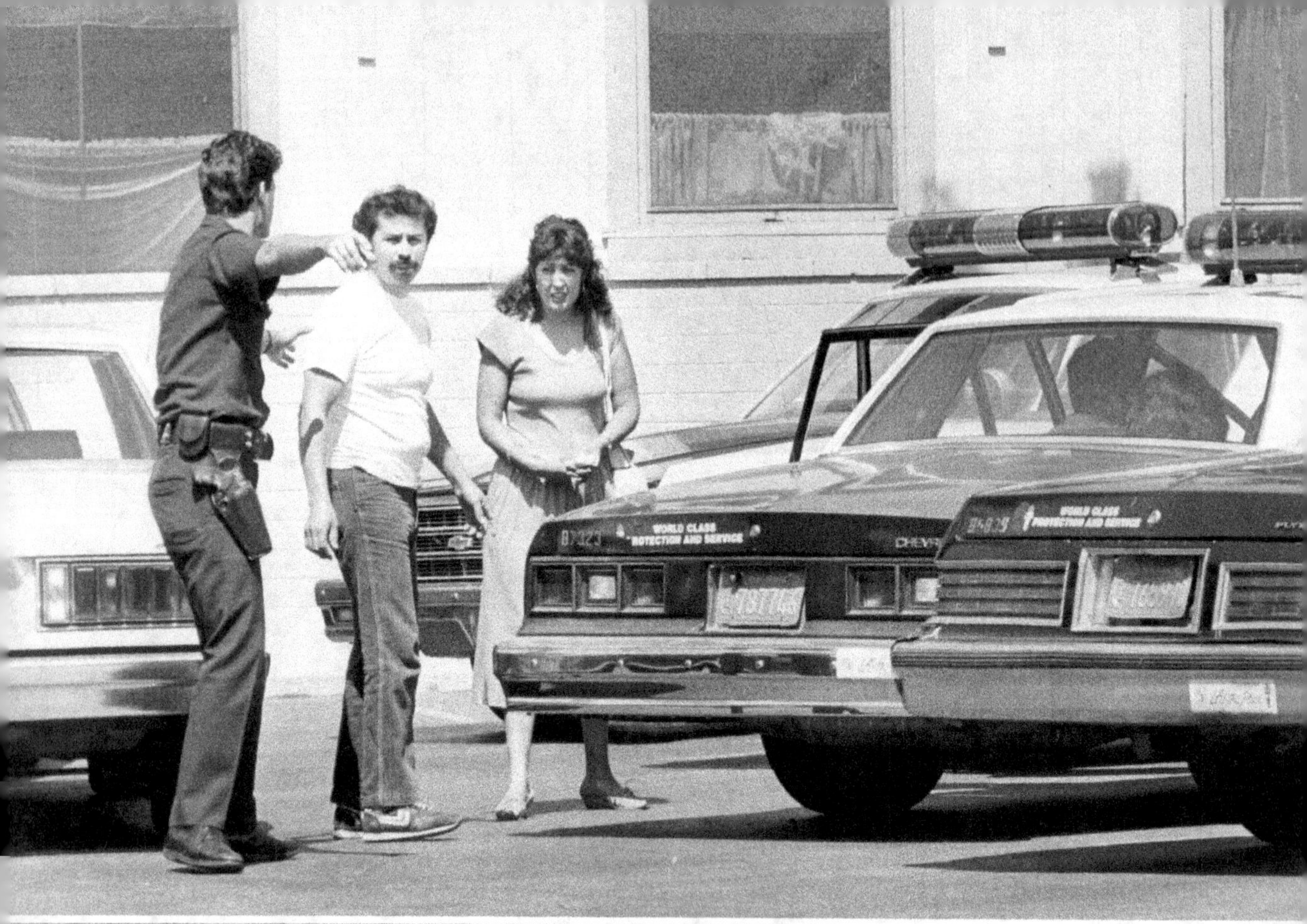
WORLD CLASS
PROTECTION AND SERVICE

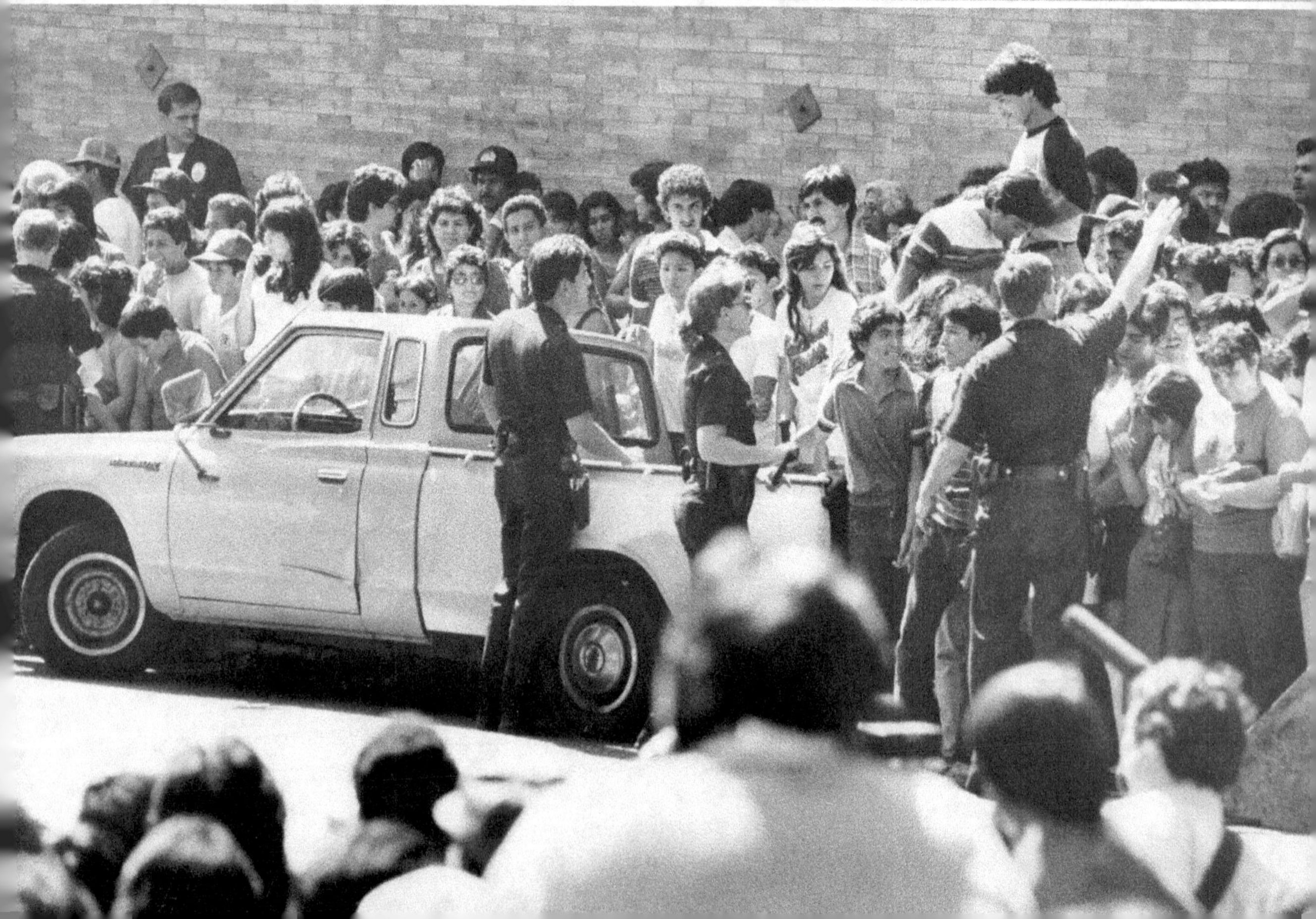

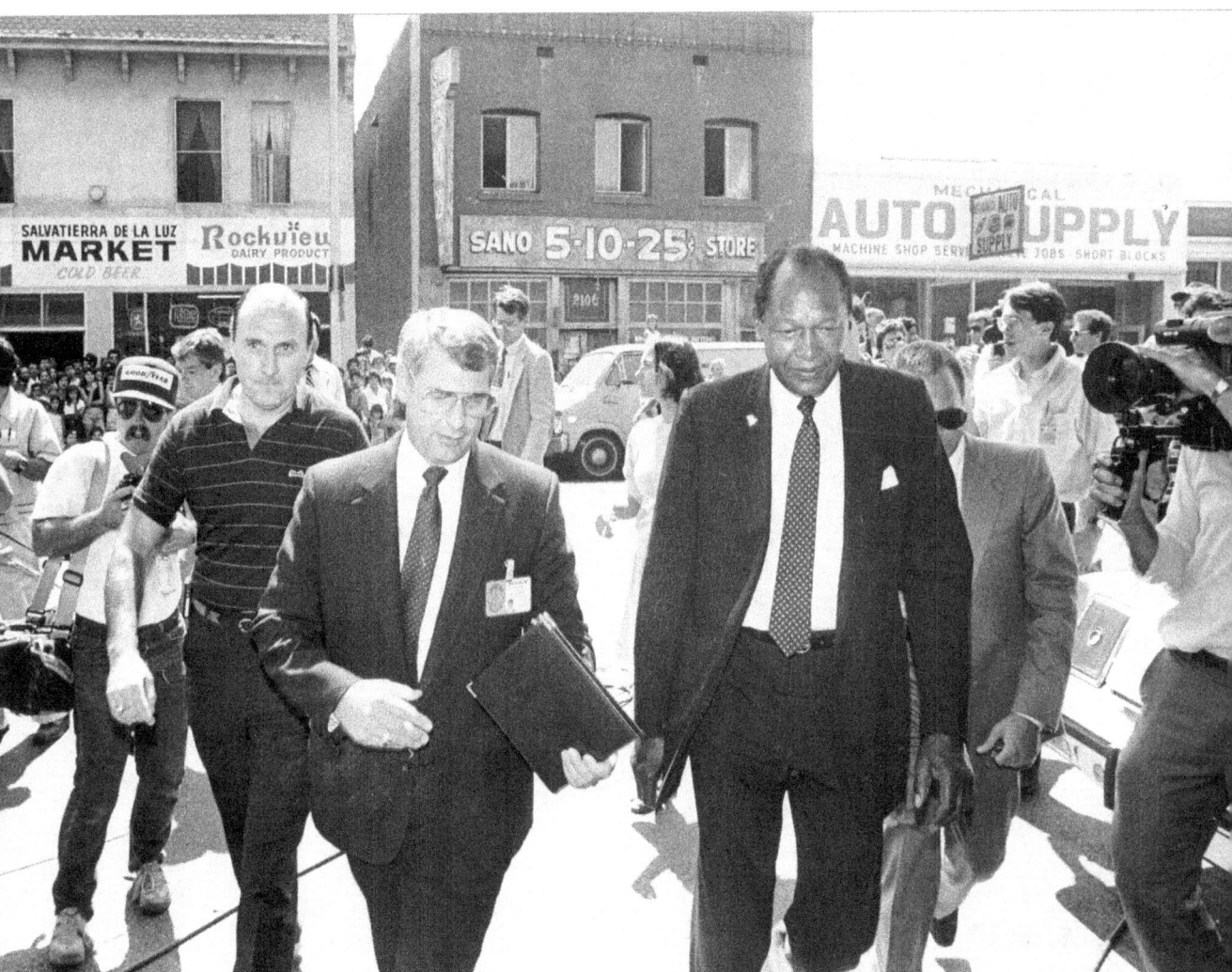

Mayor Tom Bradley visited Hollenbeck Station. (Herald Examiner Collection)

Opposite Top: The De La Torres. (Chris Gulker/Herald Examiner Collection)
Bottom: The crowd outside Hollenbeck Station. (Mike Sergieff/Herald Examiner Collection)

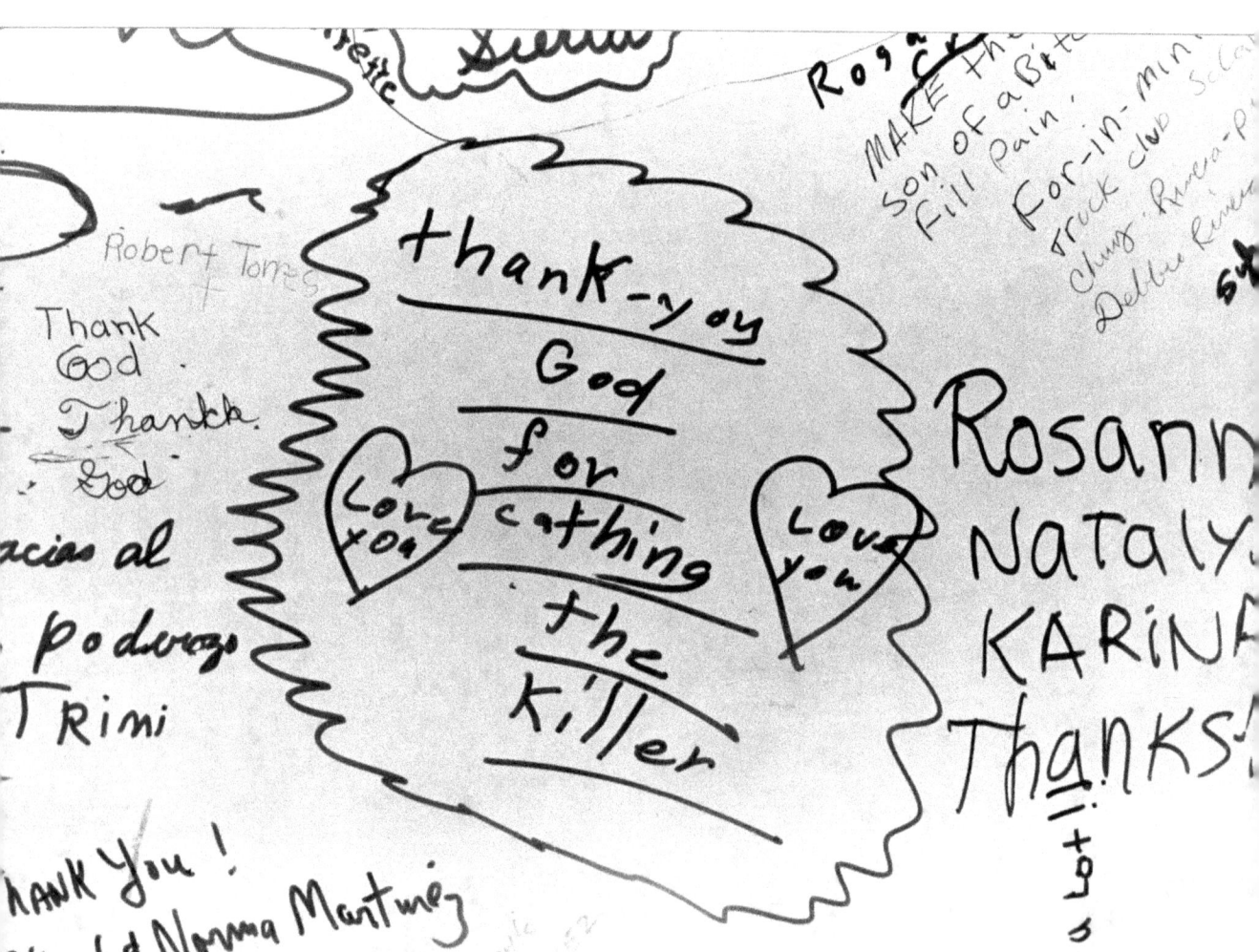

A thank you note to Faustino Pinon for his role in capturing the Night Stalker. (Dean Musgrove/Herald Examiner Collection)

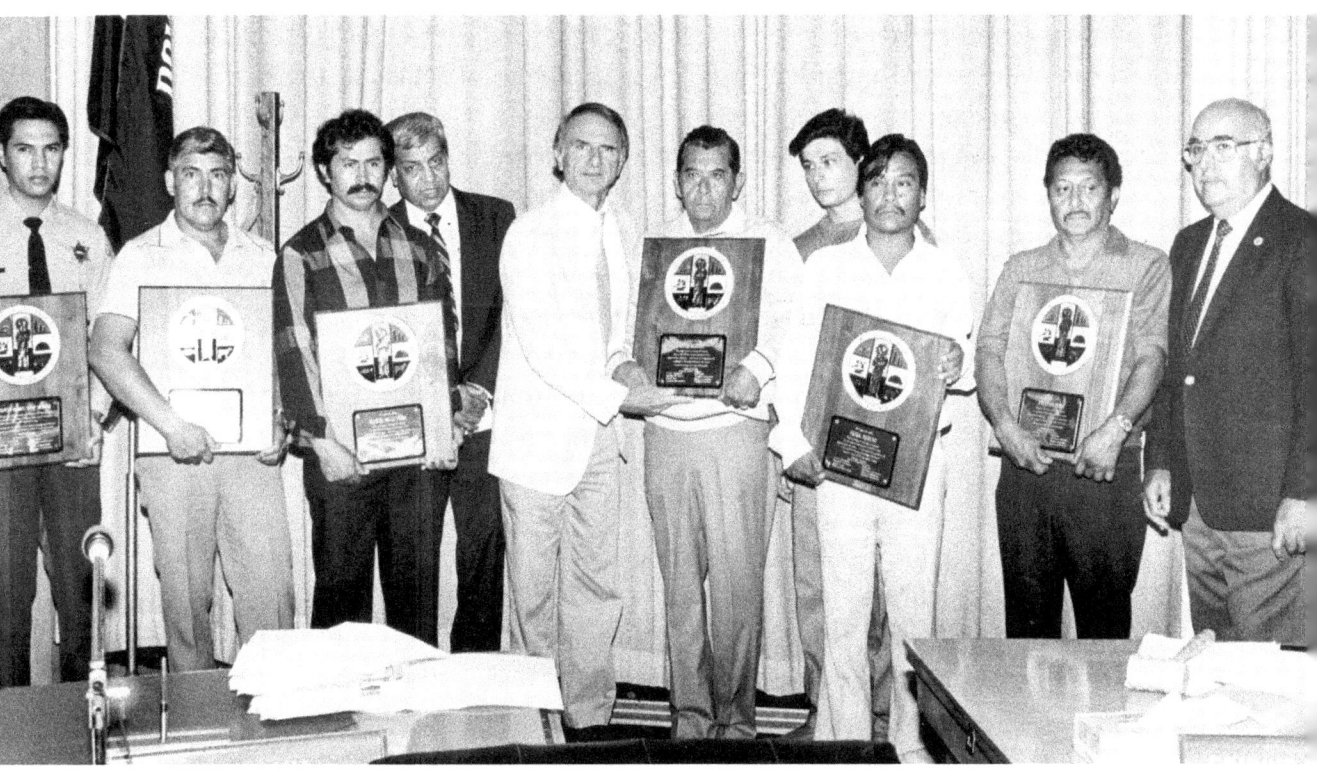

Sheriff Sherman Block (far right) met with and formally recognized those involved in the capture of Richard Ramirez. (Mike Sergieff/Herald Examiner Collection)

THE INVESTIGATION

In addition to the eyewitness testimony of those who survived Ramirez's attacks, investigators needed physical evidence to tie Ramirez to the many, many criminal charges he faced. Prior to his arrest, Ramirez was stopped by a police officer for a nighttime traffic violation and successfully fled. In the event Ramirez had discarded evidence to further avoid detection, the area of the traffic stop was searched.

Indicative of the inter-agency cooperation was the daylight evidence recovery effort at the borders of the City of Los Angeles and the City of Glendale.

Newly-hired Sheriff's deputies were brought from the training academy to assist with the search near the York Boulevard on-ramp to the northbound Glendale Freeway. The on-ramp was temporarily closed in order to provide the searching officers and deputies with a margin of safety.

Once similar shoeprints were discovered at multiple crime scenes, an effort was made to identify the type of shoe and its potential wearer. The Avia athletic shoe was the same model and has the same sole pattern as that worn by the killer.

The sole of the sample athletic shoe closely matched the sole prints discovered at multiple crime scenes. Some sole prints were left in the blood of the victims, others were recovered by making plaster casts of the sole prints found in the dirt at the curtilage of some victims' residences.

Thorough searches of the crime scenes produced important evidence that would ultimately both link the series of crimes and convict Richard Ramirez. The plaster cast is a standard technique used in the scientific solution of crimes. In order for the recovery of a latent print to be useful, it must be located by personnel processing the crime scene. Their diligence in the series of crimes ensured a serial killer was brought to justice.

This chart on page 121 detailed the shoeprint evidence collected during the entirety of the investigation. Of the 1,354 pairs of Avia athletic shoes made, six pairs were shipped to the region and only one pair of size 11-1/2–12 was known to have been sold.

Ramirez as a criminal, was also a serial burglar. Items stolen were often sold. Those engaged in this pursuit are also criminals, often referred to as "fences." Items awaiting sale or items that weren't purchased by Ramirez's fences were held in lockers at the Downtown Los Angeles Greyhound Bus Depot. It was a Ramirez's fence who revealed this practice. Following arrest, detectives found goods stolen during Ramirez's multiple burglaries stored in the bus depot lockers exactly as described.

One of the first follow-up investigations conducted after the arrest of Richard Ramirez was a visit to Ramirez's brother Ruben. Ruben revealed that his brother's personal vehicle, a green 1976 Pontiac was parked on Avenue 23 in the Lincoln Heights area of Los Angeles. After confirming the presence of the vehicle, investigators obtained a search warrant which allowed them to search and seize evidence from the vehicle. A search of the interior yielded Ramirez's fingerprints.

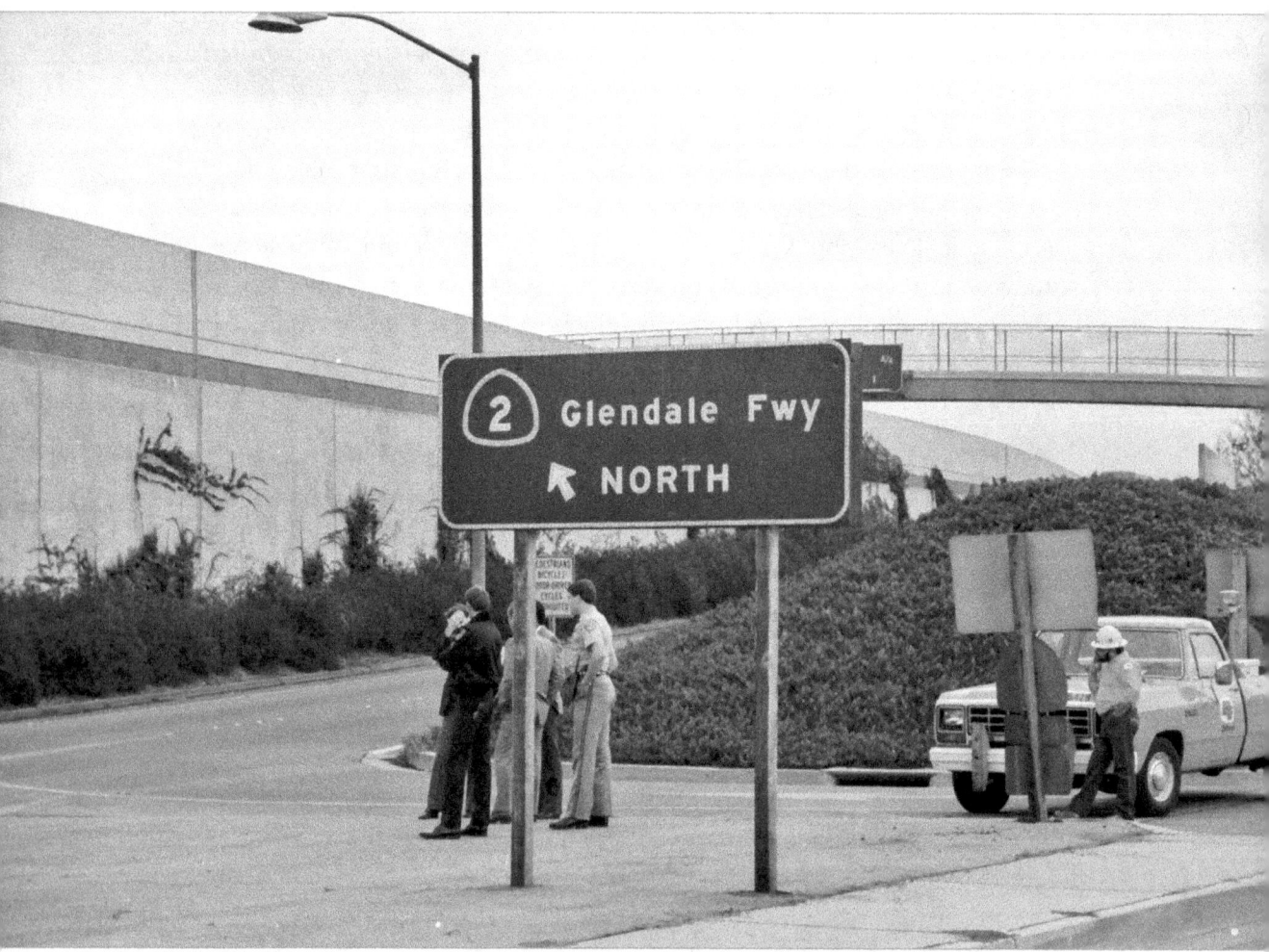

Clustered behind the freeway sign are members of the Glendale Police Department, the California Highway Patrol, the LAPD and officials from the lead agency, the Los Angeles Sheriff's Department—all were working together to search for and collect evidence. (Los Angeles Sheriff's Department)

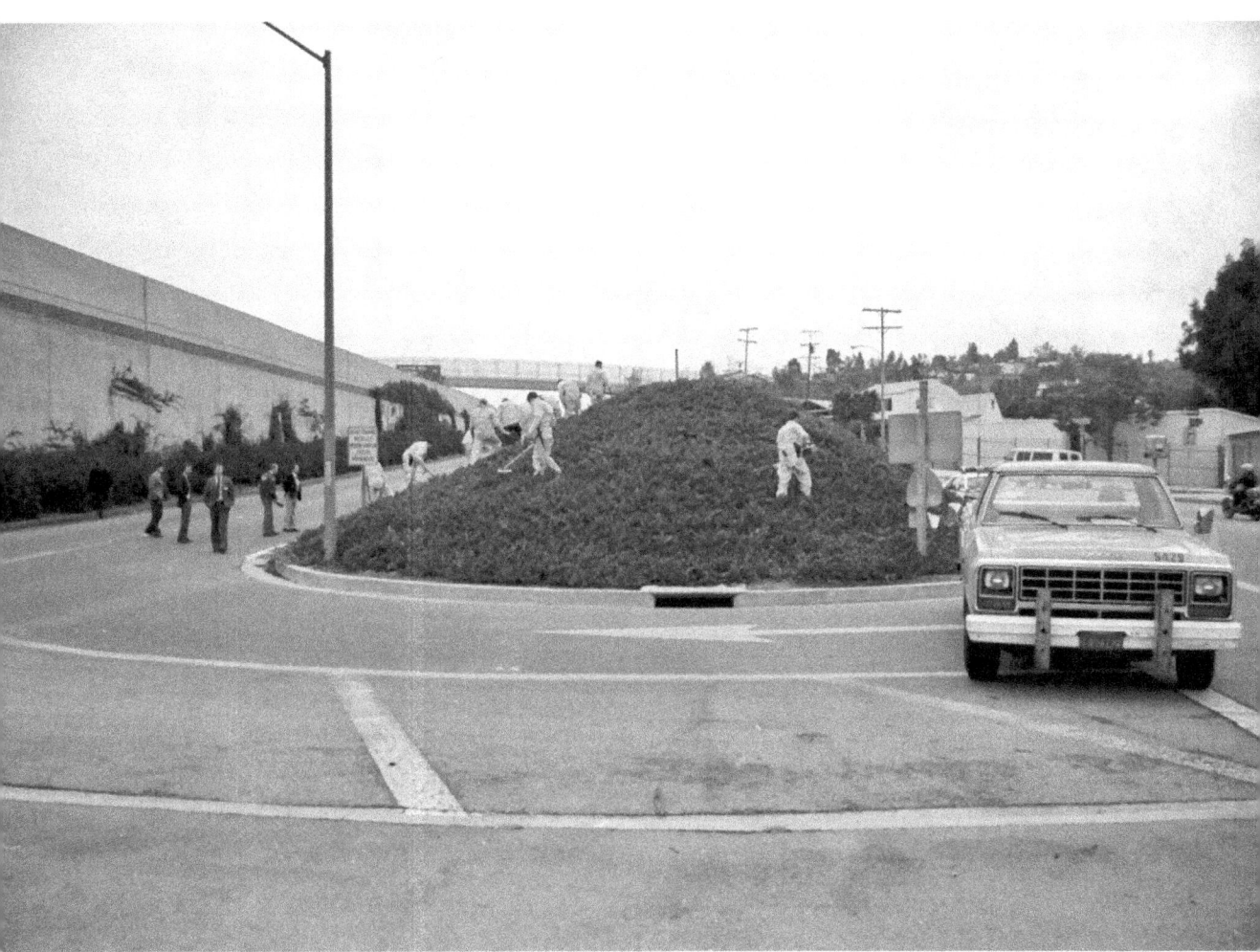

Newly-hired Sheriff's deputies from the training academy assist with the search near the York Boulevard on-ramp to the northbound Glendale Freeway. (Los Angeles Sheriff's Department)

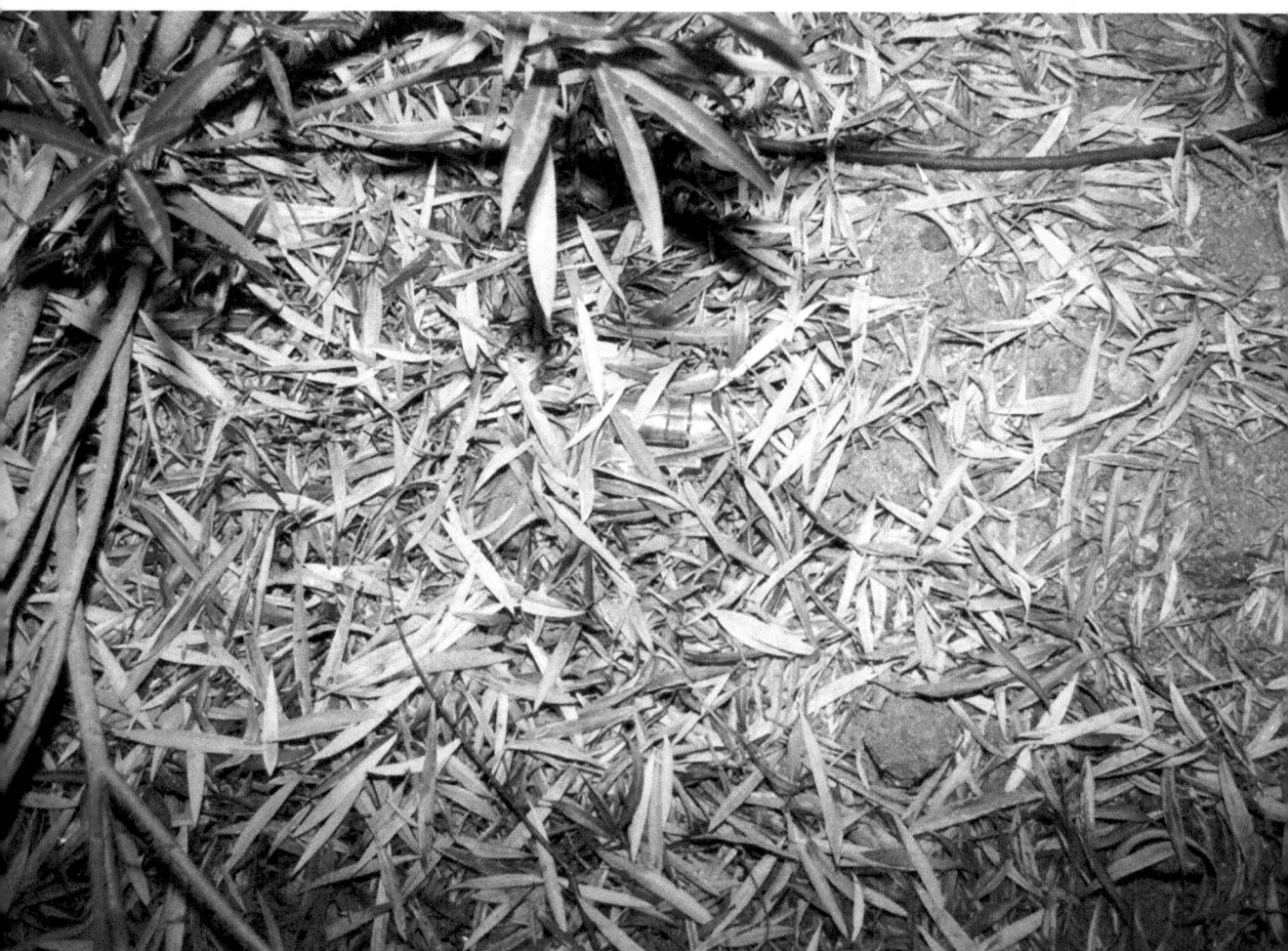

Above & Opposite: A revolver that was forensically connected to Ramirez's crimes was discovered in the growth adjacent to the freeway. (Los Angeles Sheriff's Department)

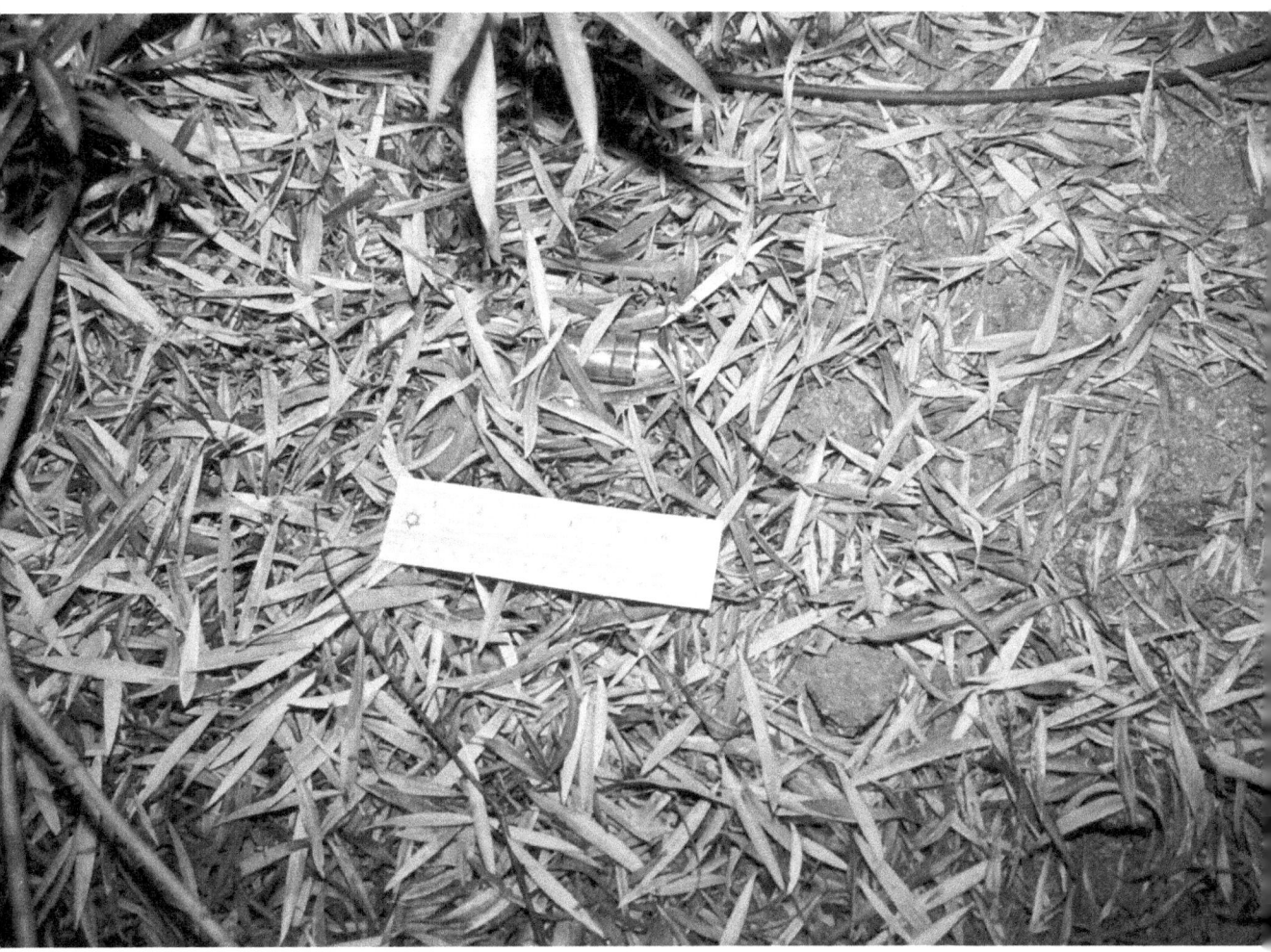

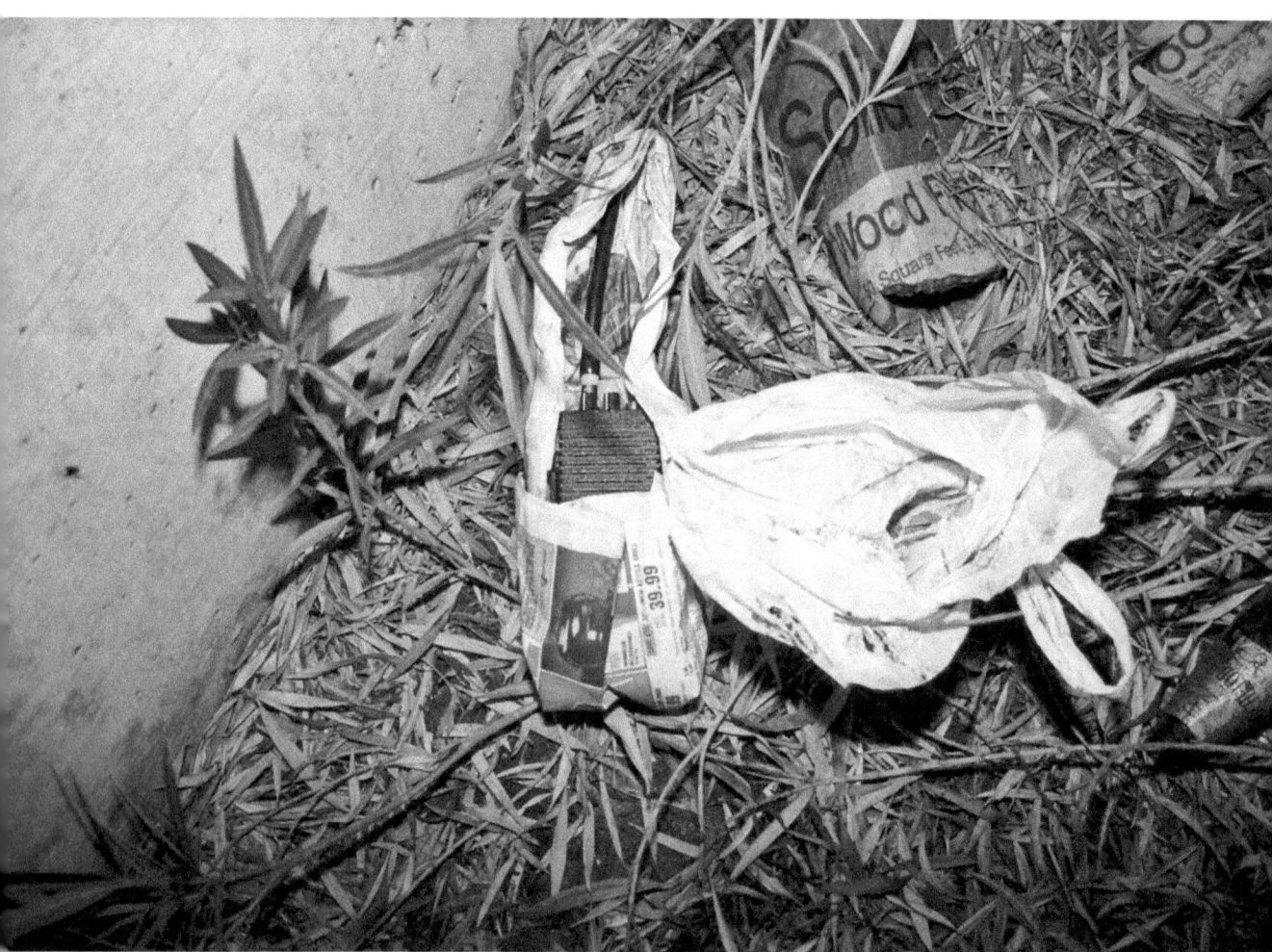

The ruler of a Sheriff's criminalist helps to better identify the location where the handgun was found. A scanner, which could be used to monitor police radio transmissions, was also found. (Los Angeles Sheriff's Department)

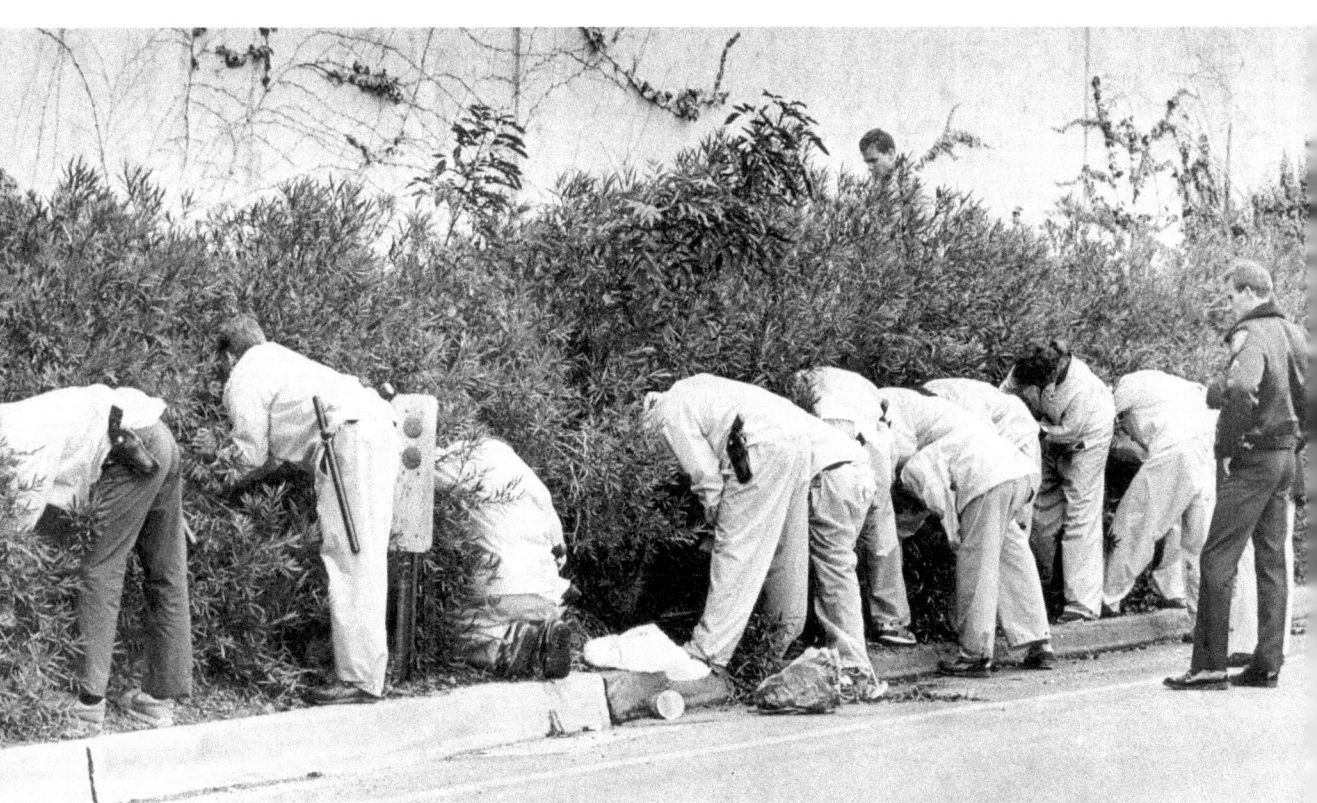

A Glendale police officer stands by as trainees from the Sheriff's academy wearing rain gear search for evidence discarded by the Night Stalker. (Paul Chinn/Herald Examiner Collection)

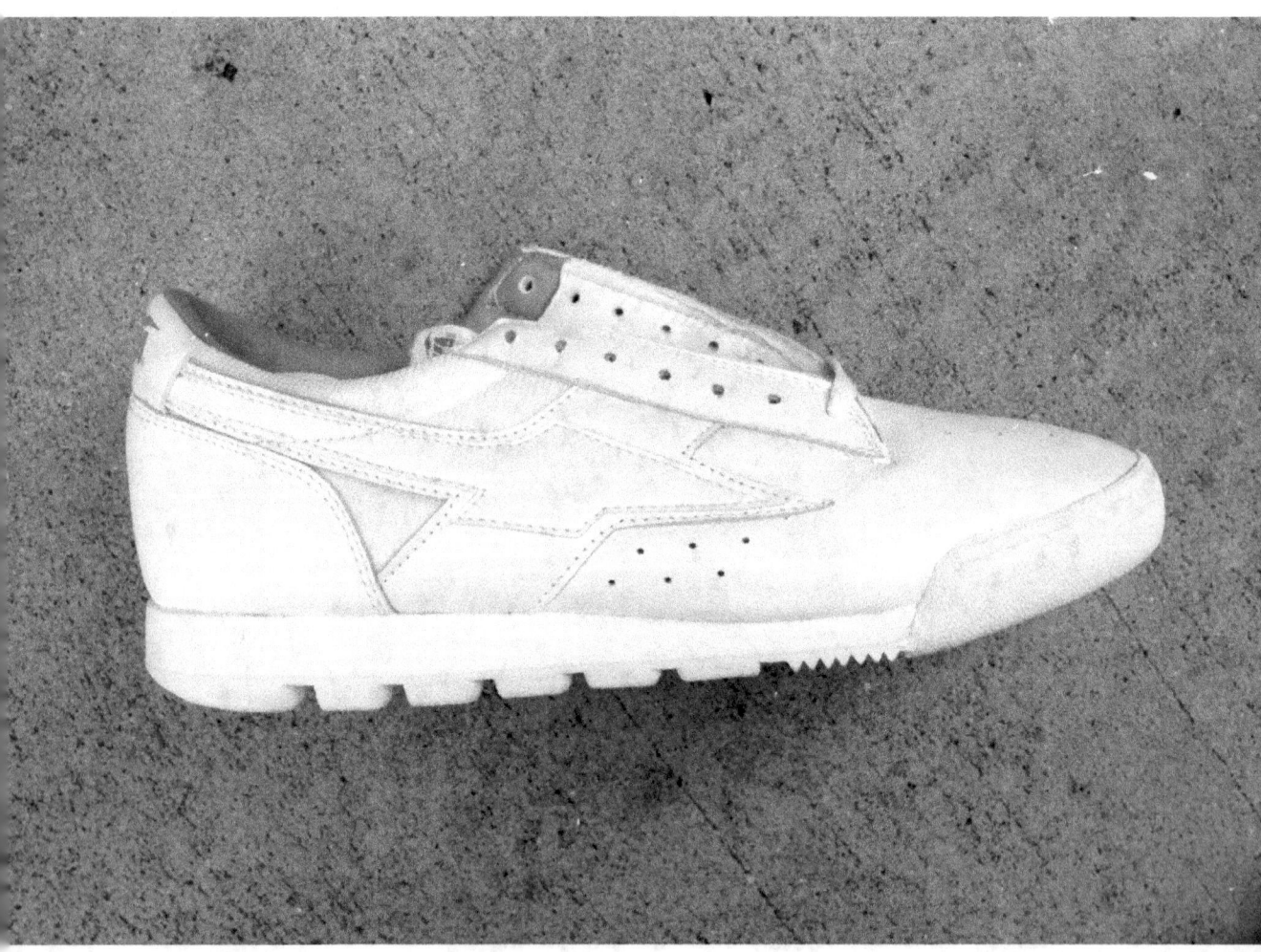

The Avia athletic shoe depicted above is the same model and has the same sole pattern as that worn by the killer. (Los Angeles Sheriff's Department)

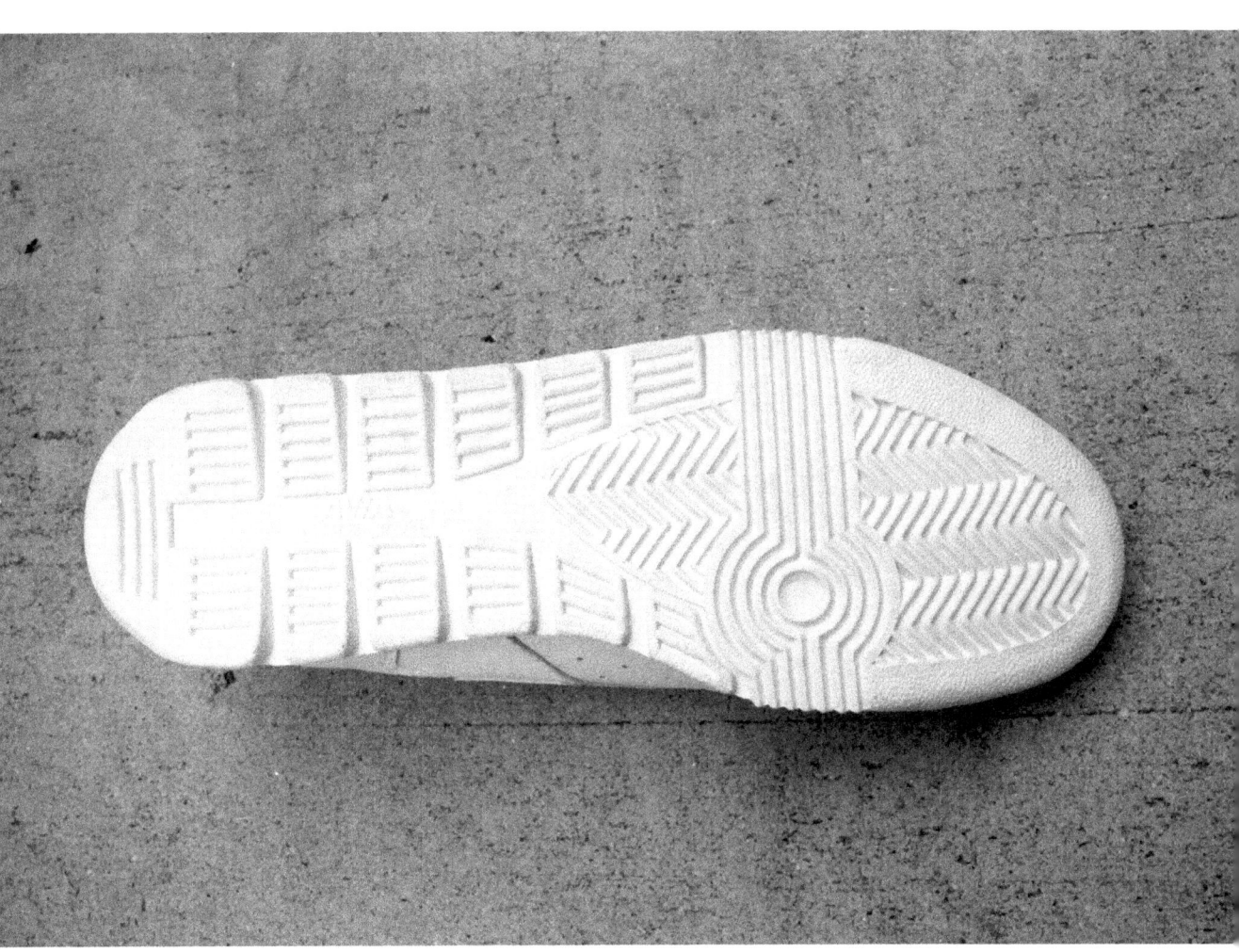

The sole of the sample athletic shoe closely matched the sole prints discovered at multiple crime scenes. (Los Angeles Sheriff's Department)

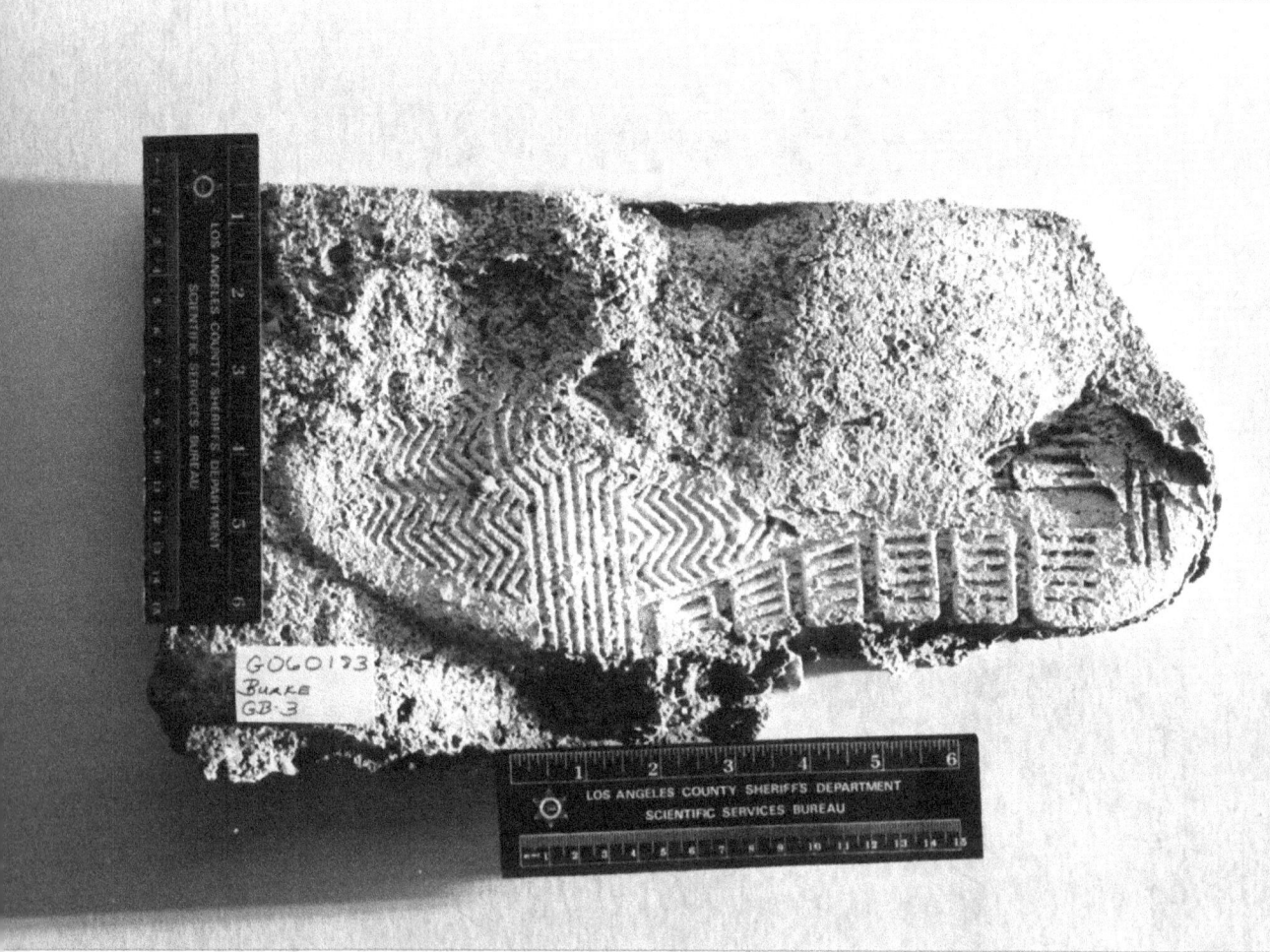

The plaster cast is a standard technique used in the scientific solution of crime. (Los Angeles Sheriff's Department)

SUMMARY OF RESULTS

VICTIM	EVIDENCE DESCRIPTION	RESULTS OF ANALYSIS
...RA, VINCENT	PLASTER CAST, RIGHT SHOE PRINT PLASTER CAST, LEFT SHOE PRINT PARTIAL PATTERN ON BUCKET LID.	AVIA AEROBICS SIZE 11½-12 AVIA AEROBICS SIZE 11½-12 AVIA CHEVRONS
...ST OLIVE ...VIA	TAPELIFT, PARTIAL SHOEPRINT	AVIA AEROBICS, COACHES or BASKETBALL, NO SIZE DETT...
...ILLIAMS	PLASTER CAST, RIGHT SHOEPRINT PLASTER CAST, LEFT SHOEPRINT	AVIA AEROBICS, COACHES or BASKETBALL, 12 INCHES IN... AVIA AEROBICS, COACHES or BASKETBALL, 12.5 INCHES IN...
...MABEL ...E, FLORENCE	PARTIAL PATTERN ON ELECTRIC CLOCK	CONSISTANT WITH AVIA CONCENTRIC CIRCLES, RIGHT FOOT. NO SIZE DETERMINED
...ON, MARY	PARTIAL PATTERN ON TISSUE. OUTLINE OF RIGHT SHOEPRINT ON CARPET.	AVIA AEROBICS, LEFT SHOE. NO SIZE DETERMINED NO PATTERN DETAIL. 12 INCHES IN LENGTH. CONTOUR SIMILAR TO AVIA AEROBICS, SIZE 11-11½
...ETT, WHITNEY	PARTIAL RIGHT SHOEPRINT ON COMFORTER	AVIA AEROBICS, SIZE 11½-12
...ON, JOYCE	2 TAPELIFTS, RIGHT SHOEPRINT 2 TAPE LIFTS, LEFT SHOEPRINT	AVIA AEROBICS, SIZE 11½-12
...ANANTH, ...IARONG	TAPELIFT, LEFT SHOEPRINT TAPELIFT, PARTIAL PATTERN TAPELIFT, PARTIAL PATTERN	AVIA AEROBICS, SIZE 11½-12 AVIA CONCENTRIC CIRCLES, RIGHT or LEFT SHOE. NO SIZE DETERMINATION CONSISTENT WITH AVIA. STRAIGHT LINE
...WATH, ELYAS	TAPELIFT, DOT MATRIX PATTERN	CONSISTENT WITH NEW or SLIGHTLY WORN STADI... SHOES, OR SHOES OF SIMILAR MANUFACTURE...

This chart detailed the shoeprint evidence collected during the entirety of the investigation. Of the 1,354 pairs of Avia athletic shoes made, six pairs were shipped to the region, only one pair of size 11½–12 was known to have been sold. (Los Angeles Sheriff's Department)

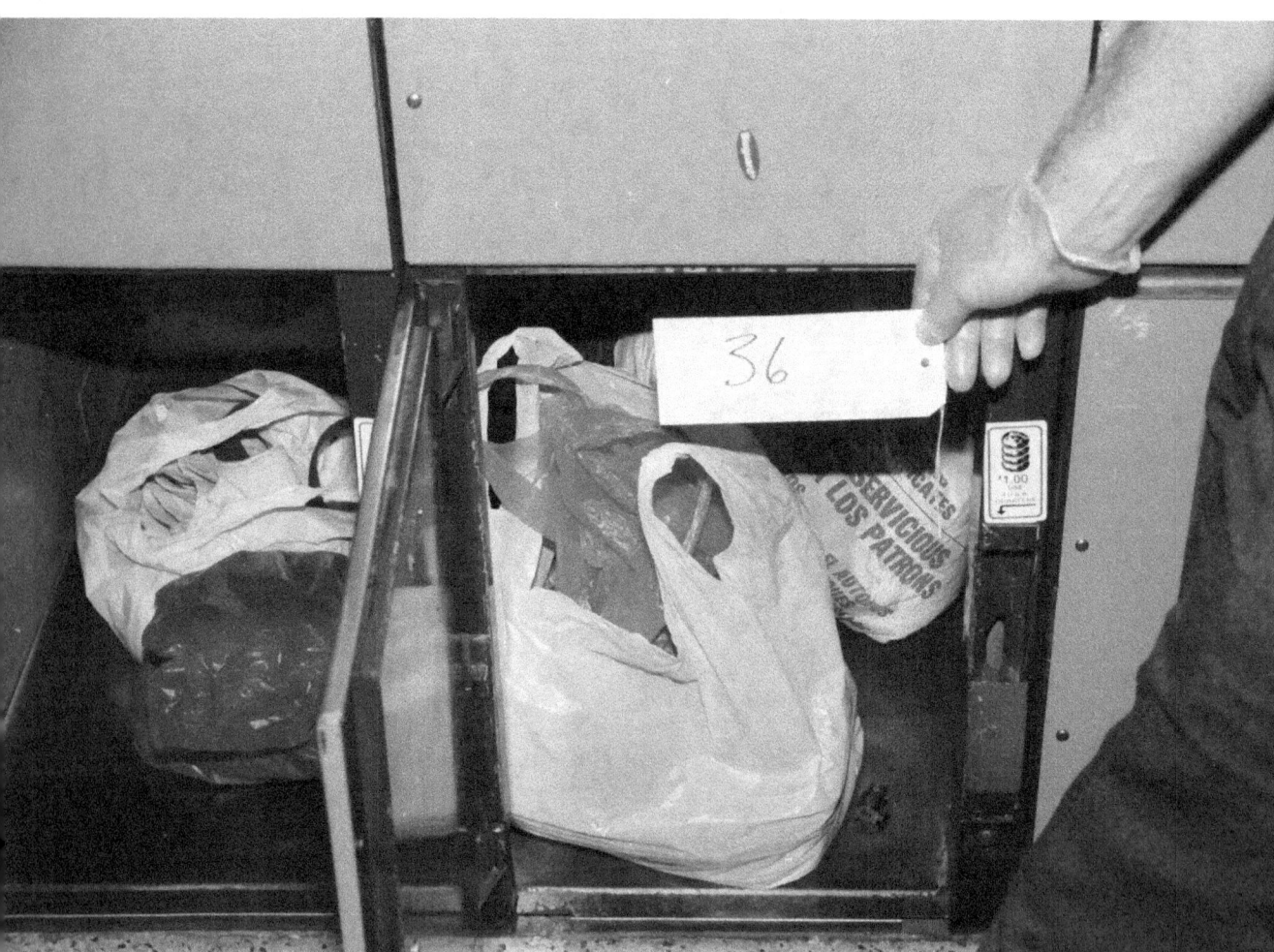

Evidence found in a locker at the Greyhound Bus Depot in Downtown Los Angeles. (Los Angeles Sheriff's Department)

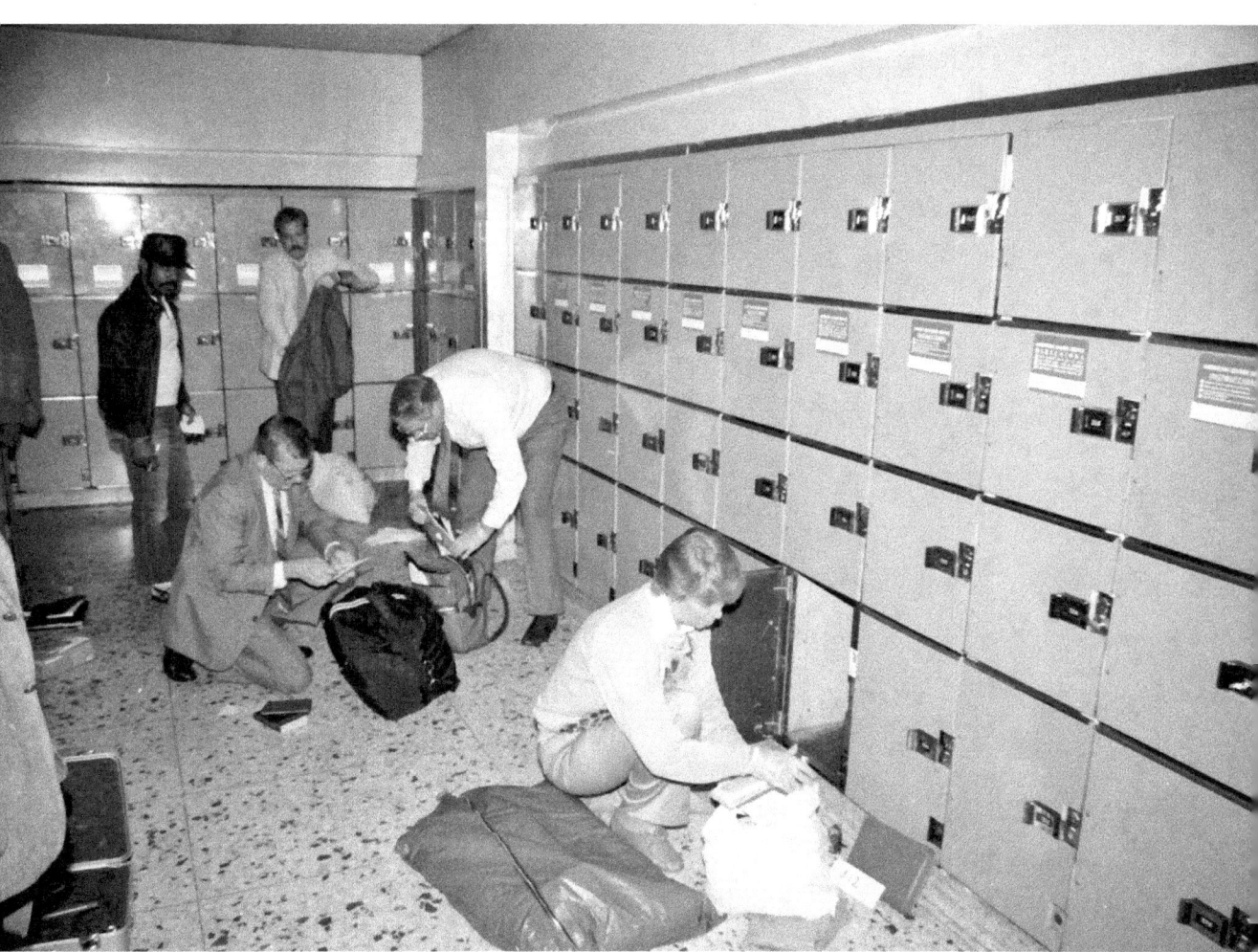

Searching the lockers proved fruitful. (Los Angeles Sheriff's Department)

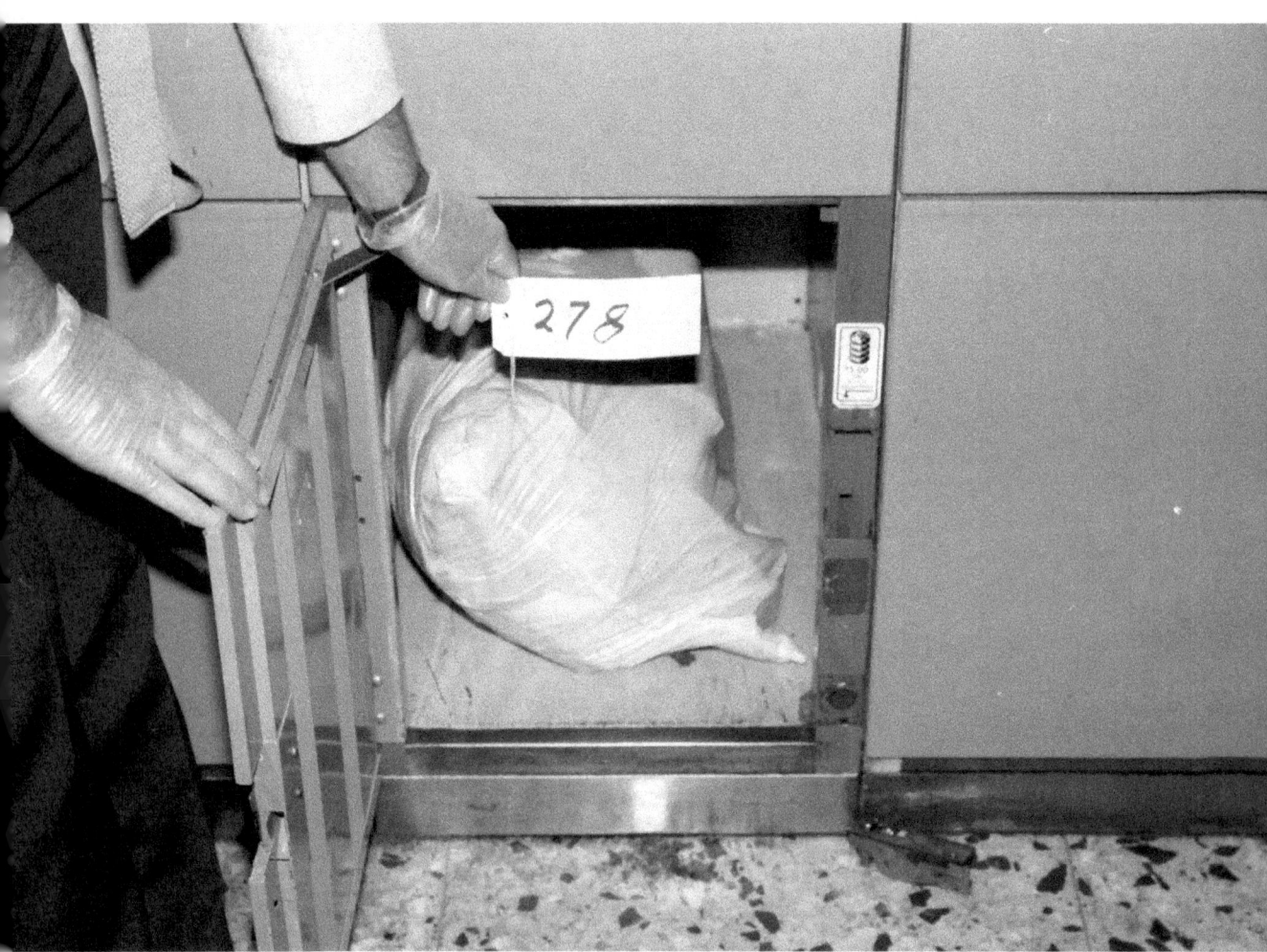

**Evidence stashed in Greyhound Bus Depot lockers by Ramirez.
(Los Angeles Sheriff's Department)**

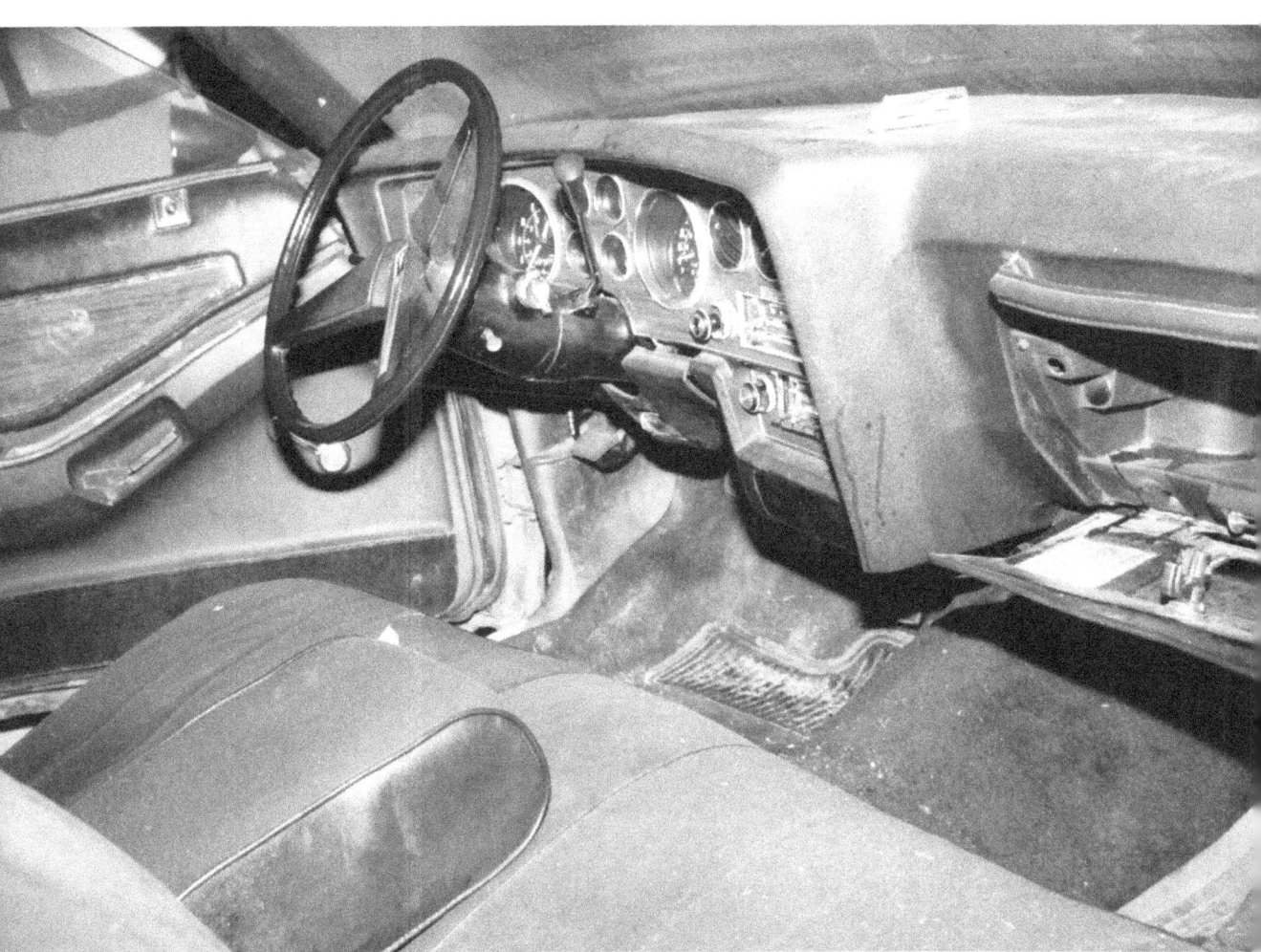

The interior of Ramirez's car. (Los Angeles Sheriff's Department)

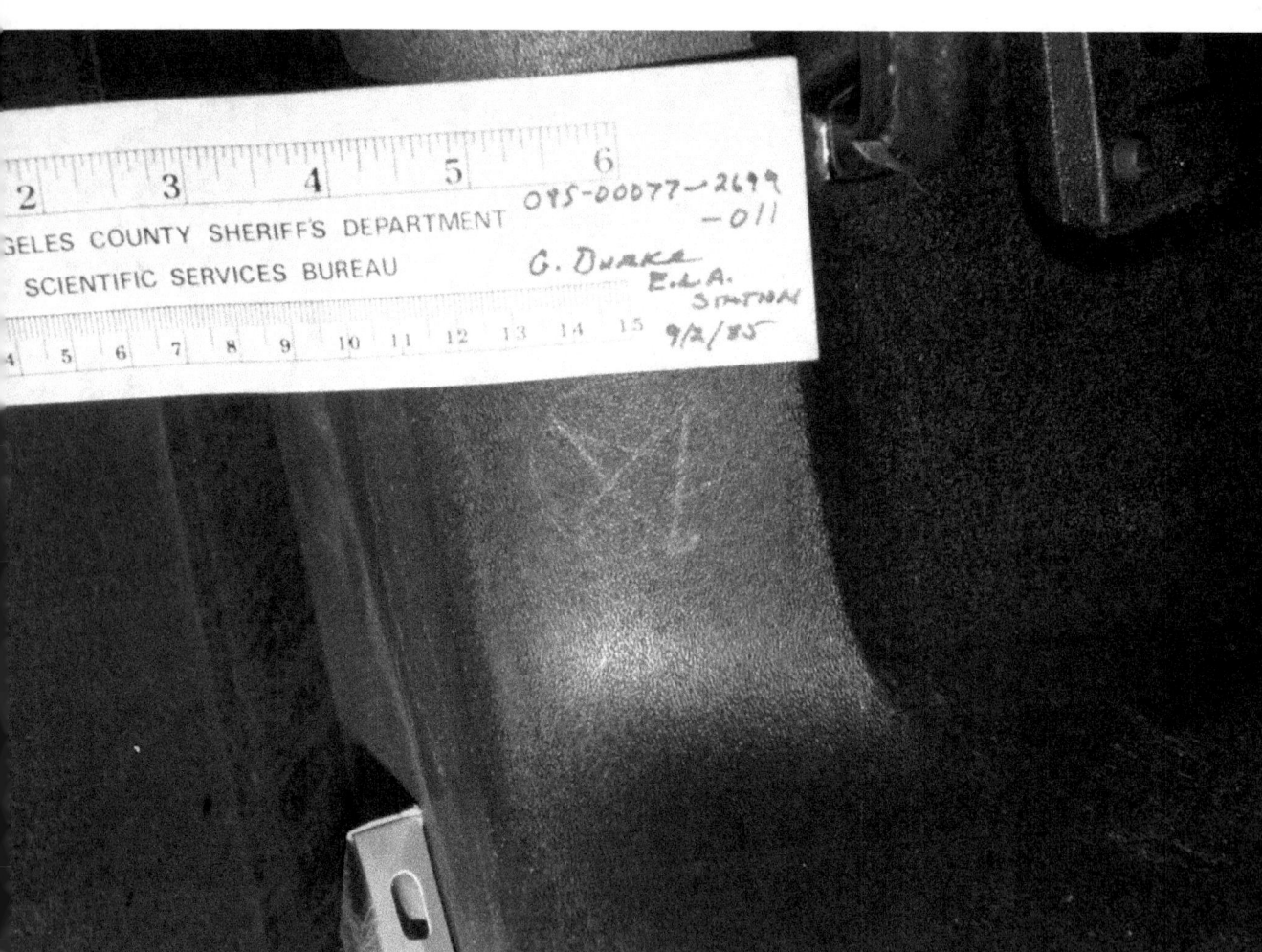

A pentagram was also drawn into the dashboard. Investigators preserved the pentagram and made it available for use as evidence. (Los Angeles Sheriff's Department)

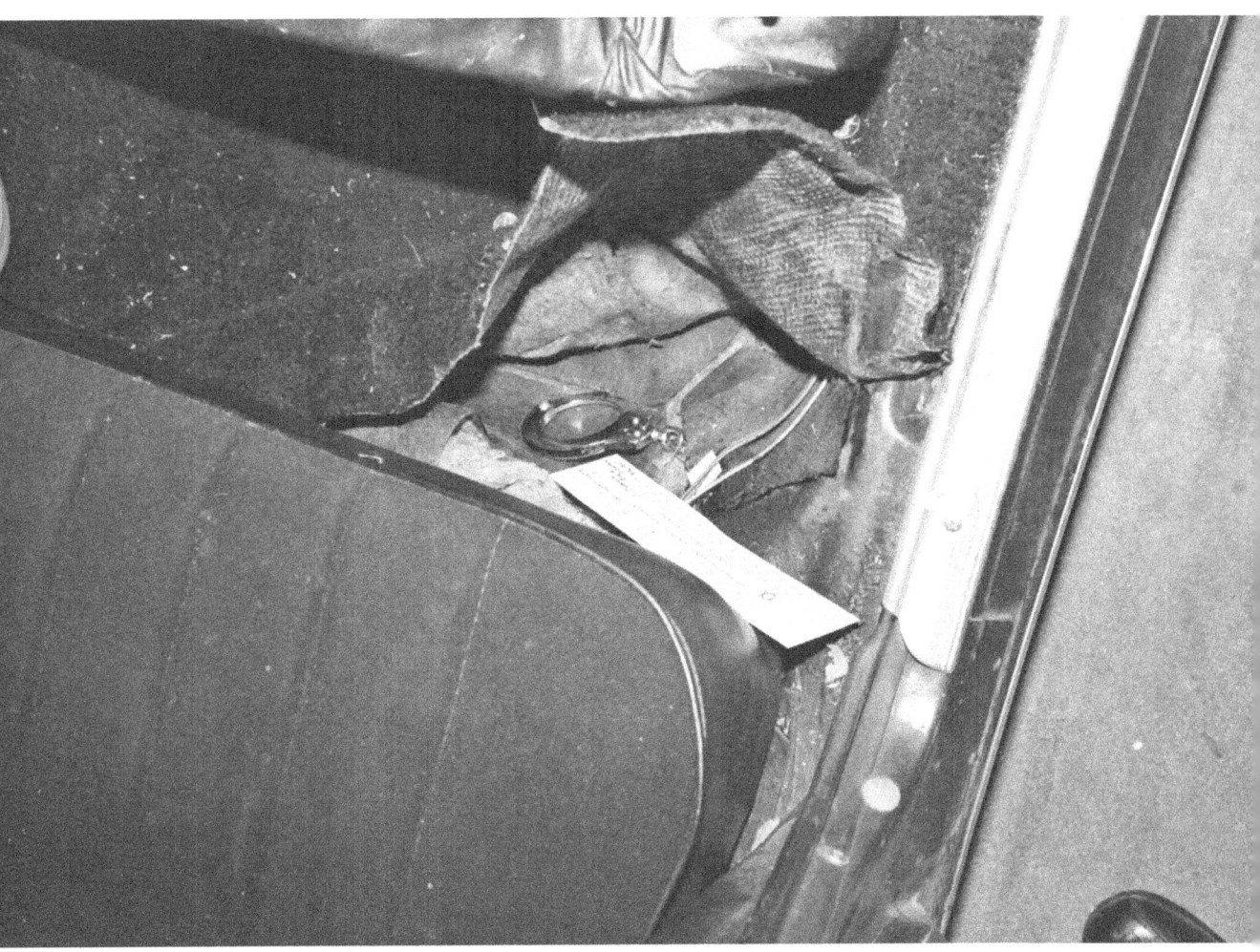

Handcuffs under floor mat. Another pair of handcuffs was also located and seized. (Los Angeles Sheriff's Department)

SEPTEMBER 5, 1985

Ramirez was said to have feared the live line-up which was held on September 5, 1985. Ramirez was concerned that the wound on the back of his head would help surviving victims identify him. Ramirez was never ordered to turn his back to the victims as they readily identified him from the frontal view. Ramirez is depicted below wearing the number two.

Richard Ramirez's criminality included robberies and burglaries. The personal belongings laid out on the tables (right) were recovered during the search of the home of the man to whom Ramirez customarily sold his stolen goods. The surviving victims and family members of those murdered were shown these tables directly after many identified Ramirez in a live line-up at Los Angeles County Jail. Many came forward to claim property stolen from them.

Live line-up, Ramirez is #2. (Los Angeles Sheriff's Department)

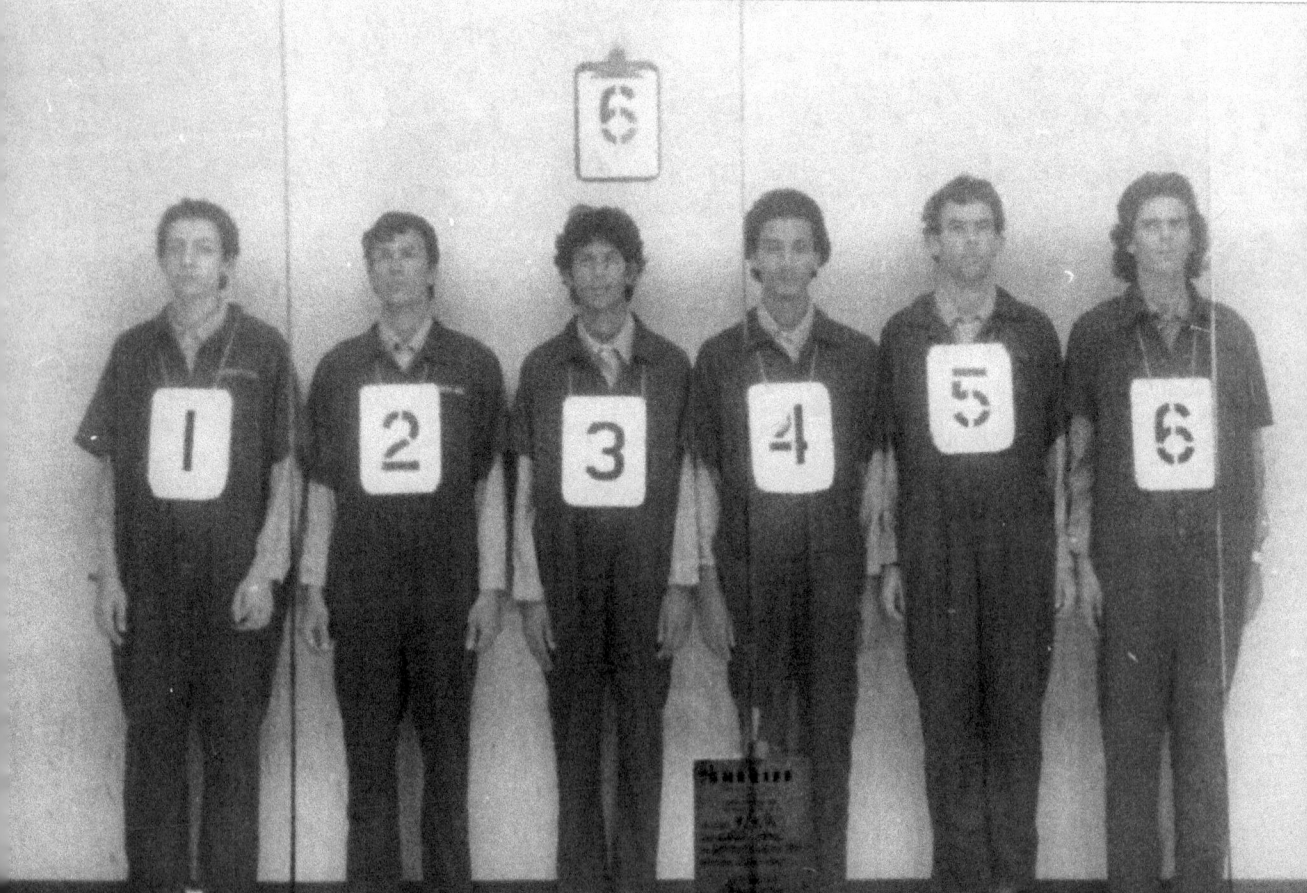

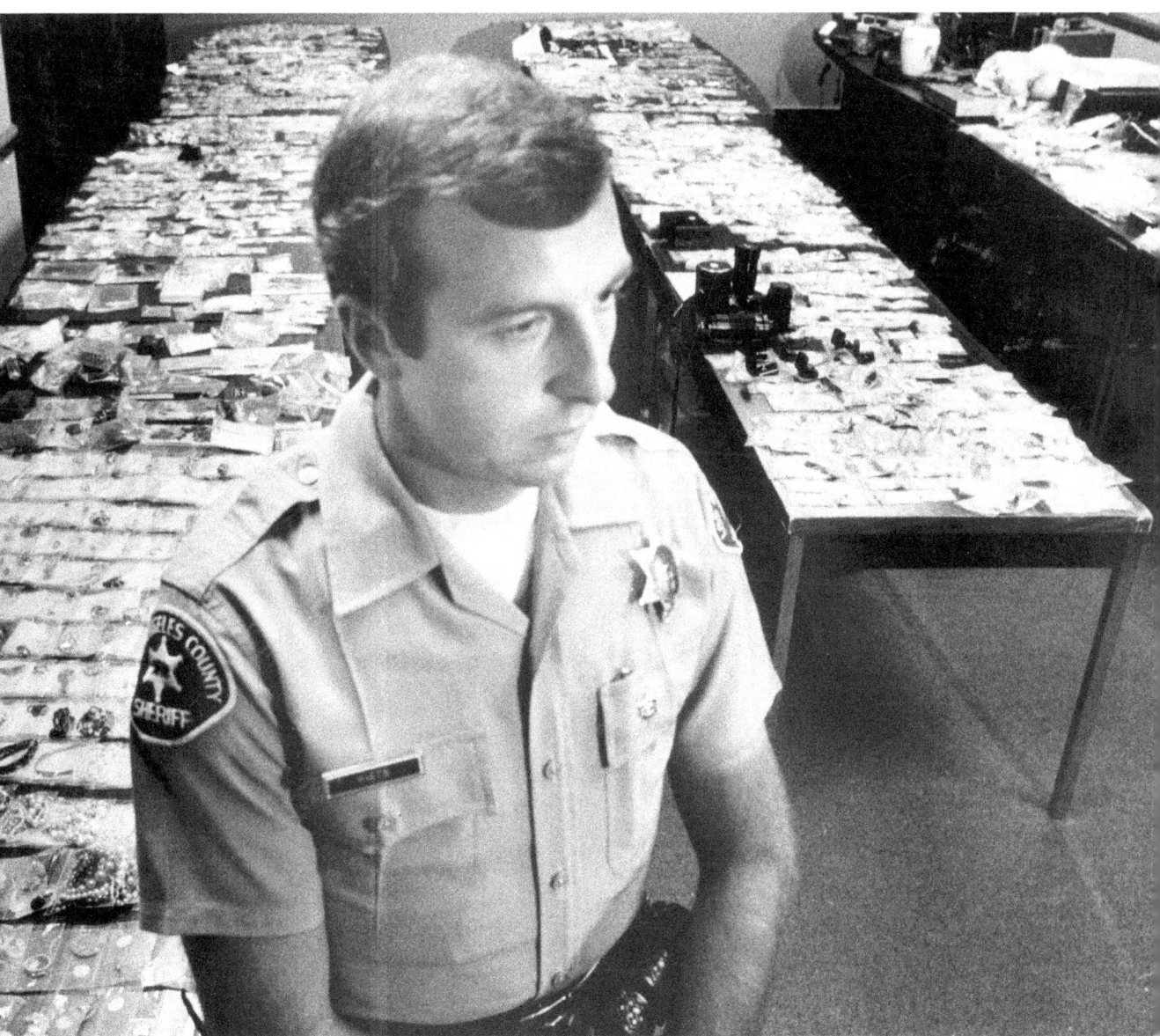

The considerable number of items displayed behind the Sheriff's deputy speaks to the level of Ramirez's criminal activity. (Anne Knudsen/Herald Examiner Collection)

ARRAIGNMENT & TRIAL

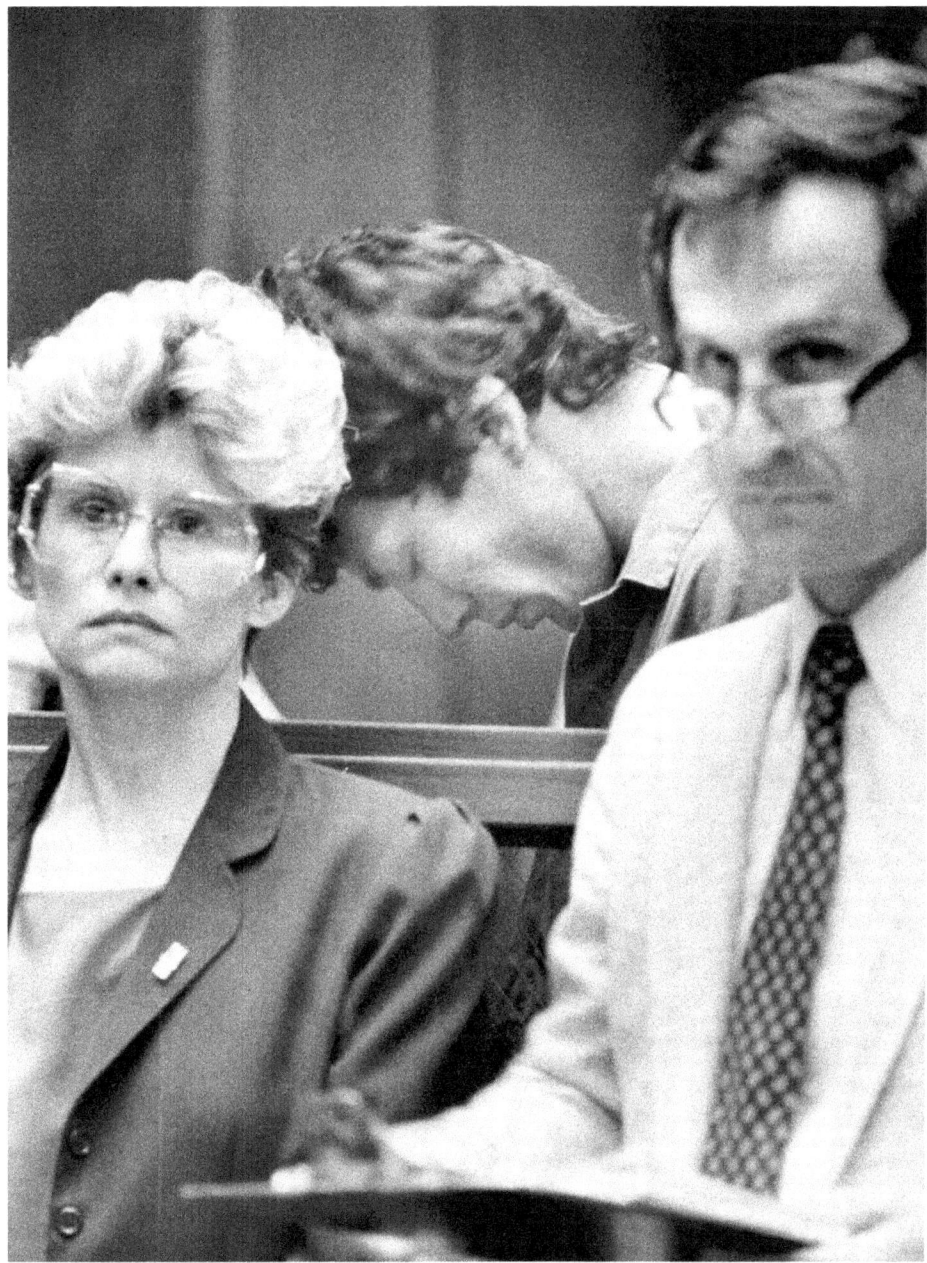

Ramirez's arraignment in the court room of Judge Elva Soper. In the coming years, a preliminary hearing, motions and a protracted trial would bring further attention to the serial killer. (Paul Chinn/Herald Examiner Collection)

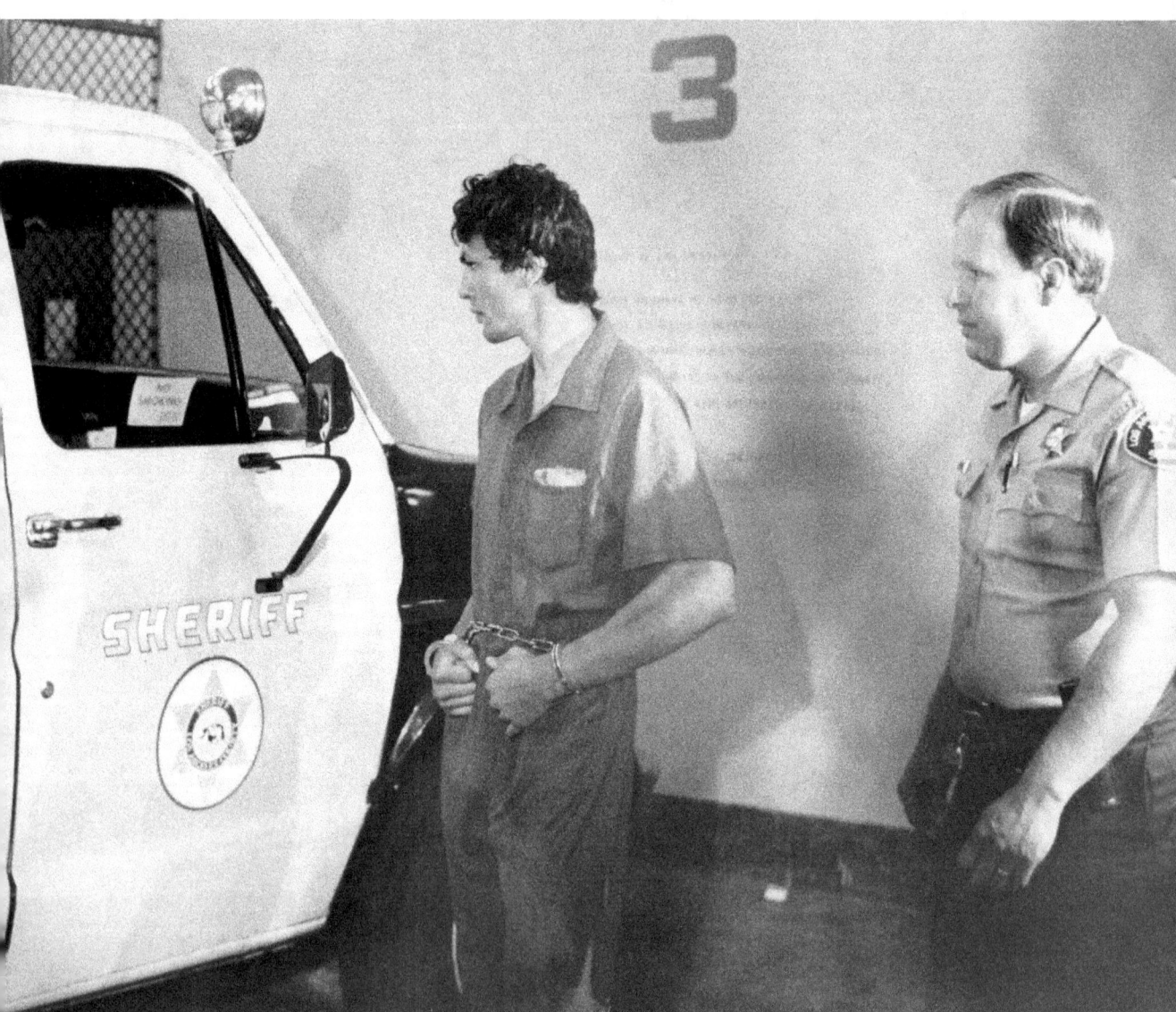

Ramirez was transported alone in a specially barred van. (Paul Chinn/ Herald Examiner Collection)

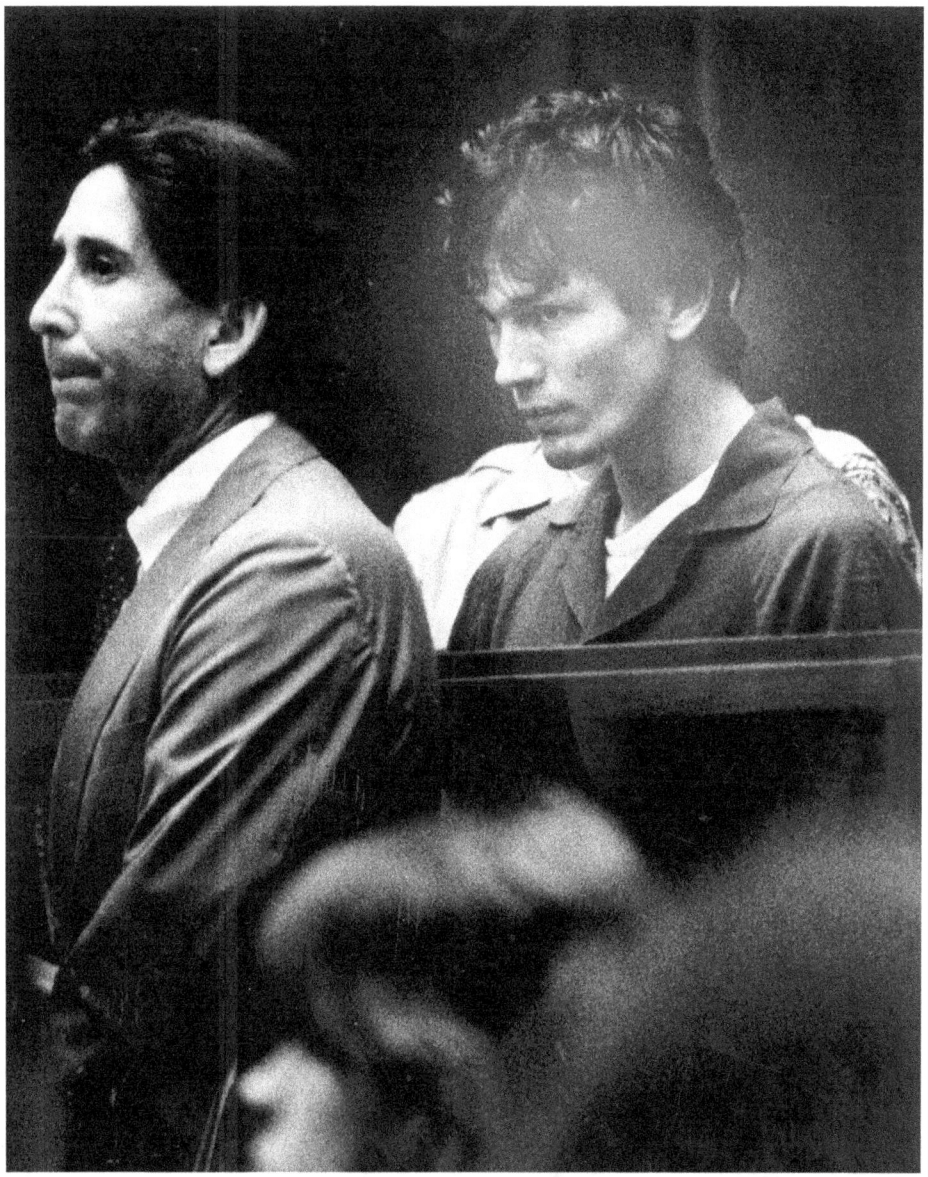

September 10, 1985: Allen Adashek was one of a string of attorneys tasked with defending Ramirez over the course of many years. During this appearance Ramirez would face a murder charge for the first time. (Mike Mullen/Herald Examiner Collection)

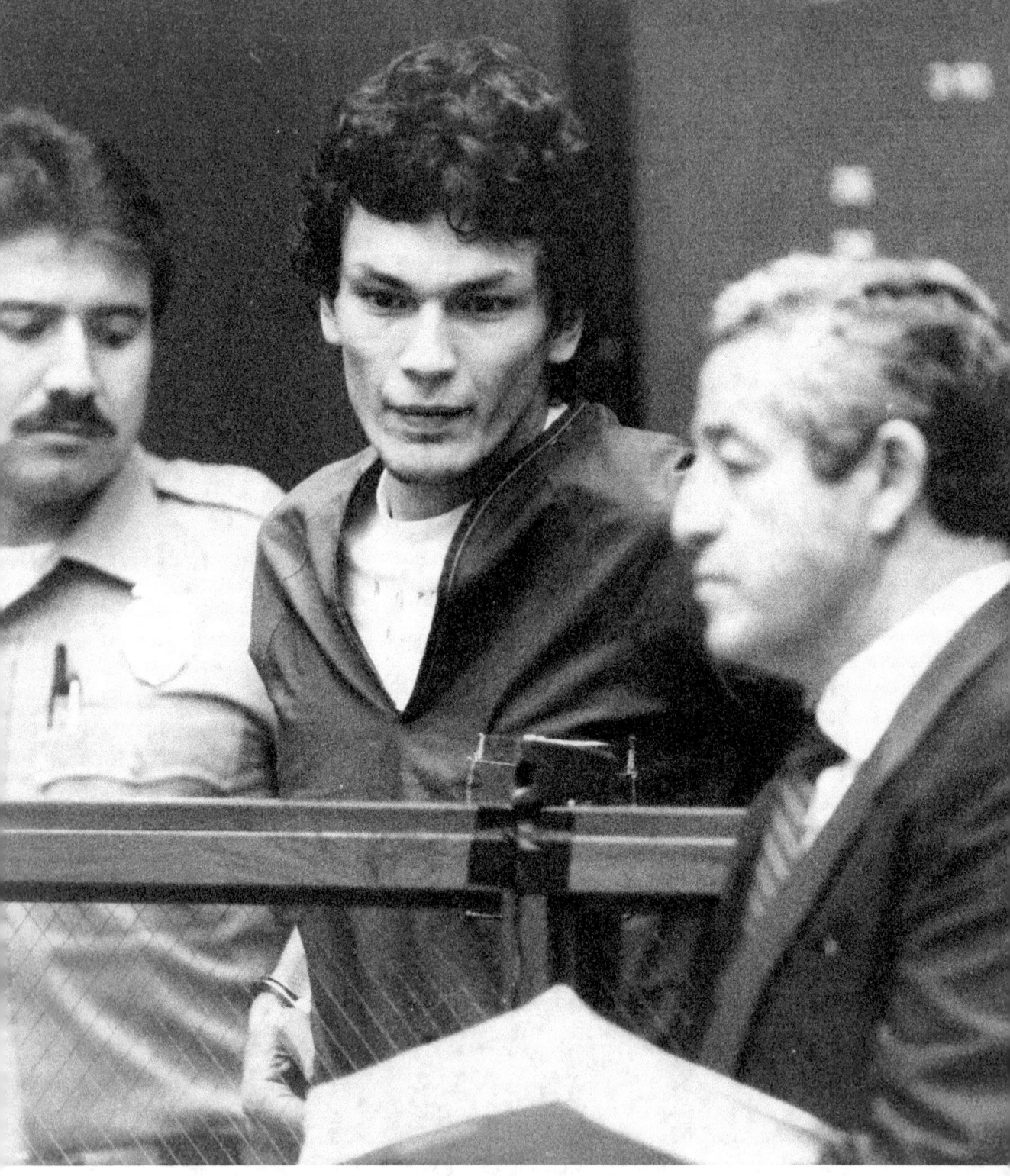

October 1985: One month later Ramirez was in court with a different attorney, Joseph Gallegos. (Michael Haering/Herald Examiner Collection)

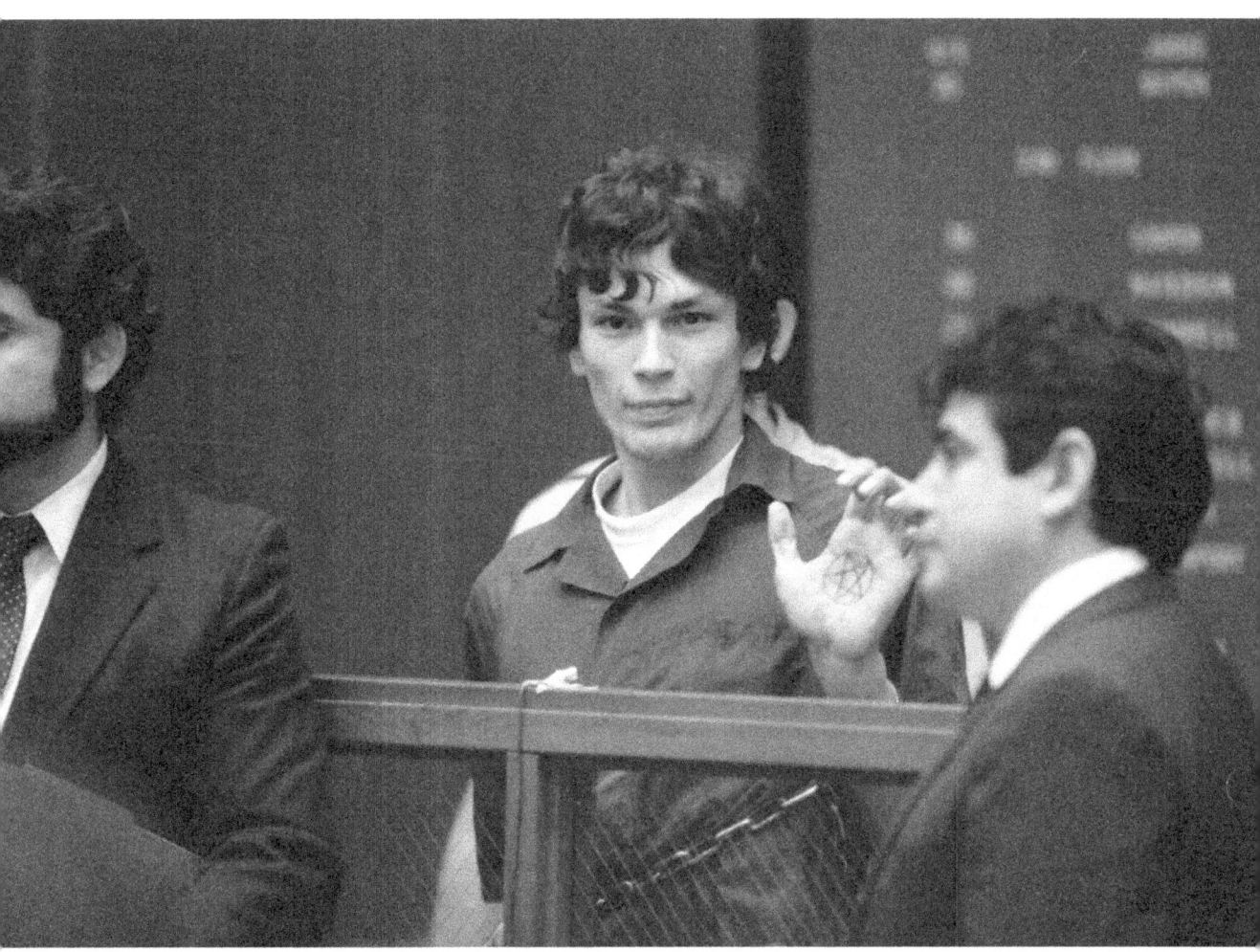

October 24, 1985: A pentagram—the symbol that linked numerous murders to satanic rituals—was flashed by Ramirez in a court appearance. (Lennox McLendon/AP Photo)

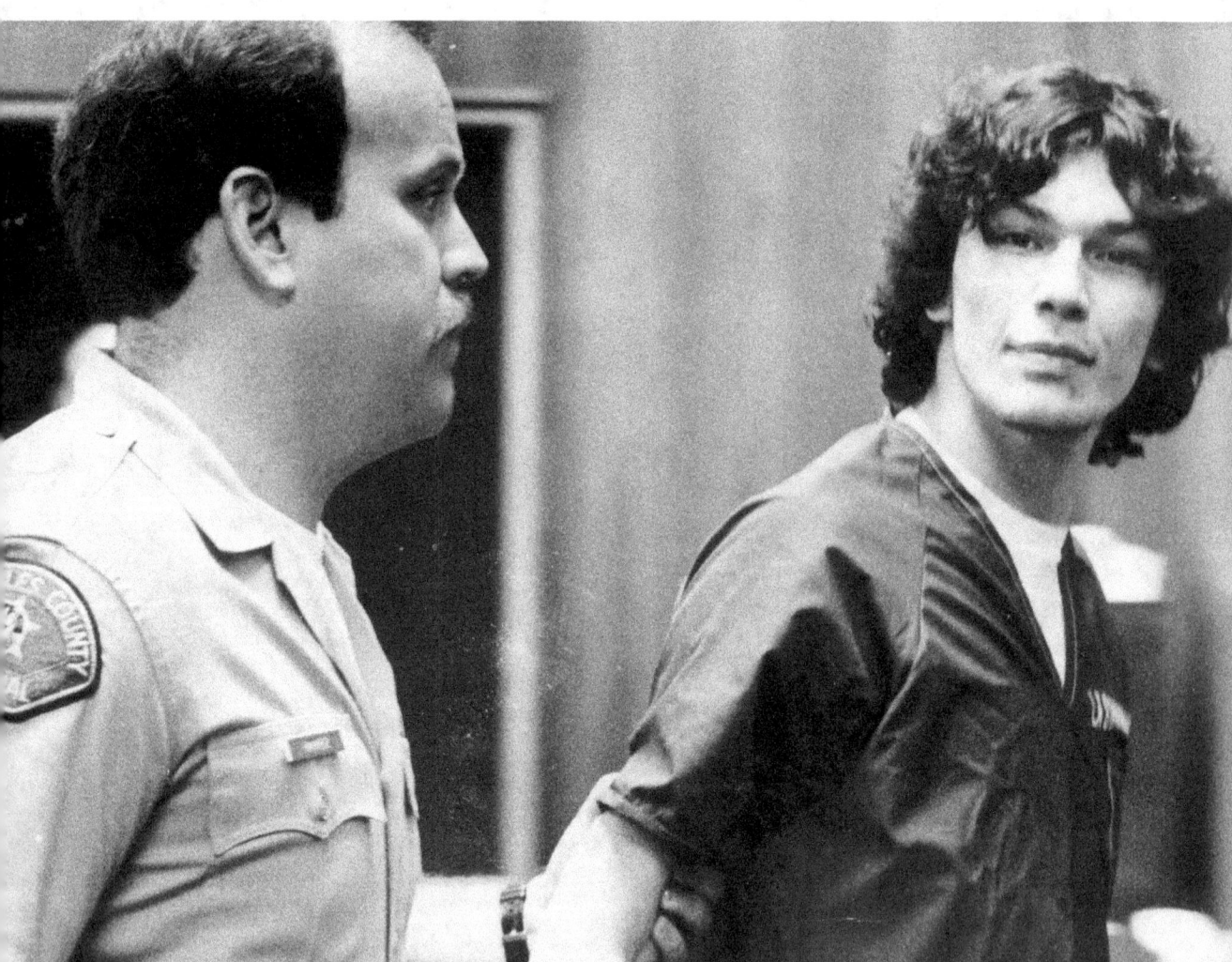

February 26, 1986: Ramirez was in court to hear that judicial proceedings
will be open to the public, a ruling rendered by Judge James Nelson.
(Michael Haering/Herald Examiner Collection)

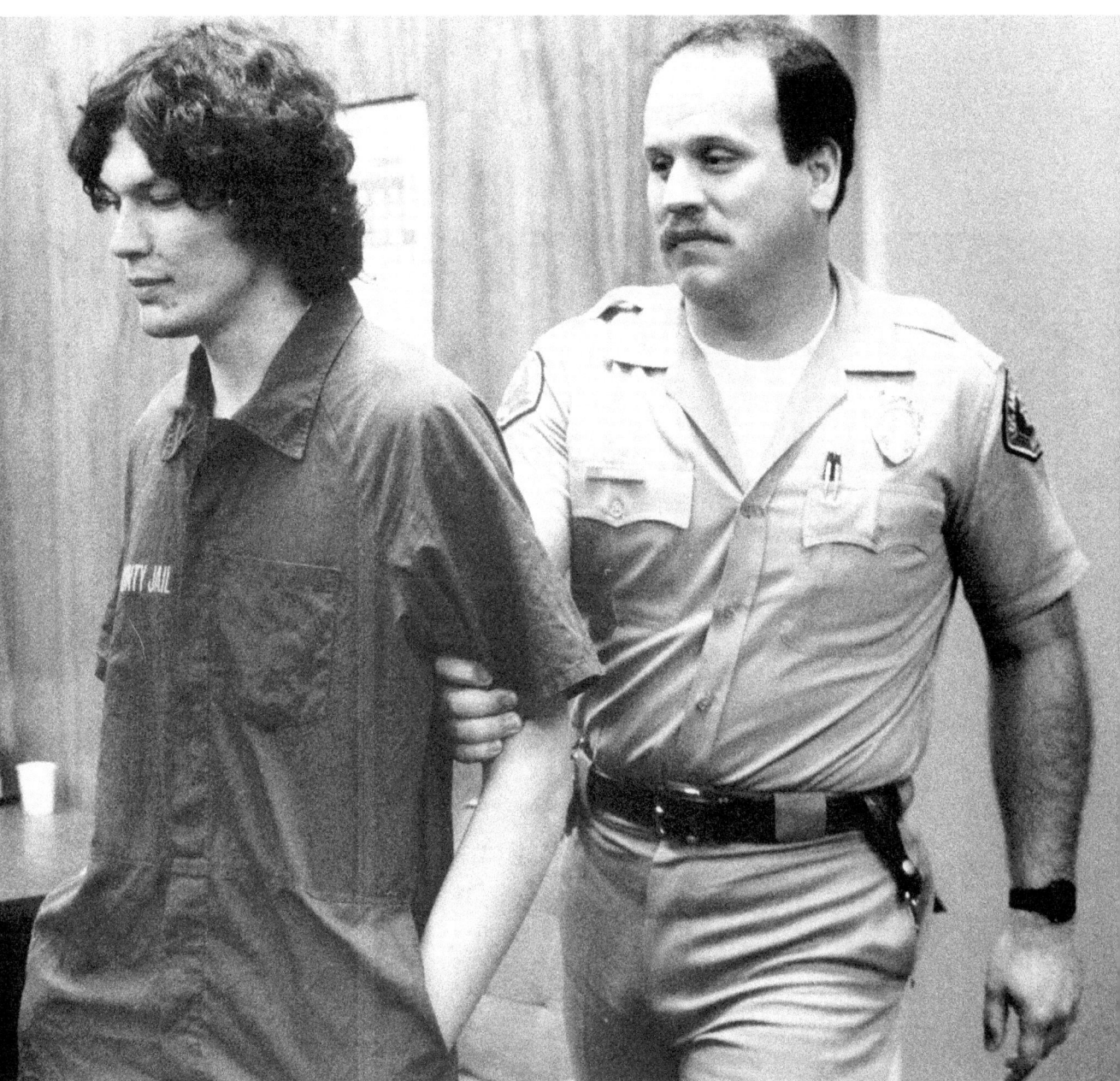

March 18, 1986: Ramirez is brought into court by a Los Angeles County Marshal during preliminary hearing proceedings. (Michael Haering/Herald Examiner Collection)

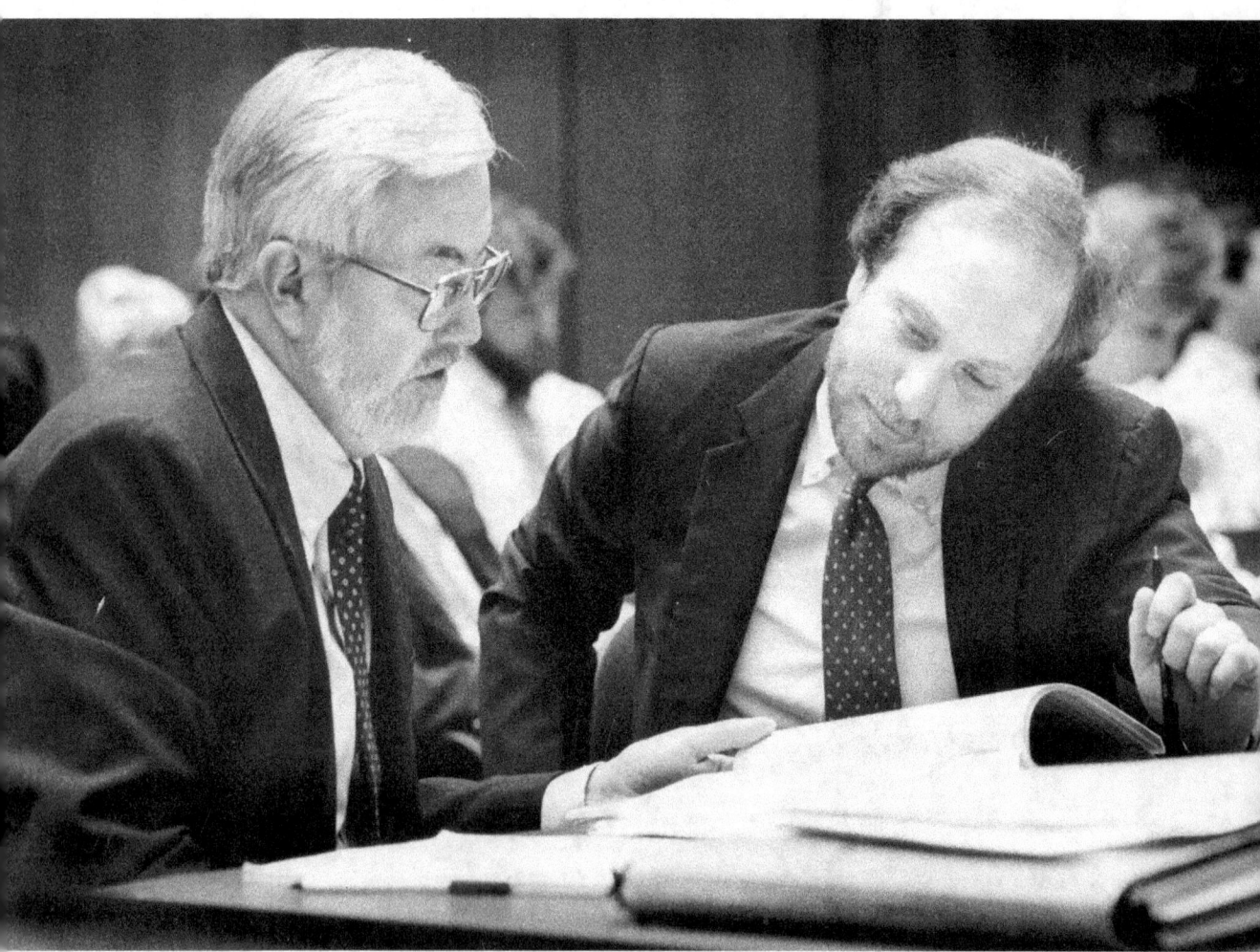

Deputy District Attorneys Phil Halpin and Alan Yochelson represented the people of the State of California in the prosecution of Richard Ramirez. (Michael Haering/Herald Examiner Collection)

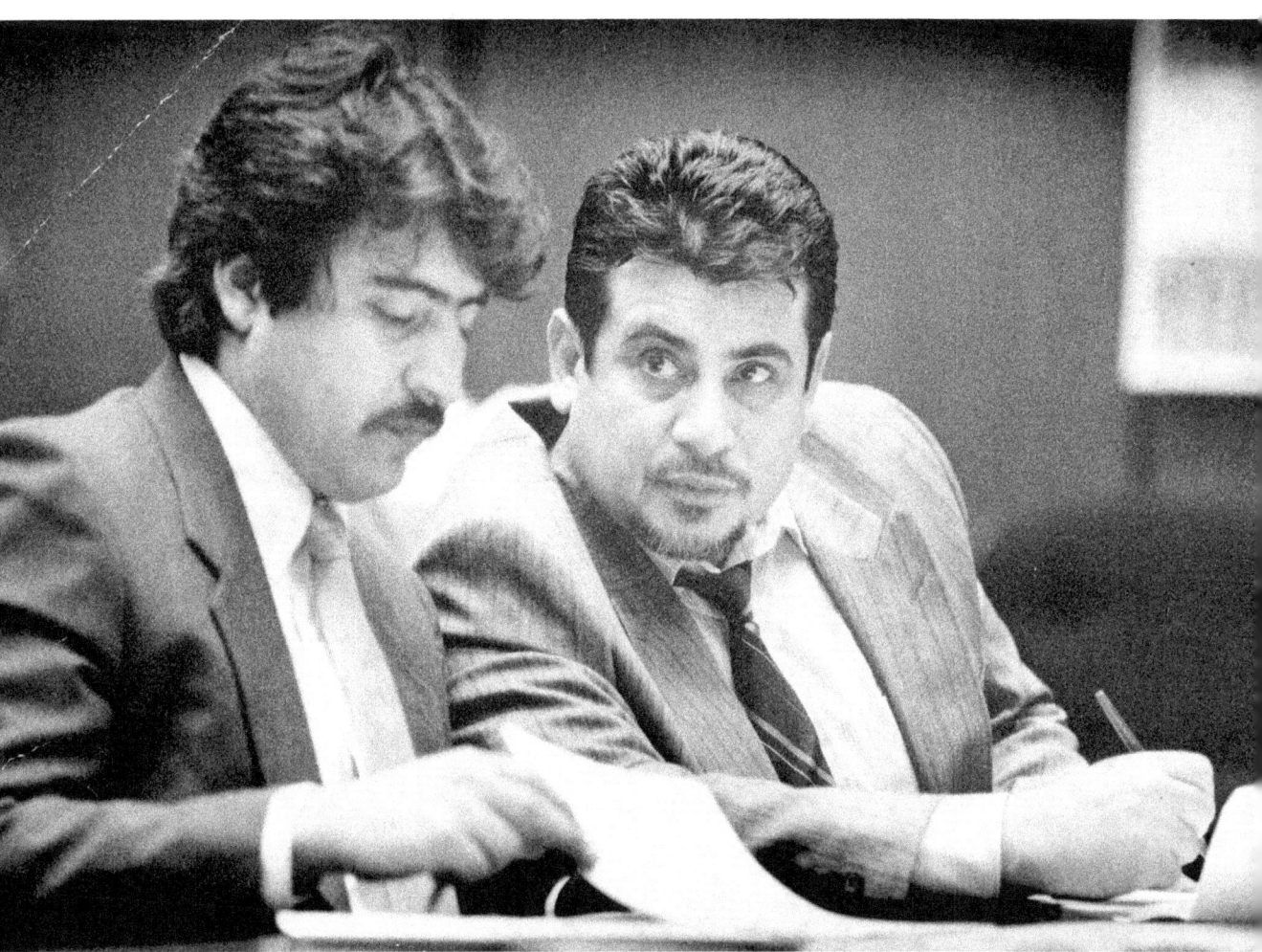

**Ramirez was defended by Richard Salinas (left) and Daniel Hernandez.
(Leo Jarzomb/Herald Examiner Collection)**

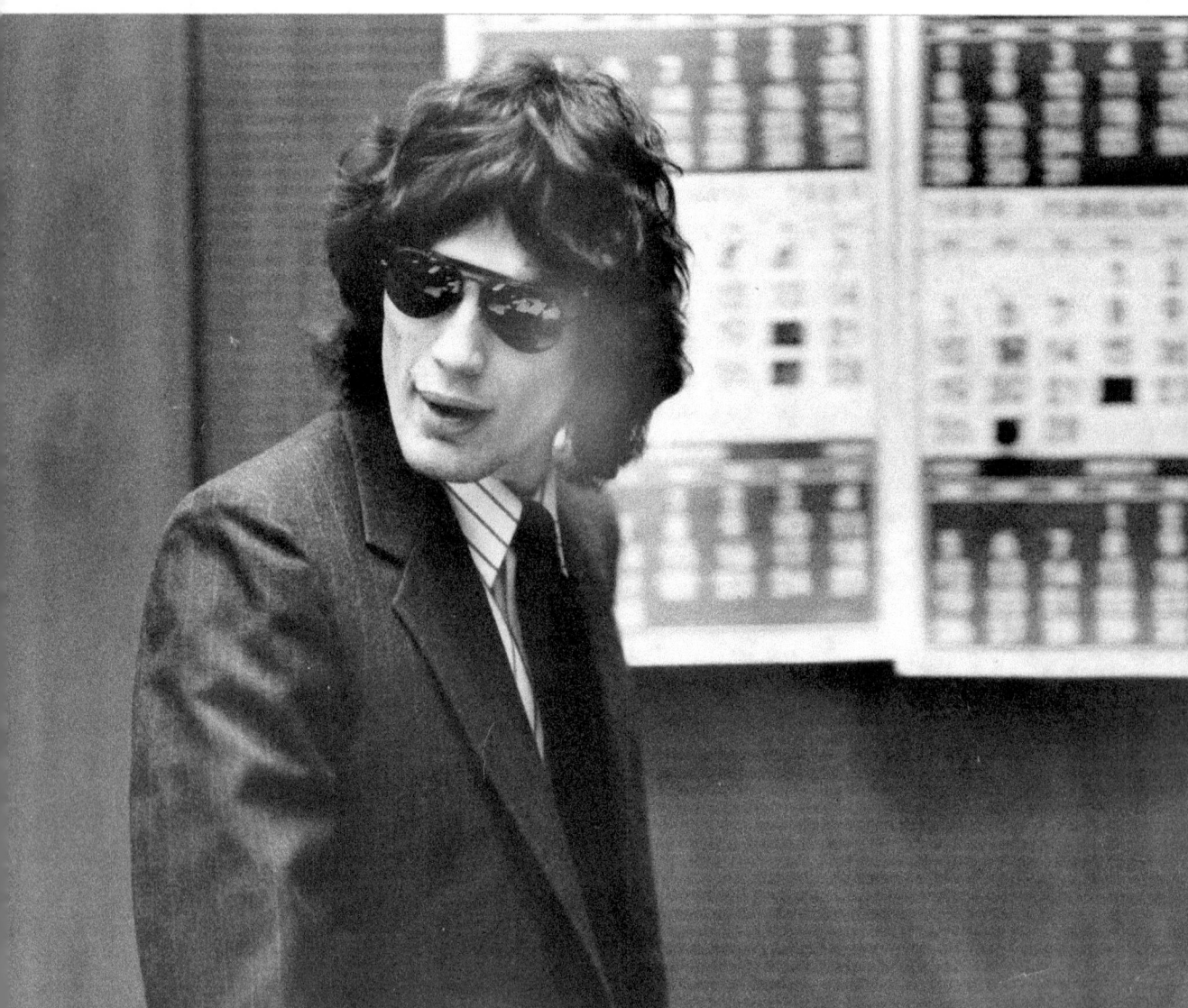

Ramirez, looking quite different than the criminal alternately referred to as the "Man in Black" or the Night Stalker. (Michael Haering/Herald Examiner Collection)

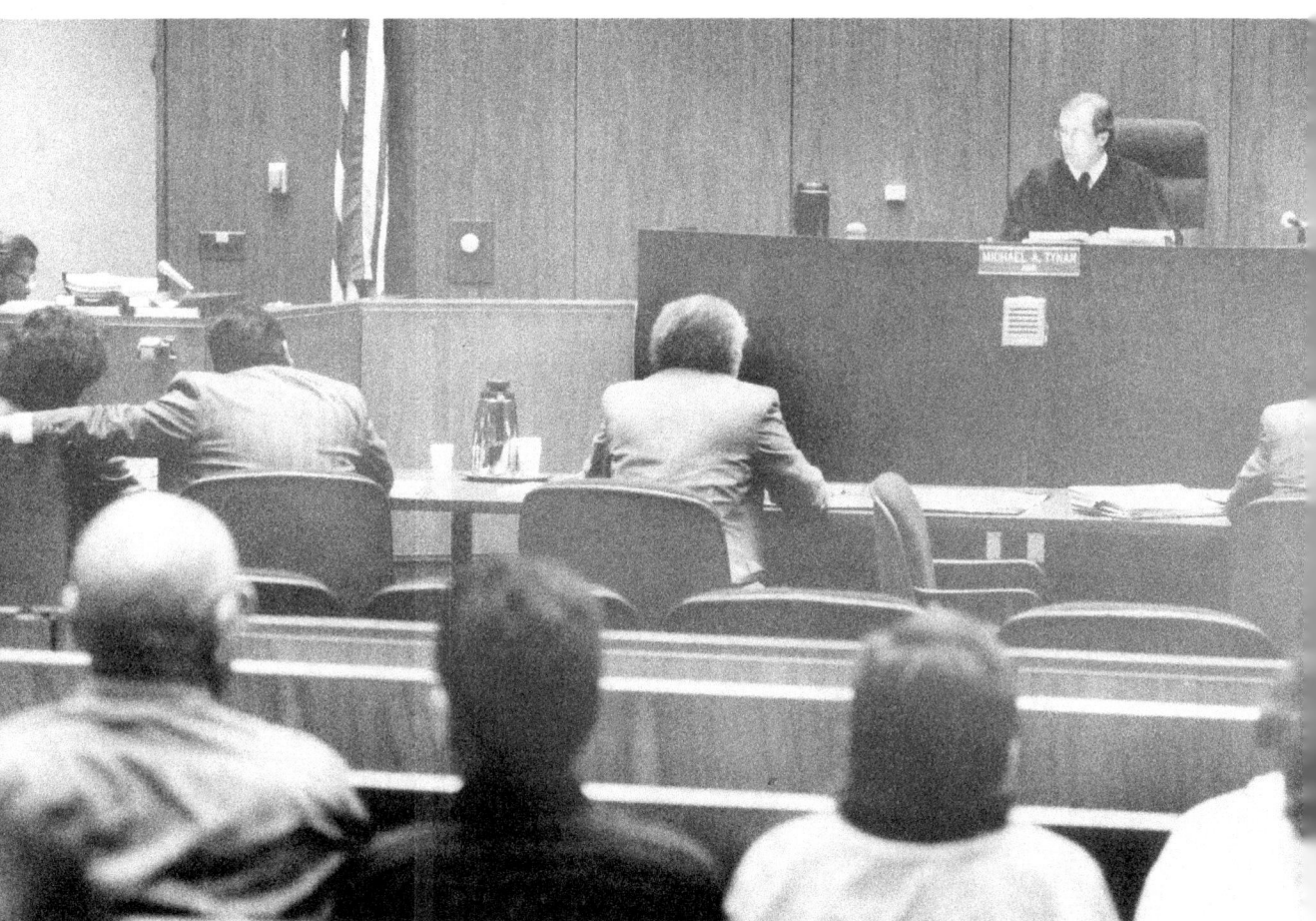

**Ramirez would face Judge Michael Tynan during the extended trial.
(Mike Sergieff/Herald Examiner Collection)**

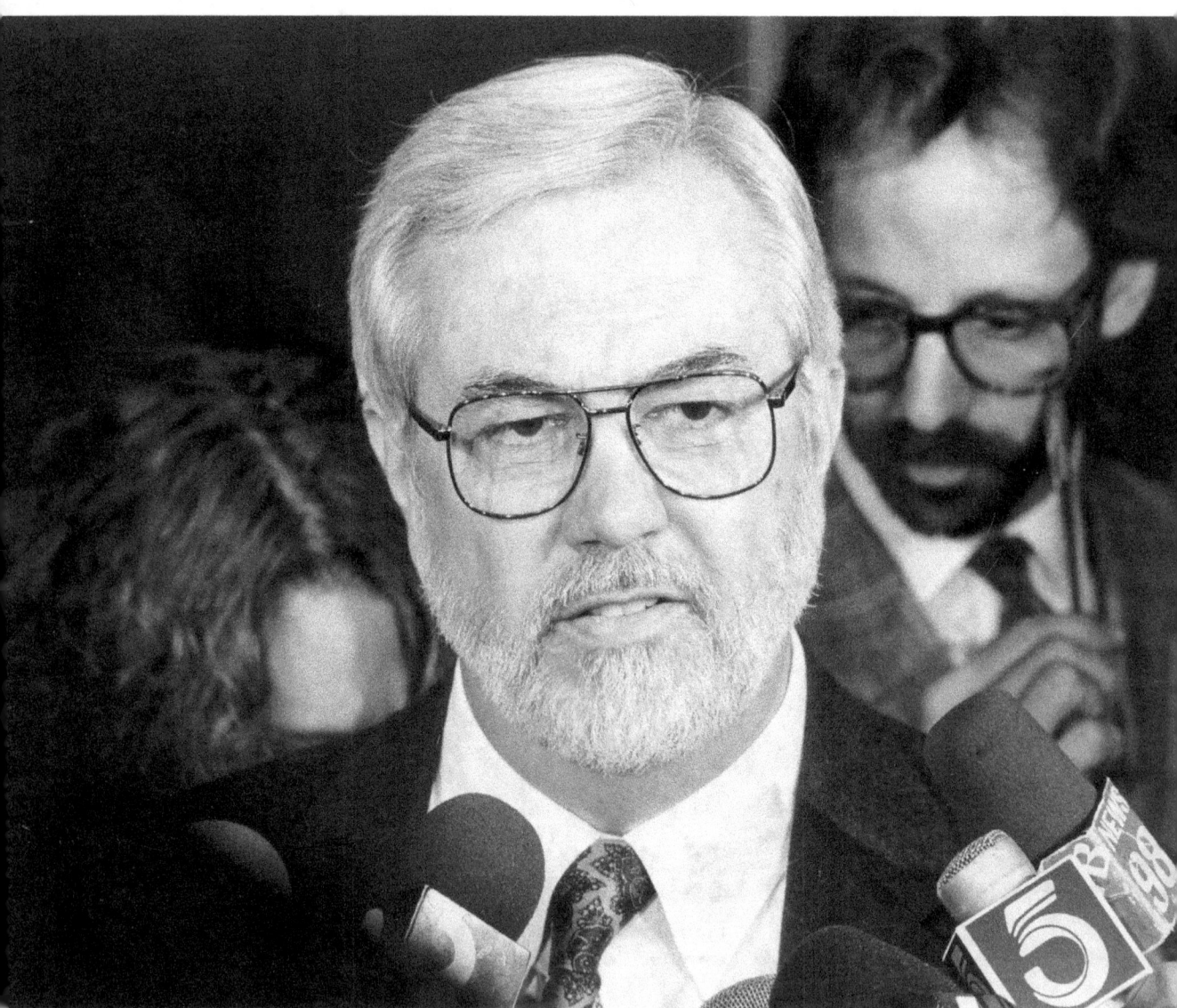

Ramirez would have to overcome the overwhelming evidence and expert trial strategy and presentation delivered by District Attorney Halpin. (Michael Haering/Herald Examiner Collection)

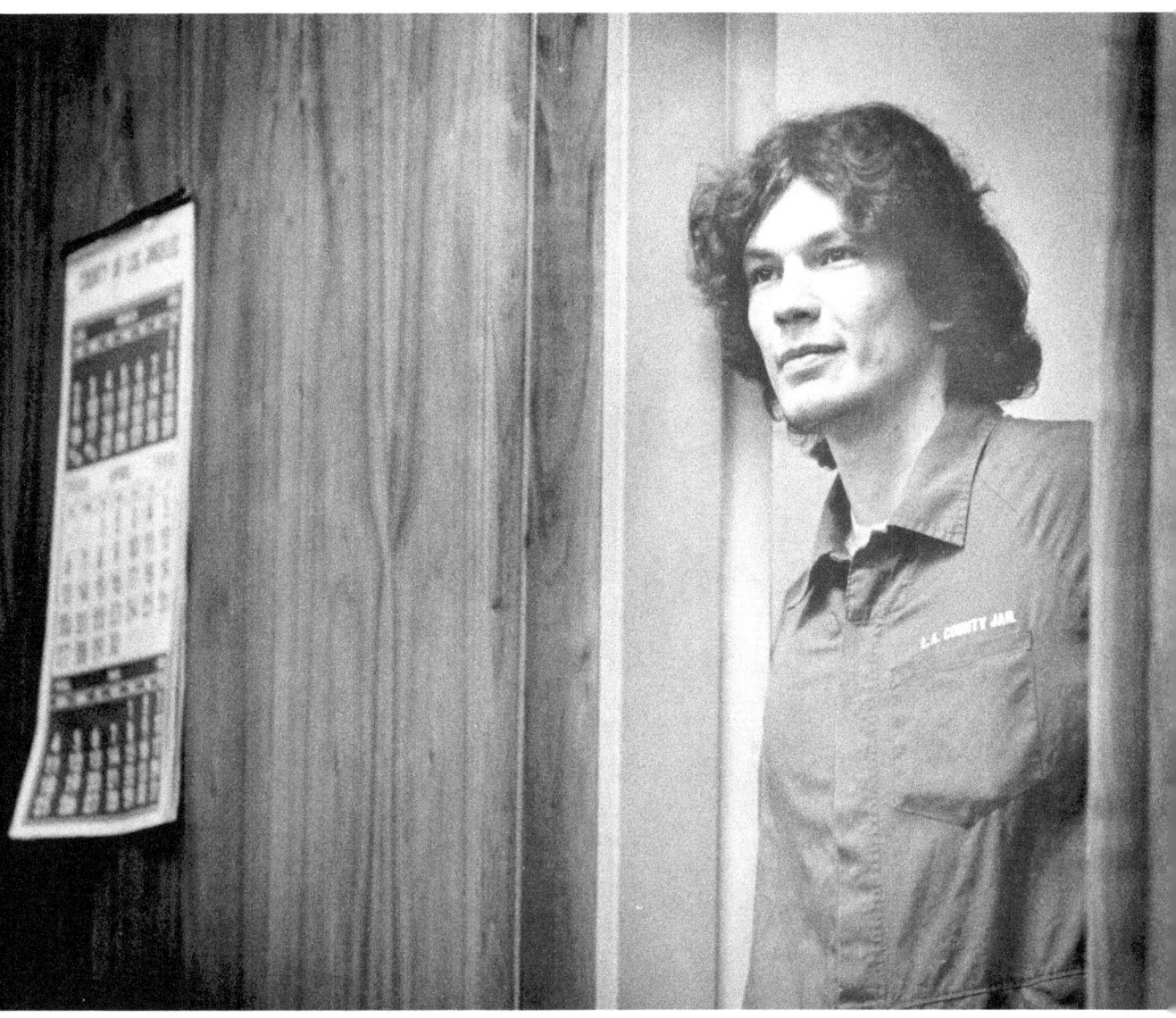

Once the jury proceedings concluded, Ramirez no longer appeared in a suit. Knowing he would likely receive a death sentence, Ramirez wore a smile while entering the court where he would ultimately be condemned. (Mike Mullen/Herald Examiner Collection)

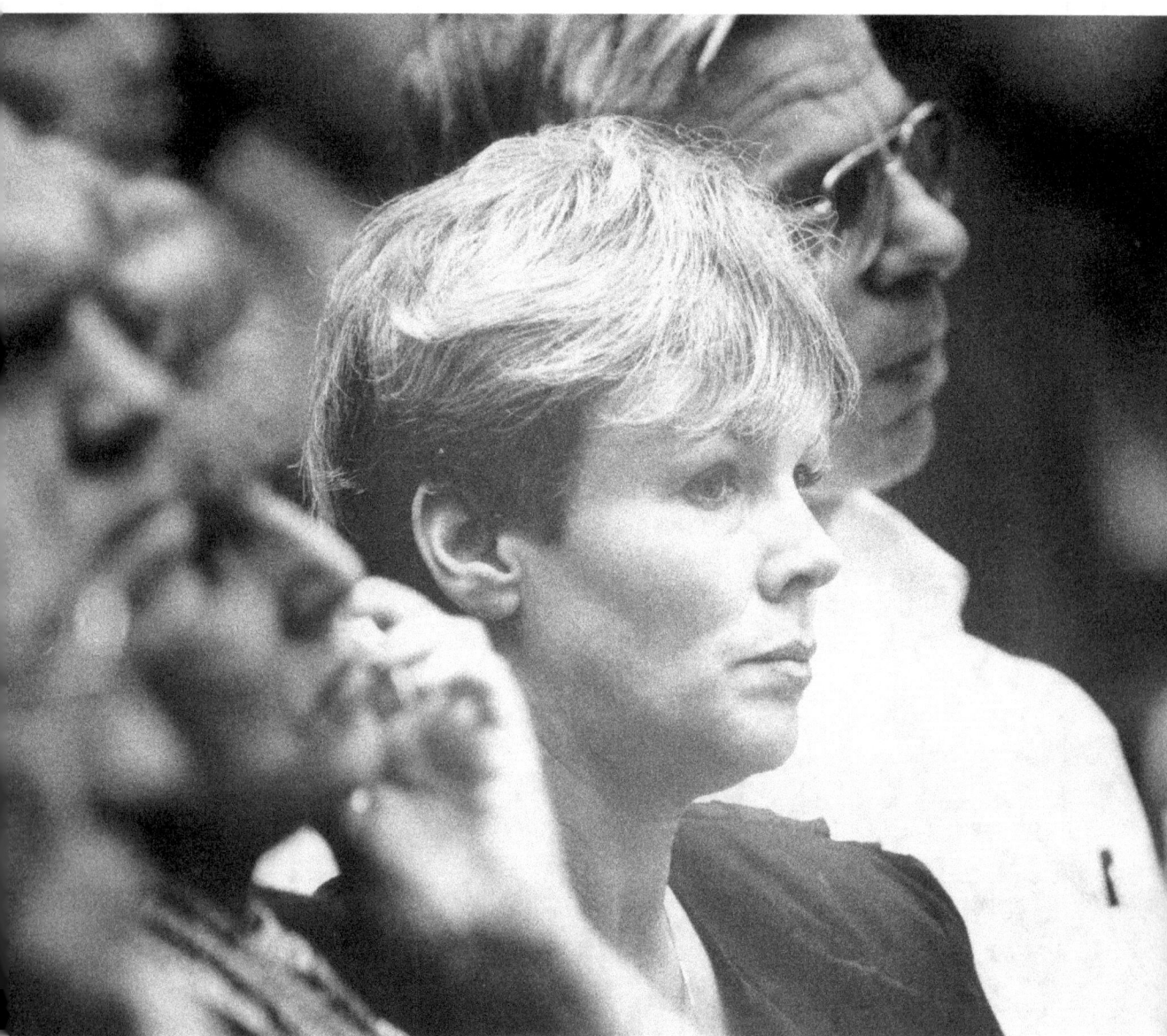

Victims and their relatives were present to witness the judicial proceedings. Judy Arnold's parents, Max and Lela Kneiding, were brutally murdered by Ramirez. Mrs. Arnold and her husband Bill were present for the reading of the verdicts. (Michael Haering/Herald Examiner Collection)

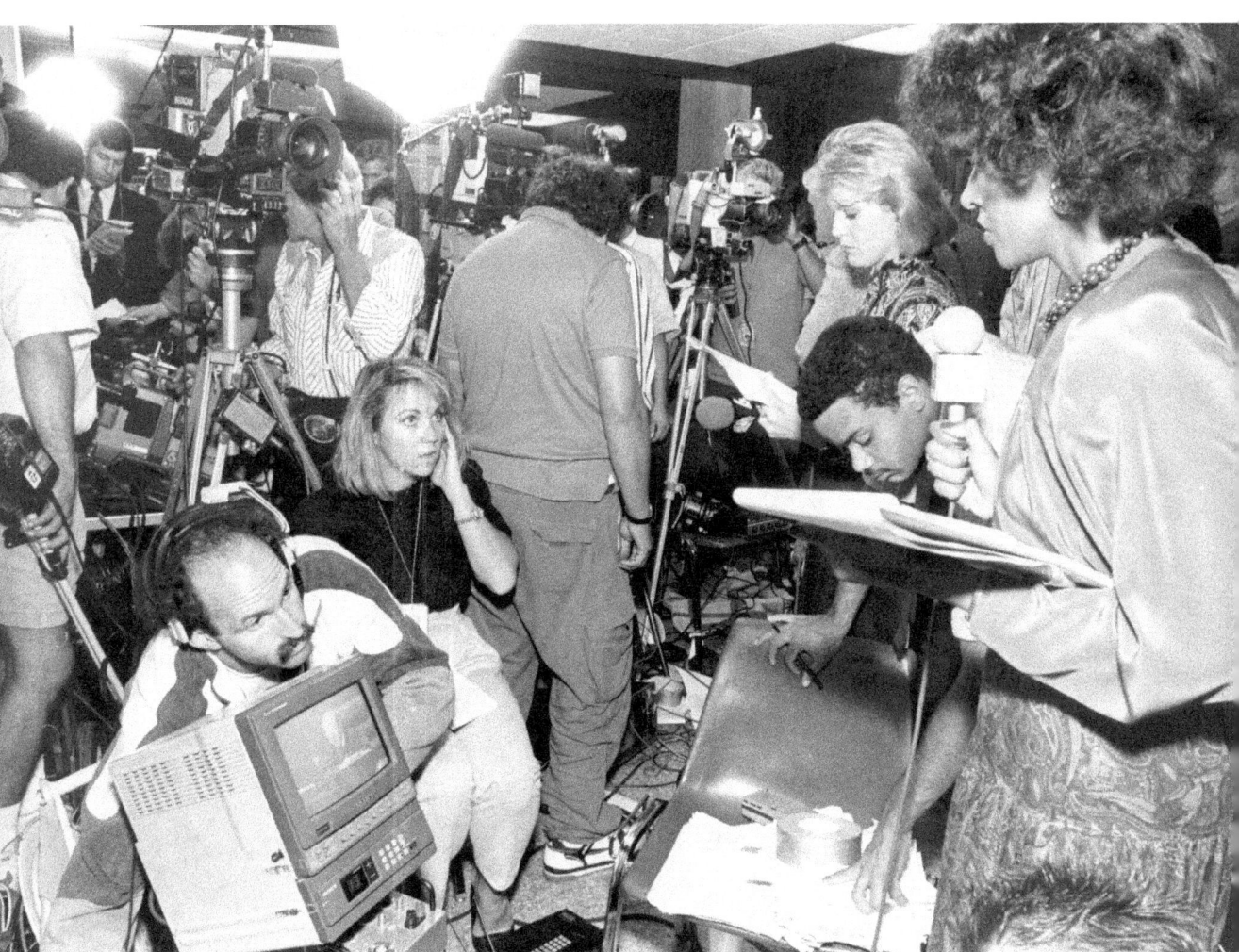

The news media massed as they awaited verdicts from crimes committed nearly five years before this photo was taken. (Akili-Casundria Ramsess/Herald Examiner Collection)

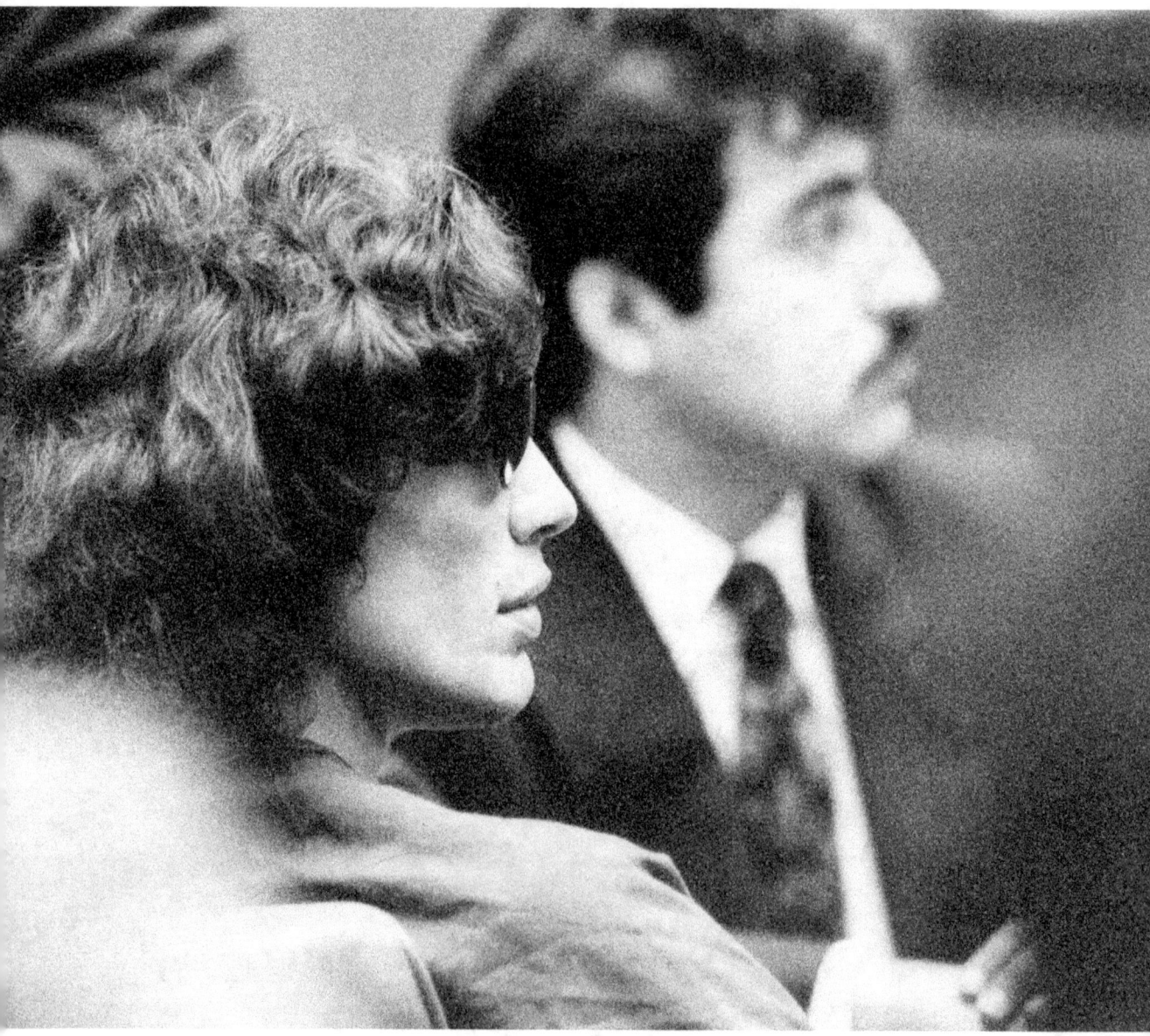

September 20, 1989: Ramirez was still wearing sunglasses on the day the verdicts were read. (Michael Haering/Herald Examiner Collection)

Opposite: The *Herald-Examiner*'s photo feature was released the day after verdicts were announced in the trial of Richard Ramirez. (Herald Examiner Collection)

FACE OF EVIL

The Terror and the Trial

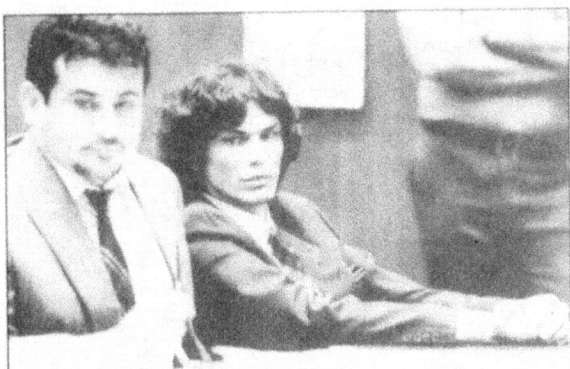

Defendant slouches in courtroom chair next to defense attorney Daniel Hernandez as his trial on the 13 Night Stalker murders and 30 related felony counts gets under way in Los Angeles

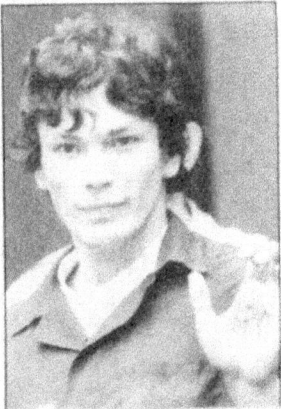

Mark of the devil: Satanism was key element of trial. Night Stalker left cult symbols and made some victims swear to Satan, and Ramirez displayed crude pentagram drawn on his palm

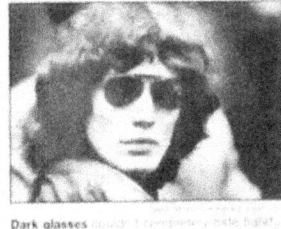

Dark glasses couldn't completely hide hateful glare from Ramirez in session court last July

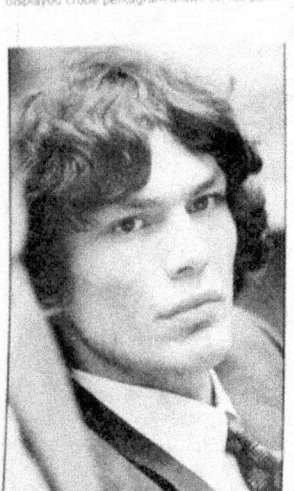

Battered and bruised Richard Ramirez is led to LAPD's Hollenbeck division booking room after capture by enraged East L.A. residents

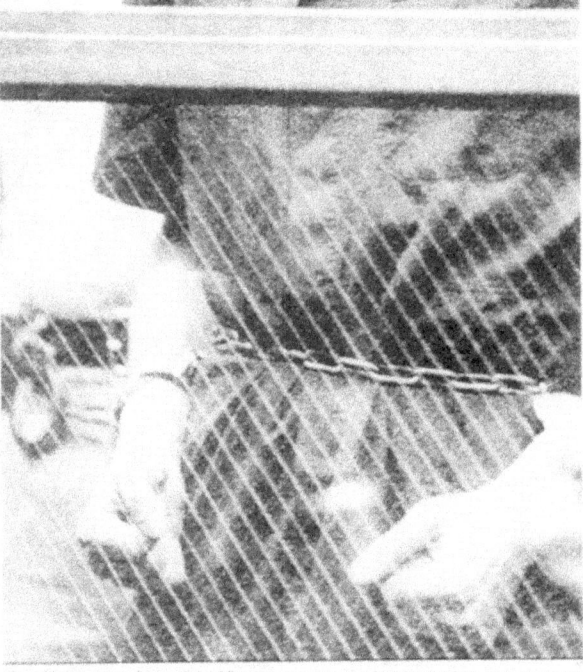

The cold eyes of Night Stalker Richard Ramirez, remarked upon by several victims, were in evidence in court appearance last October when judge rebuked him for seeking another change of attorneys

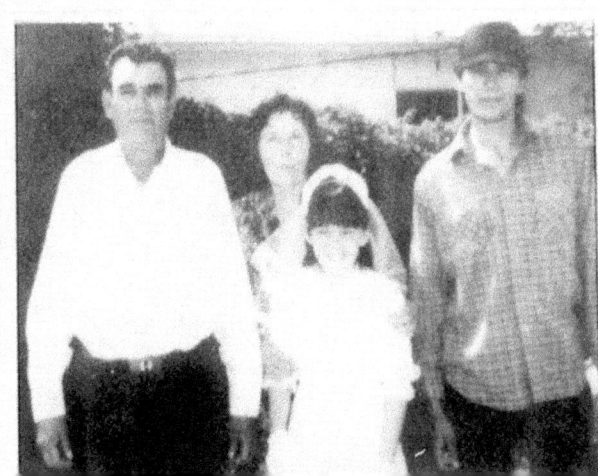

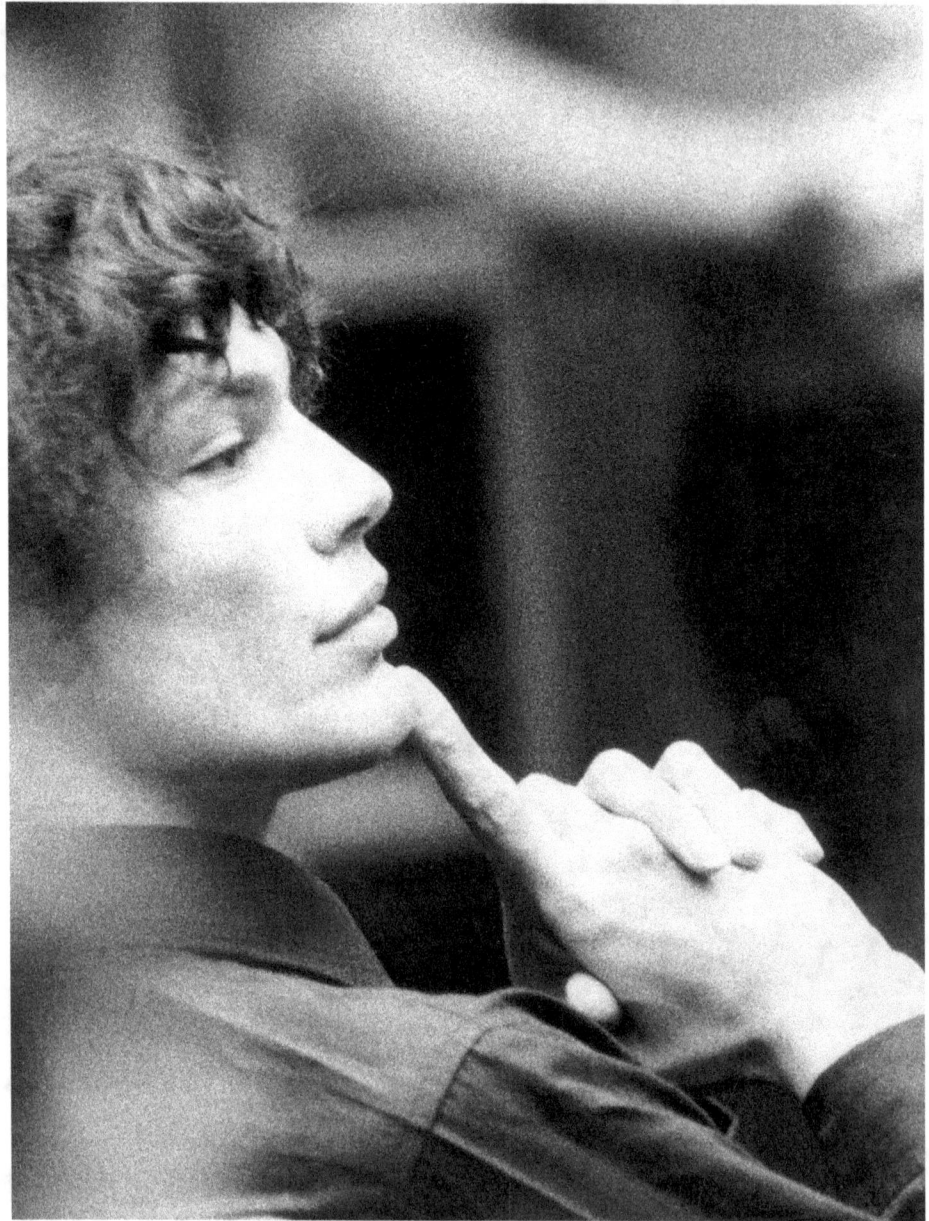

October 4, 1989: Despite an apparent pensive look, Ramirez received multiple death sentences. (Akili-Casundria Ramsess/Herald Examiner Collection)

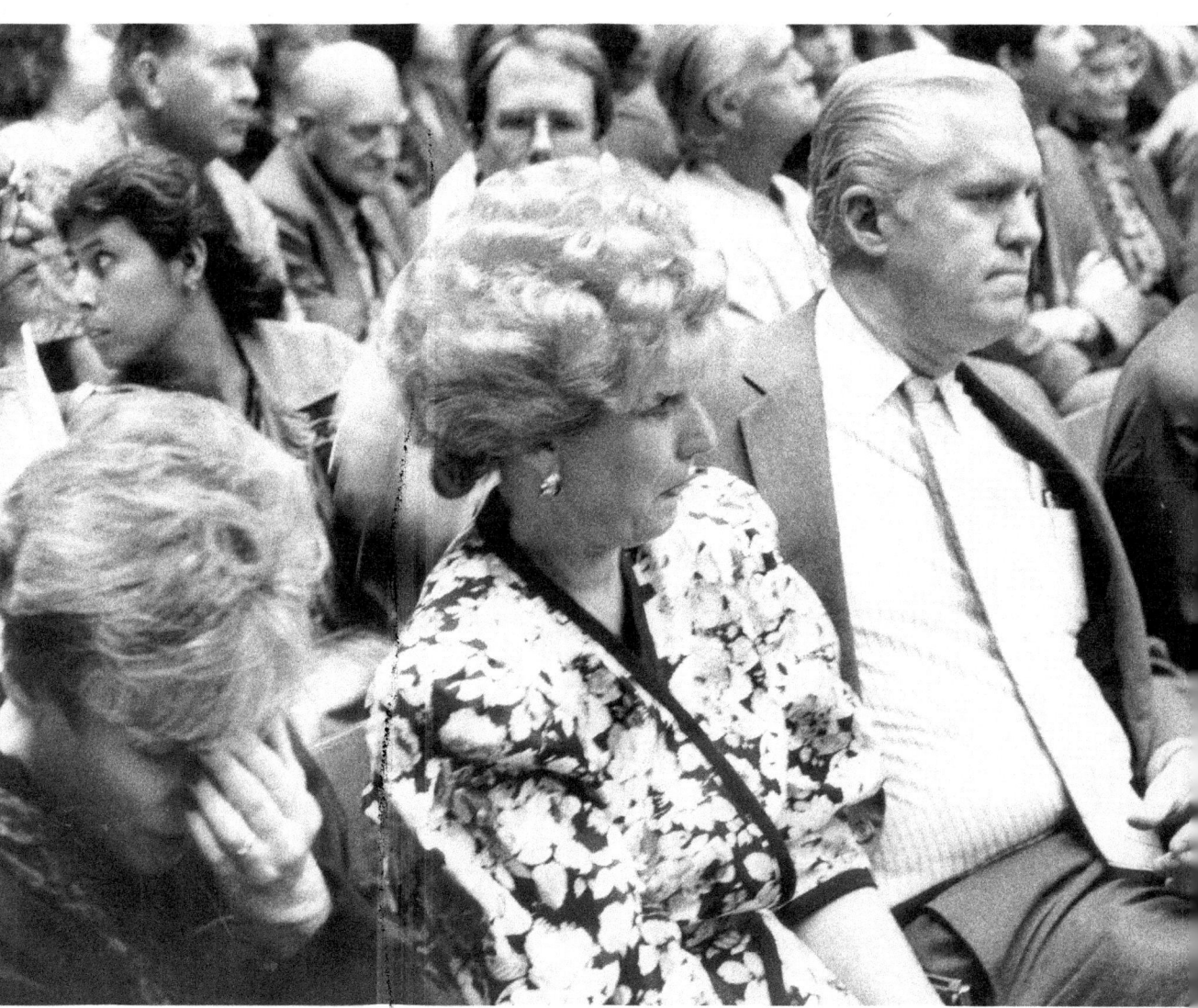

Judy Arnold and her sister Ellen Francis at the sentencing, which
included convictions for the murder of their parents, the Kneidings.
(Akili-Casundria Ramsess/Herald Examiner Collection)

EVERY UNIFORMED COP,

EVERY HOMICIDE INVESTIGATOR,

AND EVERYONE WHO WORKED

WITH GIL CARRILLO MOBILIZED

TO ENSURE THE LAST VICTIM WAS,

IN FACT, THE FINAL VICTIM.

GIL CARRILLO, LOS ANGELES SHERIFF'S DEPARTMENT

Gil Carrillo spent most of his adult life chasing killers.

Some killed friends or neighbors, others killed family, some killed rival gang members and others killed complete strangers. Still others mixed their murderous ways with crimes such as robbery. But one haunting death purveyor had a malevolent mixture of burglary, sexual assault and murder. It was serially delivered to diverse locations around Los Angeles County during the summer of 1985.

Carrillo and his partner, Frank Salerno, were hunting a single, evil human being, who fancied himself accountable to no other human. The satanic personage dubbed the Night Stalker generated fear throughout a good portion of Southern California, yet the man himself—Richard Ramirez—feared nothing.

His had a rather broadly square and pock-marked face with high-cheek bones. These facial features, coupled with a slim build rendered him nearly skeletal. At 6'1", and seemingly always clothed in black, his appearance generally ranged from neo-goth to back alley frightening. Add greasy, black wavy hair, and Ramirez was both the devil's acolyte and a walking ghoulfest. A despicably intimidating creep who preyed on those far more frail than he.

Gil Carrillo, on the other hand, was a well-dressed, highly respected and accomplished Deputy for the Los Angeles Sheriff's Department where he was assigned to its esteemed Homicide Bureau.

Carrillo had been a deputy for more than 13 years and was in his fifth year as a homicide investigator. He had seen plenty of dead folk and brought to justice those responsible for their deaths.

Carrillo was highly trained, and knew of different types of killers. Child killers, wife slayers, those who killed in the heat of passion, and those who laid in wait. Some sought a thrill, others looked for sexual gratification and the seemingly rarest of all killed in series. Most critical to the latter was intervention. If something or someone didn't stop a serial killer, the death toll would unnecessarily mount. So when a series of killings is linked, the press is on. Every

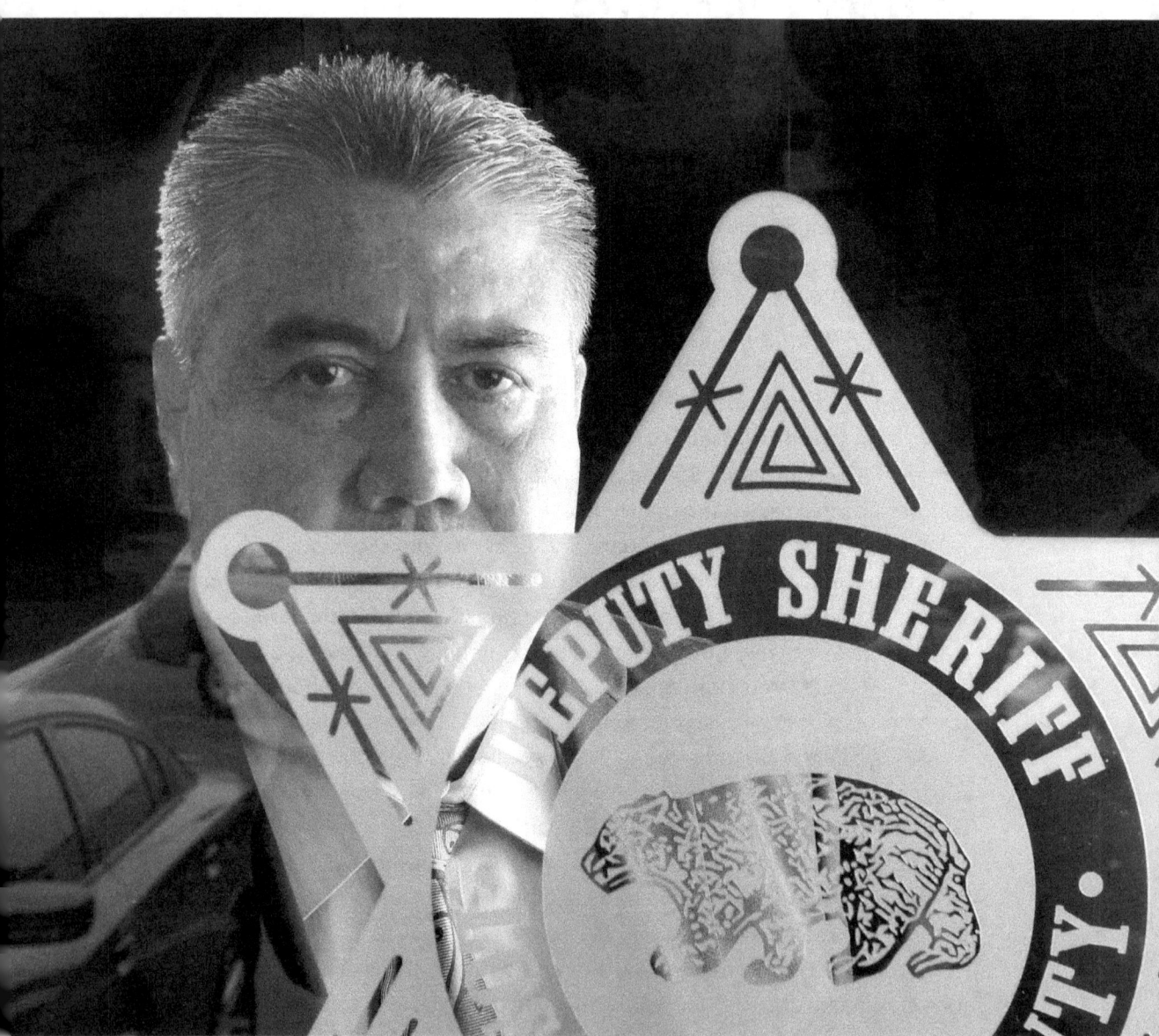

Gil Carrillo was the chief investigator for the Sheriff's Department on the Night Stalker case. (Bill Alkofer/Orange County Register)

uniformed cop, every homicide investigator, and everyone who worked with Gil Carrillo mobilized to ensure the last victim was, in fact, the final victim.

In the era preceding the collection of DNA, talented detectives like Carrillo relied on other forms of evidence to tie crimes to one another. Linkage in this case was made through latent shoeprints that showed up at crime scenes that also bore the fingerprints of the killer. The same sole impression of an Avia athletic shoe had been found at a number of crime scenes. Most of the shoe impressions were found in the ground. Sadly, in the course of brutally murdering Joyce Nelson, the killer kicked her in the face hard enough to leave a recognizable shoeprint on her face.

This shoe also made an impression on Carrillo. More than thirty years later Carrillo readily recalled that 1,356 pairs of size 11-1/2 Avia model 440 shoes were sold in California. Six pair made their way to Los Angeles. One pair was worn by Richard Ramirez.

Carrillo examined reports and crime scenes for indications that an Avia-wearing suspect had been present. All the while, he and his colleagues kept this case key, distributing it only on a "need to know" basis. By now Carrillo was expecting that Ramirez was monitoring the news media, seeking to find coverage of his many crimes.

Carrillo was right. Ramirez fled LA well into his crime spree and headed to San Francisco. On August 18, 1985, Ramirez burglarized the Pan family home and shot both residents—Peter and Barbara. Barbara was left for dead. Peter was left dead.

During the ensuing press conference, San Francisco officials announced Carrillo's case key to the media. As confirmation of Carrillo's suspicions, Ramirez, was in fact attuned to the media. His Avias were promptly dropped into the sea from the Golden Gate Bridge. A careless misstep was made in San Francisco. At best it would make things difficult for the many jurisdictions investigating Ramirez crimes. At worst the cases would never be solved.

Whatever the outcome, through his post-arrest contact, Carrillo came to learn that Ramirez enjoyed knowing and having information that Carrillo and his colleagues did not. This manifested itself in an entirely disgusting conversation wherein Ramirez questioned Carrillo about crimes where Ramirez defecated.

But leaving his feces in bushes wasn't the calling card that was prominently featured in the case that brought Carrillo's considerable investigative skills to prominence.

That distinction belongs to the pentagram. A simple encircled star was the linkage between the courtroom, criminal celebrity and the horrific crime scenes. Carrillo knew about the satanic marking during the investigation, but the public's widespread awareness was propelled by a courtroom photograph of a smiling Ramirez displaying his pentagram-adorned palm. During his trial, Ramirez also traced the symbol on the trial table.

These were observations made by Carrillo, well after his first personal contact with the gruesome devil worshipper. His first personal contact occurred when Carrillo and his longtime and deeply admired partner, Frank Salerno, attempted their post-arrest questioning.

Ramirez refused to waive his Miranda rights. The invocation of his Fifth Amendment rights meant that the two immensely talented homicide detectives would not be working their way into a meaningful conversation with the murderer. With one exception: Ramirez had questions of them.

This was an odd wrinkle, but may have been the beginning of a behavior Carrillo would experience for years to come. Ramirez enjoyed being the center of attention. Ramirez "ate up" his status as a semi-celebrity, even when on trial for his life.

Carrillo discerned a seeming courtroom routine. During his entry into the courtroom, Ramirez would scan the crowd for an attractive woman. When the proceedings allowed, Ramirez would look in her direction. Upon exiting the courtroom, Ramirez would smile at the woman he had picked out. For some this was oddly reminiscent of his victim selection. Perhaps even a substitute for picking out homes with open windows during the daytime and returning later to assault, burglarize, rape and murder.

Ramirez seemed to have abundant chat for Carrillo. At another point, according to Carrillo, Ramirez contemplated marketing a brand of sunglasses fashioned after the style of glasses he sported in the courtroom.

To keep Carrillo on the conversational hook, Ramirez once told Carrillo that he had committed four more murders in Los Angeles County that he would one day disclose to the detective. It never happened, but it was a method of ensuring that Carrillo would be an intent listener.

Carrillo, of course, recognized Ramirez's narcissism, it was a characteristic familiar to his work with homicide suspects. So, the Sheriff's homicide detective kept his conversations with the Night Stalker in balance by not bringing Ramirez satisfaction by saying anything that would make Ramirez happy or satisfied. For a cop that cares deeply for his victims and their families, his seeming care for killers is nothing more than a duty ultimately designed to serve the victims.

This case had many.

Carrillo remembers and recalls each of them with great specificity and abundant care. He retired from the Los Angeles Sheriff's Department as a homicide lieutenant who had handled more than 400 homicide cases. That's more than 400 families who lost a loved one. That's a lot of folks who made an impression on the veteran detective. They gave his life purpose, one he supported with talent and resolve. It's fitting that fate saw to it that Gil Carrillo would investigate and help successfully prosecute the Night Stalker.

In this case it's also fitting that Carrillo has outlived the pitted-face monster who summered in the City of Angels in 1985.

SLEEP SAFELY NOW,
THE BAD MAN IS GONE.

AFTERWORD

The three cops spoken of herein—Gil Carrillo, my father, and I—are all retired from law enforcement. In my retirement, I served 11+ years as the Executive Director at the LAPD Museum. Joan Renner and Mike Fratantoni were two of my loyal volunteers there. Sheriff McDonnell, for a good portion of my museum tenure, was on the museum's board of directors. Joan introduced me to Photo Friends, and I have enjoyed my time working with this dedicated group. Joan also connected me with Gil Carrillo. In his retirement, I found Carrillo still abundantly concerned for the victims in this case. His recollection of the details of the massive investigation was remarkable. Carrillo credits Frank Salerno for teaching him the finest details of homicide investigation.

I also serve on the board of directors of the Los Angeles Police Federal Credit Union where Linda Hada and Sharon Padgett spoke of their fears during the summer of '85. Both of their husbands worked diligently to administer this financial institution, Mike Padgett as the immediate past CEO and Ed Hada as the current CEO. It was my chance discussions with Linda and Sharon that helped me better understand the social impact the Night Stalker crimes brought to the region.

For those victims who survived and those souls lost to the crimes, I extend my thoughts and sympathies to each and to those important to each of you. As I mentioned in the text, less than two years after this crime spree, my roommate was murdered while serving as a plainclothes officer for the Metropolitan Division of the LAPD. While constructing this book, his killer came up for parole for a third time. I appeared at the hearing and spoke in opposition to the parole. So did my longtime LAPD partner, Detective Bob Kraus. Prior to his murder, Jim Pagliotti was another officer who scoured Hollywood on the summer nights of 1985 searching for the Night Stalker. Jim is buried in his hometown, Goleta, California, and resting eternally in a place that Richard Ramirez will never see.

ABOUT THE AUTHOR

GLYNN MARTIN is the co-author of the *Los Angeles Times* bestseller, *LAPD '53*, a work he created with world-renowned novelist, James Ellroy. Martin is also a credited contributor to *L.A. Baseball* by fellow Photo Friends Director David Davis. Following his graduation from USC, Martin spent more than 30 years in and around the Los Angeles Police Department and continues to volunteer for the Los Angeles Police Memorial Foundation. Prior to entering police work, Martin gave due consideration to life as a sportswriter, having started out as a sports reporter and photographer for the now defunct *Ledger* newspapers in Glendale, where Martin was born, raised and continues to live with his wife, two grown children and an oversized Labrador. He can be found at www.lapdhistorian.com

ABOUT THE CONTRIBUTORS

GLEN CREASON has been the Map Librarian for the Los Angeles Public Library for the past twenty-nine years and a reference librarian in the History Department since 1979. He was a co-curator of the landmark map exhibit *Los Angeles Unfolded* in 2009, and in October of 2010, he published the book *Los Angeles in Maps* for Rizzoli International. He has written about local history, maps and popular culture for local publications including the *Downtown News, Mercators World*, the *International Map Collectors Society Journal*, the *Public Historian*, the *Communicator*, the *Los Angeles Times* and *Edible Ojai*. He blogged weekly on maps for 170 posts as a columnist for *Los Angeles* magazine and is a contributor on research topics for the *Huffington Post* and *LAist*.

KATHY KRISTOF is an award-winning journalist and editor of *SideHusl.com*, a site that researches, reviews and rates online platforms that allow consumers to make money. Her features have appeared in the *Los Angeles Times, CBS News, Forbes, Kiplinger, Inc.*, and many other publications. She's the author of *Investing 101, Taming the Tuition Tiger* and *Kathy Kristof's Complete Guide to Dollars and Sense*. However, her biggest claim to fame may be that she was once a *Jeopardy* question: "Kathy Kristof replaced what famous syndicated columnist who died in 1991?" (Sylvia Porter)

ESTER PETSCHAR is native Angeleno who, as a teenager, worked for Coast Envelope Company during summer breaks from high school (working alongside one of the victims). She worked for twenty-three years for Pac Bell & AT&T Remote Maintenance & Testing Services. In 1988, she started taking art classes at Pasadena City College, followed by a two-year program at the cutting-edge school, Santa Monica School of Design Art & Architecture; followed by studies at Santa Monica College's Academy of Entertainment & Technology. Now a practicing visual artist for more than twenty-five years, she specializes in chalk street painting and very detailed small murals and portraits.

CHRISTINA RICE has been with the Los Angeles Public Library since 2005, serving as the Senior Librarian of the Photo Collection since 2009. She is the author of *Ann Dvorak: Hollywood's Forgotten Rebel* (University Press of Kentucky) and is currently working on a biography of actress Jane Russell. She has been a writer on the *My Little Pony* (IDW Publishing) comic book series since 2014, and was a contributor to the *Femme Magnifique* and *Where We Live* anthologies.

ABOUT THE PHOTO COLLECTION

The Los Angeles Public Library (LAPL) began collecting photographs some-time before World War II and had a collection of about 13,000 images by the late 1950s. In 1981, when Los Angeles celebrated its 200th birthday, Security Pacific National Bank gave its noted collection of historical photographs to the people of Los Angeles to be archived at the Central Library. Since then, LAPL has been fortunate to receive other major collections, making the library a resource worldwide for visual images.

Notable collections include the "photo morgues" of the *Los Angeles Herald Examiner* and *Valley Times* newspapers, the Kelly–Holiday mid-century collection of aerial photographs, the Works Progress Administration/Federal Writers Project collection, the Luther Ingersoll Portrait Collection, and the landmark *Shades of L.A.*, an archive of images representing the contemporary and historic diversity of families in Los Angeles. Images were chosen from family albums and copied in a project sponsored by Photo Friends.

The Los Angeles Public Library Photo Collection also includes the works of individual photographers, including Ansel Adams, Herman Schultheis, William Reagh, Ralph Morris, Lucille Stewart, Gary Leonard, Stone Ishimaru, Carol Westwood, and Rolland Curtis.

Over 126,000 images from these collections have been digitized and are available to view through the LAPL website at https://tessa.lapl.org/.

ABOUT PHOTO FRIENDS

Formed in 1990, Photo Friends is a nonprofit organization that supports the Los Angeles Public Library's Photograph Collection and History & Genealogy Department. Our goal is to improve access to the collections and promote them through programs, projects, exhibits, and books such as this one.

We are an enthusiastic group of photographers, writers, historians, business people, politicians, academics, and many others, all bonded by our passion for photography, history, and Los Angeles.

Since 1994, Photo Friends has presented a regular series called The Photographer's Eye, which spotlights local photographers and their work. In 2011, Photo Friends inaugurated L.A. in Focus, a lecture series that features images drawn primarily from the Photo Collection. We have presented programs on L.A. crime, the San Fernando Valley, Kelly–Holiday aerial photographs, and L.A.'s themed environments, among others.

With initial funding from the Ralph M. Parsons Foundation, Photo Friends sponsored the L.A. Neighborhoods Project by commissioning photographers to create a visual record of the neighborhoods of Los Angeles during the early part of the 21st century (all now part of the collection). To ensure the library's collection will continue to reflect such an important part of Los Angeles' history, a generous grant enabled Photo Friends to hire five contemporary photographers to document present-day industrial L.A.; these images have become part of LAPL's permanent collection and are available to view through the library's photo database. Photo Friends also curates photography exhibits on display in the History Department.

Photo Friends is a membership organization. Please consider becoming a member and helping us in our work to preserve and promote L.A.'s rich photographic resource. All proceeds from the sale of this book go to support Photo Friends' programs.

photofriends.org

This book was published in conjunction with a photo exhibit at
Los Angeles Central Library's History & Genealogy Department,
curated by Glynn Martin.
On display in the History & Genealogy Department (LL4)
January 17 – July 14, 2019

Satan's Summer in the City of Angels: The Social Impact of the Night Stalker
By Glynn Martin
Copyright © 2019 Photo Friends of the Los Angeles Public Library
Images © Los Angeles Public Library Photo Collection

Text: © 2019 by Glynn Martin
Foreword: © 2019 James Ellroy
In the Time of the Night Stalker: © 2019 by Glen Creason
My Childhood Summer of Fear: © 2019 by Christina Rice
Close Encounters with the Night Stalker: © 2019 by Ester Petschar
No One Was Safe: © 2019 by Kathy Kristof
All rights reserved.

Published by:

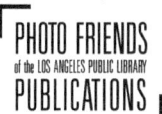

Photo Friends of the Los Angeles Public Library
c/o Future Studio
P.O. Box 292000
Los Angeles, CA 90029
www.photofriends.org

Designed by Amy Inouye, Future Studio Los Angeles

Special quantity discounts available when purchased in bulk by corporations,
organizations, or groups. Please contact Photo Friends at: photofriendsla@gmail.com

ISBN-13: 978-0-9978251-8-3
Printed in the United States

**Cover photo: Persons unexpected took up arms. (Anne Knudsen/Herald
Examiner Collection)**
**Back cover photo: A shoeprint was found during the investigation of the
Zazzara case. Similar shoe prints recovered at other crime scenes led
investigators to believe a single person was responsible for a series of
crimes. (Los Angeles Sheriff's Department)**

www.ingramcontent.com/pod-product-compliance
Lightning Source LLC
Chambersburg PA
CBHW052034280526
45791CB00010B/2965